Nhava & Sheva

BATTLING FOR THE ENVIRONMENT:

OIL, PORTS AND THE COASTLINE

Nhava & Sheva

BATTLING FORTHE ENVIRONMENT:
OIL, PORTS AND THE COASTLINE

Shyam Chainani

ACADEMIC FOUNDATION
NEW DELHI
www.academicfoundation.com

First published in 2012
by

ACADEMIC FOUNDATION
4772-73 / 23 Bharat Ram Road, (23 Ansari Road),
Darya Ganj, New Delhi - 110 002 (India).
Phones : 23245001 / 02 / 03 / 04.
Fax : +91-11-23245005.
E-mail : books@academicfoundation.com
www.academicfoundation.com

Cataloging in Publication Data--DK
Courtesy: D.K. Agencies (P) Ltd. <docinfo@dkagencies.com>

Chainani, Shyam.
Nhava & Sheva : battling for the environment: oil, ports & the coastline / Shyam Chainani.

p. cm.

Includes bibliographical references (p.) and index.

ISBN 9788171889655

1. Jawaharlal Nehru Port (India). 2. Eminent domain--India--Maharashtra. 3. Harbors--India--Maharashtra--Protection. 4. Environmental protection--India--Maharashtra. 5. Petroleum industry and trade--Environmental aspects--India--Maharashtra. 6. Shipping--Government policy--India--Jawaharlal Nehru Port. I. Title.

DDC 343.54790252 23

Printed and bound in India.

DEDICATED TO

Sohrab P. Godrej and Sadashiv Gorakshkar
Who fought so hard for Nhava

Professor S.S. Varde
Who gave his staunch support

Dr. S.C. Maudgal
Fearless fighter for the environment who stuck to his guns and bucked the system and who the system then tried to destroy

Noshir Soonawala
Who supported me to the hilt

Tatas
For their immense tolerance and help

Rehan, Vivaan, Tara, Drew, Sumair and Diya
May there still be pristine coasts and lovely green islands for them to enjoy

Emblem of Lady Khatum Marium School

Foreword

AT THE OUTSET LET ME EXPRESS MY GRATITUDE for being asked to write this foreword to Shyam's book. I am deeply honoured. Notices for the acquisition of the entire lands at Nhava initially for a regional park were received sometime in September 1970 much before I met Shyam. It would not be an exaggeration to mention that this came as a bolt of lightning. What followed was a series of meetings with different Managing Directors of CIDCO, innumerable civil servants and ultimately various Ministers from the Maharashtra Government. Wherever I turned I was confronted with a disinterested blank look, and received various sermons such as "you should be proud that your ancestral lands are being taken over for a national project, in fact you should hand them over free to the Government," another one from a Chief Engineer of the BPT who enlightened me that I should be grateful that in a matter of a few years Nhava would march into the new century as the entire area would be concreted! To him concreting an area was the ultimate symbol of civilisation! One of the Managing Directors of CIDCO even challenged my argument that our Campus had been in existence since 1910, as according to them there were no existing structures on their maps! I later discovered that they had gone over Nhava, along with ONGC engineers, in a helicopter before deciding to acquire the entire land, with maps dating back to 1870s!

I had almost exhausted all my energy and was tired of being shunted from pillar to post without even a sign of sympathy. When in December 1978, out of the blue, I received a telephone call from Shyam inquiring whether our Trust were the owners of Nhava and what were we doing to try and get it exempted? I explained to him that by June 1976 the Government had finally decided to acquire the whole of Nhava for a supply base for ONGC and our earlier petition to the then Chief Minister Shri V.P. Naik dated 11th Aug 1971 supported by various appeals from the shipping fraternity, including shipping companies, shipping unions, etc. had fallen on deaf ears! I further informed him that ONGC had already taken possession of over 54 hectares of land at Nhava and recently we had been informed that CIDCO officials would come to Nhava to take possession of a strip of land for an access road right through our Campus cutting through the corner of our Marine Museum and dismembering our Campus into two separate segments! All my efforts to divert or realign the road fell on deaf ears and I was told that this alignment was finalised by their foreign consultant and could not under any circumstances be altered! Shyam immediately managed to arrange a meeting through his contacts with the then Urban Development Secretary on 26th December, when we put forward our case. To my amazement the Secretary contacted Mr. Cheema of ONGC over the telephone who agreed to alter the road alignment without even asking or receiving permission from any foreign consultant!

Thereafter, Shyam took up the campaign to save Nhava in right earnest. On reading through this book the reader will no doubt appreciate his energy, perseverance, and dedication to a cause and his fetish for taking notes and meticulous record keeping. He must have written hundreds of letters, met innumerable civil servants and Ministers from Mantralaya up to New Delhi when ultimately Smt. Indira Gandhi, the Prime Minister, finally intervened and issued a directive to exclude the village and our Campus! In response, ONGC reluctantly decided to exclude our Campus from the acquisition. Shyam over the years, right up to his death jealously guarded against any other agency like the Coast Guard, Bombay Port Trust, Mazagon Dock, ship building yards, etc. from encroaching upon our Campus area on the north side of Nhava.

When Shyam who was a member of our Governing Council mentioned at our Annual General Body meeting in October 2009 that he was thinking of culling out some of the chapters on Nhava from his original voluminous book entitled Heritage & Environment (An Indian Diary) and inquired whether I would be interested in getting them bound in a booklet form along with our photographs for our Museum Library, I immediately volunteered to publish the booklet as part of our Centenary Celebrations programmes in 2010. He undertook to com-

Garden setting of the Maritime Museum with Rashid Yusuf (inset)

plete it by June/July so that we could print and release it sometime in September/October as part of our celebrations. In our subsequent Governing Council Meeting in March 2010 he apologised for the delay as he was pre-occupied with his efforts in preventing large scale illegal constructions at Mahabaleshwar and his efforts to battle the onset of cancer which his doctors had recently informed him he was suffering from, unfortunately none of us took this news very seriously! He persisted in his determination to complete his book which he ultimately did in December before being admitted to Breach Candy Hospital for chemotherapy. Within a couple of weeks to my horror he went into a coma and expired on Christmas day 2010!

His sudden passing away at such a young age has deprived the environment movement of a stalwart the likes of which we will not see again! Personally I have lost a friend of over 30 years and an ardent

supporter, who came to love Nhava and was willing to protect it at any cost! May God bless his soul and may his soul rest in eternal peace! Those visiting the Campus at Nhava will no doubt appreciate the fruition of his efforts as our Campus now stands as a permanent monument to his memory! It is no small matter that this book comes out on our Marine Museum Centenary.

Shri A.R.A. Yusuf,
Chairman Emeritus, SMYSW Foundation

Chairman Emeritus Rashid Yusuf wrote this Foreword in July 2011. Sadly, he passed away on June 4, 2012, and was unable to see the publication of this book- Editors

The Yusuf family emblem: Veritas Vinci (Truth conquers)

Preface

THIS BOOK IS AN OUTCOME OF MY FIRST BOOK, "Heritage and Environment – An Indian Diary", Chapter Seven of which dealt with Nhava and Sheva which obviously included the battle to save India's oldest Nautical Institute (Training Ship *Rahaman*), and the Marine Museum, both run by the Sir Mohamed Yusuf Seamen Welfare Foundation. Rashid Yusuf, Chairman Emeritus of the Foundation, asked if he could have 500 copies of the Nhava Sheva Chapter. I felt however, that the chapter needed to be expanded for several reasons.

Firstly, for reasons of time and space and because it was one of eleven chapters of the book, I had not gone into as much depth as I should have. Secondly, my colleague Deepak Bhor was subsequently able to locate some of our earliest papers which gave a lot of information on the beginning of the Nhava campaign. Thirdly, there were several items which I had not included in that chapter since they appeared elsewhere in the book. These needed to be included to make the Nhava Sheva story more comprehensive. Furthermore, there was a need for many more photographs.

I have also included discussions on several items that may, at first glance, appear to be extraneous. Foremost of these is the Jawaharlal Nehru Port (earlier called Nhava Sheva Port) which I have included since the port gravely threatened Nhava and since the campaign to save Sheva arose directly from the one to save Nhava. This also led to the stipulation of vital safeguards regarding the Bombay Port and the Bombay Mainland/Sewri Nhava bridge, which will vitally affect Nhava. Elephanta

Water Colour of clock tower at Nhava Campus

is crucial since the entire Elephanta-Nhava-Sheva triangle, along with the beach at Nagaon in Uran, are vital for the environment of Bombay and New Bombay.

In writing this current book, I have included several details, seemingly trivial, even at the cost of readability in order to try and give a fuller account of what happened, including the many pulls and pressures and the attacks which we had to face.

Personal factors, social contacts, friendships, community feelings play a vital part in all decision making and environment and heritage are no exceptions. I have tried to list these out as truthfully as possible,

Water Colour of Anchorage Bungalow, the residence of Rashid Yusuf and Family

so that this becomes as accurate a case study and history of environmental action and decision making, as is possible.

I owe a debt to HSBC – their erstwhile CEO in India Zarir ("Z") Cama who sanctioned the grant for my first book, together with Naina Lal Kidwai, the current CEO, and Malini Thadani – who made that book possible. It is from that book that the current book has sprung.

Many people including some of the key players, had given their suggestions and comments on my earlier book, where I had mentioned their names. As regards the text of this book, I owe a great debt to several people who read the entire text – Heta Pandit, R.C. Iyer (IAS Retired), Firdausi Jassawala, Meena Bhat, Dev Mehta (IAS Retired), Sadashiv Gorakshkar, and of course, Rashid Yusuf, himself.

I am grateful to Vice Admiral I.C. Rao for his repeated interactions and detailed expert comments on the Bombay Port chapter, to Major General S. "Bobby" Dutta for looking at the Bombay Port chapter, to Hema Ramani for her notes regarding the Right to Information chapter, to Thomas Mathew for assisting me greatly with information regarding the Union Department of Environment in its earliest days, and to another good friend who served for many years in the Ministry

Nhava reservoir depicted in a watercolour

of Environment & Forests and who shared his thoughts with me, but who did not wish his name to be mentioned.

My thanks are also due to my staff team – Sridhar, who had to decipher and type thousands of pages of my handwritten drafts and work on weekends and holidays, Yogesh for filing the many hundreds of source documents and producing them at appropriate times, Laxman and Swapna Pingle for their assistance in typing, for the Bibliography and for typing hundreds of pages of handwritten notes for the sources, Hema Ramani and Nudrat Sayed for the index, together with Deepak, Jagtap, Ravi and Jagat.

For the photographs and co-ordination, I am indebted to Bertie D'Souza of Business India, Heta Pandit and Makrand Baokar.

Perhaps my biggest debt is to my cousin, *Business India* Publisher Ashok Advani for agreeing to publish the book and providing staff support.

This book is therefore a considerably expanded and modified version of the chapter of my earlier book.

Shyam Chainani

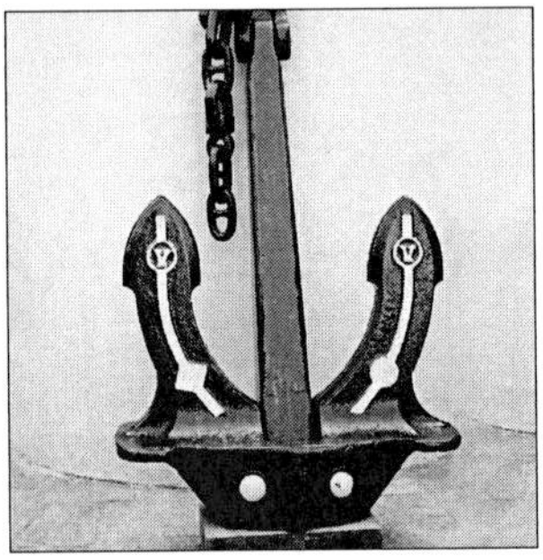

Nhava

FROM HISTORY LESSONS IN SCHOOL, I seem to remember Mary, Queen of Scots, as having said that when she died, 'Calais' would be found engraved on her heart. Similarly, for many years, I used to say that Nhava would be engraved on mine.

We have been involved in a continuous bitter battle, almost a war, since May 1978, to save Nhava. Side by side with that have been major efforts and battles to protect Sheva, Nagaon beach in Uran, besides other areas on the coast, and also to obtain space to create parks and gardens in Bombay city. These efforts put us in sharp conflict with some of the most powerful organisations in India, including the Oil and Natural Gas Commission (ONGC) and the Union Ministry of Petroleum and Chemicals. They also pitted us against the Union Ministry of Shipping & Transport, the Bombay Port Trust (BPT), the Jawaharlal Nehru Port Trust (JNPT), the Coast Guard, the City and Industrial Development Corporation of Maharashtra Limited (CIDCO) and also powerful business groups. These battles have involved several chief ministers of Maharashtra, several cabinet ministers, both at the State and the Centre, and three prime ministers – besides civil servants at the highest level in the Prime Minister's Office and elsewhere.

Powerful though the above agencies are, oddly, battling them never seemed to be an impossible task. I was ignorant of the governmental setup and did not know how difficult it was to upset the whole process of budget approvals, sanctions to construction, tenders and contracts, and so on. In addition, I was much more brash and far less tactful those days, ready to say pretty much anything to anybody, and confident that we would succeed, at least partially. My ignorance of what I was up against helped. Would I have attempted to wage the same battle today?

The battles were fought in the initial first year under the banner of the Save Bombay Committee (of which I was the honorary secretary) and since then, for the last thirty years and more, by the Bombay Environmental Action Group (BEAG), of which I have been the honorary secretary since its inception as the Bombay Bachao Committee in 1977 and around which my life has revolved since then.

The beautiful island of Nhava is virtually unknown even though it is within Bombay Harbour and only 14 kilometres from the Gateway of India. This pear-shaped island, 2 kilometres long and 1 kilometre wide, with an area of approximately 126 hectares (311 acres) along with a mangrove area of 36 hectares, is part of Greater Nhava which is almost four times as large, with an area of about 1,600 acres. It lies 1.5 kilometres east of Elephanta Island. To the south of Nhava, less than 1 kilometre away, across the Sheva creek and also close to Elephanta, lies Sheva, where the Jawaharlal Nehru Port has now been built.

On Nhava are located India's first Nautical Training Institute, the Training Ship *Rahaman*, and India's first Marine Museum. The first was established a century ago, and the Museum was founded a couple of years later. Both are managed by the Sir Mohamed Yusuf Seamen Welfare Foundation, which is run by Rashid Yusuf, with aid from his family members. Nhava was, till the mid-1970s, a lush, green, virgin area covered with mango and coconut trees, together with dense mangroves in the intertidal areas. I have always felt that if ever natural and man-made heritage both blended together harmoniously, this was such a place.

The Hindu names of Nhava were Devadevi and Nhave. The Portuguese called it Ilha de Patecas or Watermelon Island, with another name probably being Salvageo. The island was supposed to yield nothing but firewood, which would indicate its heavily wooded nature. In 1782, it was ceded by the Peshwas to the English by the Treaty of Salbai.

In 1848, one Haji Mohamed Joosub (who is said to have been a seafarer and/or a shipowner) together with his family, comprising his elder son Cassum and other son Hasham, migrated to Bombay from Surat. Cassum entered into shipping with a coastal passenger service, subsequently extended his horizons to run ships for the Haj pilgrimages, and gradually built up an enviable reputation. His was a sole proprietary concern and after his death, since no one in his family was interested in the enterprise, it gradually ceased to exist.

Hasham Joosub (subsequently spelled Yusuf) however, was more interested in intellectual pursuits and started a bookshop. In 1865, Joseph Augustus Shepherd, a Scotsman, who had been Manager of the Bombay Coast and River Steam Navigation Company that had been liquidated in 1863, approached Hasham with a proposition to initiate a ferry service in Bombay harbour. Perhaps because of his brother's involvement and fame in shipping, Hasham agreed and, along with Shepherd, formed what was subsequently named as the second Bombay Steam Navigation Company (BSN) with the purchase of *SS Lady Nyasa* which had belonged to the famous African explorer, Dr. David Livingstone. A year earlier, this vessel had been purchased by the Bhavnagar Durbar and was now up for sale in Bombay harbour. Shepherd later became the proprietor of J.N. Shepherd and Company, which subsequently became the managing agents of the BSN.

Hasham was not just an ordinary shipowner content to sit on the shore. An evocative description of him is given by T.S. Sanjeeva Rao in the January 1979 issue of *Indian Shipping & Shipbuilding*, some extracts of which are reproduced below:

> On the rocky coast skirting the Dharamtar Creek, 32 km. from Bombay, there is a small white tomb, which is frequently visited by fishermen and sailors living nearby. If you ask them about the tomb, they will say it is of the Bahadur Sailor Sahib, a brave young seaman of Bombay, who lost his life in the creek. They may tell you no more, for it is over a hundred years since the young man died and the memory of his exploits, legendary at one time, has gradually faded. Few remember that the young man was not only one of the early builders of the Konkan ferry services but also a daring sailor who lost his life while charting the Dharamtar Creek which had been unexplored till then.
>
> The young man was Haji Hasham Yusuf, the founder of the second Bombay Steam Navigation Company, and the brother of the better-known Bombay shipowner, Haji Cassum.
>
> Hasham did not live long enough to see the growth of the company he founded. It had been proposed to extend the harbour services of the new Bombay Steam Navigation Company to the higher reaches of the Dharamtar Creek, above Nigde village. Reports said that there were hidden rocks lying within the bend of the creek and it was decided to explore this region. No charting had been done in this area till then. Hasham took up the task and dived into the creek to fathom the depth at the place

Left: Haji Hashan Joosub (Yusuf)

Right: Haji Cassum Joosub (also known as Agboatwala)

> where the rocks were supposed to lie. What happened exactly is not known, but Hasham did not come up; three days later his body was found in the creek. An adventurous spirit had found its home in the waters it loved.
>
> Hasham, the brave sailor ancestor of the family, has not been forgotten. To his fond memory have been erected ... a beautiful tank at Nhava for the use of the island's inhabitants. Looking at the limpid waters of this tank, one remembers again the gallant sailor who over a hundred years ago gave his life to the cause of Indian shipping.

The article contains an error; Haji Hasham was a middle-aged man when he made the fatal dive on 25th September 1868; legend has it that he hit his head on the submerged rocks. The water reservoir, 200 feet square in area (more than 3 ½ acres), was built in 1917 by his grandson, Sir Mohamed Yusuf, at a cost of Rs. 5.80 lakhs, a large sum of money in those days. More than 90 years later, it still survives, hauntingly beautiful, adding a touch of romance, an evocative memorial to the rare combination of booklover and dashing seaman, who died a true sailor's death.

At the time of Hasham's death, his eldest son Ismail was a minor, and Hasham's brother Cassum, known as Haji Cassum Agboatwala, managed the affairs of the BSN. In due course, when Ismail became an adult, he took over the company's management and is said to have "ably carried on" Hasham's tradition. In 1898, after the retirement of Shepherd, the company became, as claimed by the Yusuf family, the first Indian-owned shipping company on the west coast of India. One of its employees, Mohamed Amir Miya of Surat, had the distinction of being the first Indian Master to be granted the Indian Coastal Trade Certificate issued by the Board of Trade. His was Certificate Number 1.

According to Rashid Yusuf, scion of the Yusuf family, the shipping enterprise went through many ups and downs partly, if not mainly, caused by unfair competitive tactics employed by the famous British India Steam Navigation Company Ltd. (B.I. Company) which, by 1914, was the world's largest shipping company. A brief mention of the B.I. Company is necessary here. By 1914, after it had merged with the world-famous Peninsular and Oriental Steam Navigation Company (P&O) in 1913, it became the world's largest shipping company. Its story makes fascinating reading, while its actions to smother competition, especially Indian competition, have been glossed over by its historians and make depressing reading. Today, the methods used by them would be frowned upon, if not termed illegal.

Ismail Yusuf decided to retire and in 1906 converted his company into a limited company. Not wanting his son to enter shipping, and wishing to invest in land, he sold three-quarters of the shares to Killick Nixon and Company, a well-known British firm of Bombay, who became the managing agents. He however retained a quarter of the shares in the company, along with a seat on the board.

The BSN Company plied to a number of places on the Konkan coast and it is claimed that they were the first to open up the area to steam navigation. An advertisement issued around 1937 by Killick Nixon tantalises one with evocative visions of the Konkan Coast:

> The steamers of the BSN CO. LTD., which ply along the West Coast of India, offer a very attractive sea holiday to persons who have only a limited time at their disposal.
>
> Between Bombay and Goa there are nearly a dozen places such as Rewdanda, Janjira, Harnai, Dabhol, Jaygad, Ratnagiri, Viziadrug, Dewgad, Malwan and Vengurla where one can spend a short holiday amidst scenery not met with elsewhere in India.
>
> Further south are Karwar, Kumta, Honawar, Bhatkal, Malpe and Mangalore, each noted for its enjoyable climate and attractive scenery. The famous Gersoppa Falls can be visited within the short space of a day from Kumta. The return trip from Bombay takes barely a week.
>
> The Calicut Extension brings within easy reach of passengers the Malabar Coast reputed for the luxuriance of its palm trees

> and the enchanting scenery of the backwaters. This is also the cheapest means of communication to Ootacamund and other famous hill stations of the South which are now increasingly patronized by the people of this Presidency.
>
> The frequency and regularity of the passenger service is said to have earned for the company the title of the "P & O of the Western Coast". It was claimed in the 1930s that because of this, a number of new ports were opened, and that the present prosperity of the Konkan is due to their enterprise.

Sadly no passenger ships ply on the west coast today and people can no longer enjoy the best way to approach these beautiful, historical places. A third Bombay Steam Navigation Company is sorely needed. Even if today's "yuppies" may not be interested, there are many others who are, and who will patronise such a service.

Haji Ismail Yusuf concentrated on land and property and he, and later his family, were among the largest landlords in Bombay, owning thousands of acres with extensive landholdings in Borla in Salsette; Powai; Kanjur in Thane district; Nhava and Gauhan in Panvel district; along with many buildings in south Bombay and in the centre of the city such as at Flora Fountain (Hutatma Chowk). Subsequently, after Independence, these lands were either encroached upon, or taken over under the Land Ceiling Act, or acquired for public purposes, including for IIT Powai, etc. If these lands had even been left partially unbuilt, they would have provided huge green lungs for Bombay!

Haji Ismail Yusuf was the head of the Sunni Muslim community in Bombay and contributed generously to a number of charities throughout the Bombay Presidency. He gave a large donation for a public hall and also established a free orphanage. He died on 20th September 1912. His only son, Mohamed Yusuf, continued the charitable tradition. In 1914, he sold his one-fourth share in the Bombay Steam Navigation Company Ltd. and gave the entire proceeds to the Governor of Bombay for the establishment of the Ismail Yusuf College at Andheri. This was the first college in the suburbs and, though being the first Muslim college in Western India, it catered to all classes, castes and creeds. He also established a marine college (more of which later) and a sanatorium at Worli Point in memory of his son Hasham who had died at a young age. Mohamed Yusuf was knighted in 1915, though in 1937, responding to the nationalist movement, he sought to renounce his knighthood.

Left: Sir Mohamed Yusuf

Lady Khatun Marium Yusuf

History

Records on this subject are not very precise, but it appears that in 1868, the BSN ships were being attended to on Nhava. In 1883, Ismail Yusuf obtained Nhava Island, together with lands on the mainland, on a 999-year lease from the then British-controlled government. As to how this happened, one account was given by Heta Pandit, writer and activist, who wrote in *the India Magazine* of February 1984, "At a nominal 'quit rent' of Rs.1,600, the entire island comprising two square kilometres of marshy land were leased to Yusuf for development in the way he thought best. At that time this was not an extraordinary proposition. Yusuf mobilised all available resources to transfigure the island into a unique combination of forested woods and rice plantations."

Heta Pandit added that "Yusuf's efforts were not confined to the island alone. With the help of two earthen dams, 1,400 acres of marshy swamp was converted into prime agricultural land. This land was cultivated by local inhabitants and half the produce from the paddy fields was given to the Yusuf family. In return, the two dams were maintained regularly...free medical benefits, pensions for the aged and the disabled in the village, and a home for widows of seamen who died in service, were some of the perquisites offered to the residents of Nhava."

Nhava's beauty has been admired by many over the decades. On Christmas day of 1931, the Chief of Ichalkaranji visited Nhava, and was so delighted with all that he saw that he felt that a brief illustrated account needed to be printed. He therefore asked G.C. Bhate, former Principal of Willingdon College at Sangli, who had also visited Nhava, to write a brief account. Bhate's first impressions were that "the distant view of Nhava is simply charming.... All the while admiring the beautiful panorama presented by the pretty island ..." There was also the mansion, almost a palace, of noble proportions called Samander Mahal (Sea Palace), built by Ismail Yusuf's son, Mohamed Yusuf. This was described by Bhate as the "Castle-like palace of the Ameersaheb". In the palace "was the Divan Khana or Durbar Hall of the Ameersaheb. Here were kept the seignoral symbols of the family. This is indeed an artistic and richly painted hall of fine proportions."

Every one of the more than one hundred visitors I have taken to Nhava and everything I have heard from visitors taken by others, is that they all came back with happy memories. Leo D'Costa, an architect and classmate of Rashid Yusuf at the Sir J.J. College of Architecture, described his first visit in 1953, writing in the *Centenary Souvenir of T S Rahaman*:

> Rashid invited a few of his school friends and myself for a mid-term break to Nhava; the journey (trip) was made by launch from Mazgaon pier and had to be timed to catch the high tide, as the landing at Nhava had to be made on the sea wall in front of the Anchorage Bungalow which was only possible at high tide. The contrast to Bombay was immediately noticeable, no noise, no pollution, peace, and tranquillity. As soon as we had settled in we decided to explore the undeveloped part of the Island facing Elephanta, now occupied by the ONGC, which was overgrown with trees and scrub; armed with shotguns, needless to say we bagged nothing, but adventure and excitement was provided by an encounter with some venomous snakes which we luckily avoided.
>
> The Nhava of those days was considerably less developed, the older buildings having been in existence for quite some time included the Samander Mahal, Marine Museum, Anchorage Bungalow, the hospital and some staff and trainees' accommodation, and the maritime training facilities.
>
> There were no motor vehicles on the campus. The ambulance complete with the customary red cross was a manually operated rickshaw, now housed in the hospital entrance as a relic of those days. As would be expected for such a remote location, services and facilities were a bit scarce compared to what a city-dweller might expect! The electric supply was a bit erratic with the single cylinder diesel generator supplying limited electricity from 6 p.m. to 10 p.m. every night and on request extending the period of lighting for special occasions.

Wrote Dr. Frans de Zwart, an Australian friend of Rashid Yusuf, who visited Nhava in 1977: "When I first visited Nhava in 1977, it did not look 'inspiring' at the time, not well maintained: old timber beams were lying around and some buildings were in disrepair; there was a lot of rubbish as well. The general, somewhat uninviting impression was further dampened because the white-painted, cement-rendered walls had been blackened by the algae which accumulated during the wet season. Despite this the former glory of the place was obvious, partially hidden and yet enhanced by the lush tropical vegetation."

This feeling of dismay was perfectly understandable from an Australian with expectations of a far higher standard of living. But 33 years later, in the *Centenary Souvenir*, Dr. de Zwart wrote: "Now at the Centenary, after having personally witnessed the progress over 33 years, I am truly amazed at how much has been achieved by so few. The buildings are painted, the roads clean, the trees and gardens tastefully maintained. The accommodation of the staff and trainees is comfortable, a superb library has been built. Sporting facilities include a full-size football ground, an athletic track and volleyball courts. Quality food is provided by the students of the Catering School, the first teachers have completed a full circle, i.e., started at Campus in Grade I and have now returned as teachers. An authentic ship's mast and ship's bridge, obtained from the nearby ship demolition yards, grace Nhava, *T. S. Rahaman* is on the international radar screen!"

In spite of all the destruction in the 1970s and thereafter, Nhava is still very beautiful. More than 50 years after Bhate, Heta Pandit wrote:

> There was a light drizzle as we jolted down the kuchcha road to Nhava. The vast expanse of the green and blue panorama was soon transformed into the murky grey and brown of a monsoon haze. Mudskippers on the glistening shores brought the static mangroves to life as we reached the village, two-and-a-half hour's drive away from the city of Bombay.
>
> The drizzle stopped as suddenly as it had begun. The fresh sea breeze blew the remnants of the monsoon clouds away as bright sunshine sparkled on soft feather-down grass. And the Arabian Sea, so still, allowed but a solitary dhow to knife through it.
>
> A pair of chestnut-headed bee-eaters were preening themselves, perched on the pathetic lopped-off branch of a mango tree. From the gardens of the training ship *Rahaman*, India's oldest nautical training establishment, white-breasted waterhens attracted our attention with loud creaking and clicking calls and almost immediately stopped feeding on the vegetation

Nhava Island as viewed from the sea (approaching the sea wall)

in the open and sought cover in the tall monsoon pasturage.

Scanty mangroves on the east side of the road prompted us to explore possibilities of regenerating them artificially. Their thinning down was obviously due to unnatural conditions and their reintroduction would, perhaps, offer a more hospitable habitat to winter migrants. Inland, century-old mango trees stood amidst stalwart coconut palms, and the spellbinding green of these ancient trees triggered an air of expectancy – a hunch that they were hiding history.

Nhava Island was known to sailors and others as Hog Island but no one knows how it got this name. Rear Admiral Sridharan wrote that it was "so named because of its hog-back hill feature". Another reason for the name was given by N. Lishman, reproduced in Ruttonjee Ardeshir Wadia's book on the *Wadia Master Builders*. He writes:

> How the Hog Island came to be possessed of such an extraordinary name is a question that puzzles many. There are no hogs on the 'Island' – nor is there anything to show that at any time was the island populated by swine. The derivation was, therefore, possibly taken from the old custom of hogging or cleaning a vessel with hog bristle brushes: although the term 'hogging' is generally meant to describe what happens to a vessel when it runs ashore and is supported at the centre only, the ends falling, causing the keel to break, 'thus hogging the vessel'. The origin of the name will in all probability remain a mystery.

The Bombay Sailing Association in their booklet which lists sailing sites in and around Bombay, makes no mention of Nhava's beauties and attractions; their description only says that the Anchorage is exposed to the north-west and can be uncomfortable with a west north-westerly or westerly wind and, further, that in certain conditions of wind and tide, there can be a nasty sea.

I had sailed past Nhava many times while cruising or racing around Elephanta, but it was not till I landed at Nhava that I appreciated its beauty. I was enchanted by its South Seas Island type of loveliness. Since it was just a brief visit, I did not see, till much later, the historic structures which include the palatial mansion, Samander Mahal, the Fatima Banu Hospital and the Marine Museum, which by then were under dire threat. These had, and still retain, an exotic charm. In a complete mistranslation of its name, I used to call Nhava 'a pearl without price'.

Nautical Institute/ Training Ship *Rahaman*

Ismail Yusuf had experienced considerable difficulty in getting suitable recruits from the seamen community for training as deck hands and officers for his ships, since the recruits available from the Konkan and Gujarat coasts were largely illiterate. This led him to establish a Marine School in 1910 at Rashid Mansion at Worli Point in Bombay, with nine orphan boys on its rolls. However, Worli Point was considered unsuitable for sea training due to the presence of rocks close to the shore. After the death of Ismail Yusuf in September 1912, Mohamed Yusuf shifted the Marine School to Nhava. In 1915, Haji Ismail's house on Nhava along with its extensive garden was presented by Mohamed Yusuf to the Marine School and now houses the Marine Museum.

In 1918, about 650 Indian seamen, mates and captains submitted a petition to the Governor of Bombay for the establishment of a full-fledged training college to train Indians in seamanship. This petition was turned down by the Government. Thereafter, pursuant to a Legislative Assembly Resolution moved in January 1922 by Sir P.S. Sivaswamy Aiyar, the Indian Mercantile Marine Committee was formed on 3rd February 1923 to investigate how best to promote an Indian mercantile marine establishment. In April 1923, the Committee visited the Seamen's Training School and Orphanage at Nhava, which by then had 300 trainees. The Government initiated negotiations with Sir Mohamed Yusuf about the conversion of the Nhava School into a full-fledged training establishment, under government auspices. However, negotiations floundered because of the government's insistence that Sir Mohamed Yusuf hand over effective control of the college to the Government's Marine Department, which, not surprisingly, Sir Mohamed Yusuf refused to do.

Thereupon, the petitioners approached Sir Mohamed Yusuf to upgrade the Marine School into a full-fledged maritime training establishment. He readily agreed, and in 1925, renamed it the Marine College. The College was granted affiliation by the Bombay University and classes were conducted up to the matriculation level to enable students to qualify for the Home Trade Certificate of Competency. The College claims to have trained officers for India's mercantile marine, though only for coastal trade, well before the famous Indian Mercantile Marine Training Ship *Dufferin* (the nursery of many of India's top naval and merchant marine officers, which commenced training in 1927).

In 1929, Sir Mohamed Yusuf, along with V.A. Pitale, the principal of the College, visited various training schools in the United Kingdom and Turkey in order to study first-hand the methods of imparting marine training. On his return, he established a trust, known as the Sir Mohamed Yusuf Trust, of which 15 percent was set aside for the charitable institutions on Nhava.

With 375 students on the register of the Marine College, many of them were trained as ratings for the mercantile marine. Subsequently, in order to impart practical sea training, two sail training vessels were also acquired. For those not interested in a sea career, classes were also conducted in crafts such as weaving, tailoring, carpentry, tin smithy and metal work.

The Bombay Steam Navigation Company was also a pioneer in training deck officers and engineers, both for the Home Trade and Foreign Going Certificates. They established two training ships, *Irrawadi* and *Bahaduri*. Deck apprentices were trained on the *Irrawadi* which was employed in the passenger and cargo coastal trade. *Bahaduri* was attached to the shipyard of the company where regular study classes were held to give practical training in the workshop, imparted by former officers of the Royal Indian Navy.

In 1949, the Government of India amended the Indian Shipping Act 1923, and assumed powers to set up training establishments for seamen officers following the recommendation of the Merchant Navy Committee. A scheme for training sailors was brought into force with the setting up of training ships at Calcutta, Vishakhapatnam and Naulakhi in Gujarat. This led to a decade of great uncertainty for *Rahaman* since, being a private charitable institution and not under government auspices, it was denied recognition for training by the Government Seamen's Employment Offices.

After protracted correspondence and the visit of Shipping and Transport Minister S.K. Patil to Nhava, in 1959, the Institute was finally recognised and a special scheme was approved stipulating a Joint Selection Board consisting of an equal number of representatives of the Directorate General of Shipping and the Nautical Institute for registration by the Director of Seamen's Employment. This would enable the trainees to be recruited as deck hands in the merchant navy.

This was a huge step for *Rahaman*.

In 1967, a Government Expert Committee under the Chairmanship of C.P. Srivastava was appointed to go into the question of unemployment among Indian seafarers. The Committee Report recommended that "the Nhava Institute could provide suitable premises for the establishment of a full-fledged Ratings Training establishment under Government auspices."

The Nautical Adviser, Captain M. S. Patel, was deputed to discuss the matter of taking over the Nautical Institute with Abdul Rahaman but like his father, Abdul Rahaman too declined. The Shipping Ministry thereafter decided to commission a floating ship, *Training Ship Rajendra*, at Bombay. This was finally inaugurated in 1972.

In the 1960s, the Nautical Institute, as the Marine College was now known, moved into a portion of Samander Mahal, which, on the death of Sir Mohammed Yusuf in 1965, was presented by his son Abdul Rahaman to the Institute. On the death of Abdul Rahaman in 1968, his son Rashid Yusuf gave the name *Training Ship Rahaman* to the Nautical Institute, by which name it is known till date.

The main building of the Nautical Institute remained in Samander Mahal for over four decades, after which it moved into more modern premises. Samander Mahal, the "Ameersaheb's Sea Palace", now houses a flourishing school of over 800 students – children of the staff and surrounding villages – from the primary level to the 12th standard.

A low point of the Institute was in 1968, when because of poor prospects of employment, the Directorate-General of Shipping restricted the training at *Rahaman* to 30 sailors a year.

The Hydraulic Lift

An interesting historical feature on Nhava was the remains of a 19th century hydraulic lift.

According to N. Lishman, at that time "the immense machine was looked upon as the most gigantic affair of the kind that had ever been erected and even now there are not to be found in the world many lifts so powerful" and that "after a heavy and careful test...The lift being

Hydraulic Lift, 1872 (Drawing courtesy Greenwich Maritime Museum, U.K.)

pronounced a success was considered worthy to take its place amongst the wonders of the world and bring the number up to ten."

The Diamond Jubilee Booklet brought out by the Nautical Institute in 1970 states:

> In the year 1864 the British Government acquired lands on the north-western tip of Nhava for the purpose of a hydraulic lift in anticipation of the increase of shipping expected by the opening of the Suez Canal. In 1869 when the Canal was finally opened for traffic, Bombay was immediately declared as the port of disembarkation for all troopships from England to India. Hence, the proposed dock scheme was handed over to the then Bombay Marines and on 16th September 1872, the Governor of Bombay declared open the hydraulic lift at Hog Island as a dry dock for troopships from England. This lift was a unique feat of engineering skill and was claimed to be capable of raising a 25,000-ton vessel high and dry, without the slightest danger, no mean achievement in those days. Towards the end of 1872 the governor and a large party of invitees were taken in a large vessel to see the working of the wonder lift. However, as ill luck would have it, the vessel instead of being lifted clear off the water, nearly went down to the bottom, together with the Governor and his distinguished guests. From that day onwards the lift was looked upon with suspicion, and finally abandoned by the government. The remains of the lift can be seen even today, near the landing jetty.

Sadly, the Diamond Jubilee Booklet became out of date with-

> in less than a decade; one of the first things destroyed by ONGC on Nhava through land reclamation was the remains of this historic relic. Till then, the hill together with the old stone jetty adjacent to the site of the hydraulic lift, was a lovely tranquil piece of rural Maharashtra with an exquisite sea frontage. Ironically, the board giving the statistics of the lift was returned to Rashid Yusuf.

Threats

The socialist policies followed after Independence had a major impact. Heta Pandit wrote in *the India Magazine*:

> After Independence, when the Indian Government passed the Tiller's Act in 1956, each farming family received sole property rights over the patch of land they tilled. The Yusuf family were deprived of their share of the rice harvest, and consequently ceased to maintain the dams. The farmers failed to organise themselves into cooperatives and both government and the tillers neglected the periodic maintenance that was required. Finally both the dams were breached and rich agricultural land went back to salt. Ironically, the government has now passed the Khajan Lands Act, by which fifty percent of the revenue derived from agricultural produce of reclaimed land is retained by the government. A case of the bullock-cart wheel hobbling to full circle!
>
> In this case, however, the government has so far failed to replace the old dam constructions and the ultimate losers are the two thousand tillers of Nhava who had lived for over twelve decades in united harmony with their environment.

An unexpected benefit of the loss of the agricultural lands was the creation of several hundred acres of mangroves.

Ismail Yusuf had made a wonderful decision when he chose Nhava. This idyllic spot and other beautiful areas across the harbour, have for long attracted covetous eyes with plans, which have destroyed much of their beauty and charm. It is ironical that Nhava's assets, including the depth of its available water, has made it especially vulnerable.

In 1946, the Government of India constituted a committee, with Admiral Sir John Grace as Chairman, to look into various issues concerning the Naval Dockyard in Bombay. The Committee found that the present Bombay site of the naval dockyard was unsuitable for several

Vice Admiral Manohar Awati visiting the Marine Museum, Nhava

reasons. The first was that because it was "closed in by the city, development or expansion" was "out of the question."

The second reason was that the expansion southwards of the commercial dock was prevented by the Naval Dockyard. Thirdly, the expansion of Bombay together with the increased cost of living "close to the dockyard area has forced the work-people to move further and further away from the dockyard and transport is not adequate at the present time". Fourthly, the present site was "very valuable by virtue of its position in the city of Bombay and should earn a fair amount annually if offered to commercial purposes". Fifthly, the construction of Ballard Pier had appreciably increased the siltation rate inside the dockyard breakwater, making it a major problem.

The Committee observed that "Bombay is an unsuitable base from which to carry out an intensive training programme. Experience has shown the impossibility of keeping ships divorced from dockyard and depot, and the readily accessible distractions of a large city would prevent proper concentration on training and competitive sport. Esprit de corps could never be adequately fostered under such conditions. Bombay can therefore be eliminated as a squadron training base, together with Madras, where, as has already been decided, no naval organisation will be maintained." These points are all as true today as they were six decades ago.

The Committee examined various options including that of a completely new location for the dockyard. The Committee was not able to carry out a thorough exploration of the Indian coast line. However, the members received advice from several Royal Indian Navy officers about the disadvantages of west coast ports due to silting and of east coast ports due to sand movements. (This last seems odd since a large number of ports are now being built on both the coasts.) The general view, which was the conventional one, was that Bombay harbour would have the most advantages and the least disadvantages.

The Committee recommended that a new dockyard be built on a site between Nhava Island and Sheva, which are both eastwards of Elephanta Island. (This would be roughly where the Jawaharlal Nehru Port – earlier called Nhava Sheva Port – was later built in the 1980s.) The serviceable machinery was to be transferred there within five to seven years. The reasons given were the available depth of water near Elephanta, the fact that the area is sheltered by Elephanta Island and, being up harbour, the incoming swell of the sea during the worst periods of the south-west monsoon would be appreciably reduced. A village for housing the work force with schools, hospitals, shopping centre, etc. was proposed on Nhava, with officers' residences being located on Sheva, where high ground overlooking the proposed site was available. Fuel storage sites were also available on Sheva. Sacrilegiously, the Committee proposed that the Armament Depot be located on Elephanta Island (now a World Heritage Site), where the sixth-century Elephanta caves are situated. The members did not seem to have even thought about the impact this would have on the caves, especially if there was a disaster.

The proposed shift to Nhava Sheva was not accepted by the Government. This was not because of environmental concerns for Nhava, Sheva or Elephanta but for several other reasons, including the lack of facilities such as electric power, fresh water, and road and communication facilities. Above all was the prohibitive cost of building a new dockyard afresh, along with dislocation to India's premier naval yard, which was a strategic risk.

In 1948, in consultation with the British Admiralty, the Government of India appointed the internationally renowned technical consulting engineering firm of Sir Alexander Gibbs and Partners of the United Kingdom. The consultants gave their final report in May 1950 in which they recommended firstly, that the existing land area of 39 acres of the Dockyard be increased to 120 acres by reclamation (mainly close to the Gateway of India), with offices, workshops, victualling stores and other

T.S.Rahaman College of Advanced Maritime Studies & Research

buildings being built on the reclaimed area. In addition, there should be a 3,200-foot-long breakwater to form a tidal basin which would increase the protected water area from 24 acres to 150 acres.

The idea of a shift to Nhava Sheva was revived by Vice Admiral Daya Shankar, one of the earliest Indians to join the navy's engineering branch as an officer. In his *Memoirs and Memories*, he wrote about the period between 1952 and 1954 when he was industrial manager of the Naval Dockyard and concerned about its future, and specifically its expansion plans:

> The Consultants had left a chart of Bombay harbour in my office and my attention was drawn to the Sheva-Nhava creek, with its deep water, hills protecting the area and a large tract of open land beside the creek. The Naval Armament Depot at Karanja was not far and there was space available for a Naval Store Depot and a Spare Parts Centre. But there was no link with the city.
>
> I thought over the idea for several days and formed the idea that we could, without disturbing current activities in the **Naval Dockyard, set about planning from scratch a newer and more orderly layout for Sheva-Nhava**, to be built stage by stage, so that the present Yard would be used for normal docking, but the new Yard would undertake major refits and/or re-equipment. There was enough space for housing as well, both

for Dockyard and other staff. The main problem was transport. While in good weather fast craft could be used, there would be problems during the monsoon.

After a few days, I consulted Mr. Parmanandhan, giving him a brief resume of my thoughts. While he agreed that there were many advantages, the proposal would meet stiff resistance, quite apart from the cost factor. The men would feel isolated from their relatives in the suburbs of Bombay, even if a rail link was built. Then there was the matter of facilities for education and health care.

Perhaps I had been subconsciously influenced by my vision of a Karwar-like base. So, while I agreed with what Mr. Parmanandhan had said, I tried out the idea on the Captain Superintendent. He felt the area was too remote, with lack of communication, and stressed that opposition would be strong. He pointed out that in the UK, all three major dockyards were in large cities: Portsmouth, Chatham and Devonport. I realised that it was not worth spending more time on the idea, even though in the long term it was a sound suggestion.

Less than fifteen years later, yet another plan to take over Nhava surfaced. On 6th June 1966, B. Sheshagiri Rao, writing in *The Evening News of India*, reported (emphasis added):

> The BPT which has been considering the establishment of a satellite or an adjunct to the exisitng port at Nhava Sheva or Hog Island, as it is also called, eight miles north of the harbour, has now definitely decided on this step.
>
> "The Government of India too has favoured the choice of the site as the most suitable for a variety of reasons. The natural deep waters around Nhava Sheva, its accessibility to the hinterland, the virgin land in the mainland to which the Hog Island could be easily linked, are among the favourable factors.

A very serious concrete threat, the most persistent and most potent of all, then and later, was from CIDCO, the planning and development authority of New Bombay, the new city being developed across the harbour from Bombay. As part of their project, CIDCO planned to acquire the whole of Nhava. A set of acquisition notices dated 13th September 1970 were received in November 1970.

Various pleas were made, right from 1971, including by Sheshagiri Rao in the columns of the *Evening News*, to leave out at least the Nautical Institute premises from the acquisition. In his above-mentioned article, which is appropriately entitled "Nhava Institute needs all help"

The George Campbell Library on the Nhava Campus

he wrote that he was in favour of both the New Bombay project and the Nhava Sheva Port. However, he felt that "the central core of the Sir Mohamed Yusuf Charitable Institute's campus at Nhava embracing within its fold the training institute, the orphanage, a museum, the trust offices, groves of trees, strips of green, a full-fledged garden and a swimming pool, should be left undisturbed". He added that the Institute "set in sylvan surroundings with an idyllic atmosphere and far from the madding crowds" had been "rendering yeoman service to society for over 60 years".

Sheshagiri Rao returned to the charge seven weeks later in another article entitled "Spare the Nhava Campus". He wrote that he was "perturbed by the news that the Maharashtra Government, after all" had decided to acquire the Nhava campus. He added that "the campus provides all amenities a township is entitled to. Nhava is a beautiful place and the campus is situated on a lovely spot, with a pleasant climate. An enchanting island, it stands as a sentinel to Bombay harbour."

He went on to say:

> The Central Government, shipping authorities, the shipping industry as a whole and seamen's organisations have all expressed themselves in favour of retaining the campus.
>
> The nautical institute has the unique distinction of not only being the first and only one of its type in India, but also the first to have trained Indians as ship masters.

> It is pertinent to note that even today it is the only private school recognised by the Directorate-General of Shipping in the entire country and the only centre for pre-sea training of seamen in Maharashtra. On the west coast, there is only another institution of its kind at Navalakhi, in Saurashtra, which is run by the Union Government.
>
> The Nhava institute was founded for the benefit of poor and orphan boys of the seafaring community of Western India by that great nationalist, the late Sir Mohamed Yusuf, a pioneer in Indian shipping. The entire island was purchased by the Yusuf family late in the 19th century.

At that time, I had nothing to do with Nhava but when I came across these articles, and the probability that a beautiful heritage site could be destroyed, I felt a sense of helplessness and sadness.

Rashid Yusuf wrote later that in May 1971 they had received a notice under Section 6 of the Land Acquisition Act whereby the entire island was notified for acquisition for a public purpose. On 10th August 1971, a petition was addressed to Chief Minister V.P. Naik appealing to him to release the land occupied by the various charitable institutions. This petition had been supported by various officials and non-officials along with many villagers. In September 1971, at the Nagpur Session of the Legislative Assembly, B.K. Boman Behram and G.N. Banatwalla raised the subject, at which point the Chief Minister undertook to review the situation after CIDCO's Development Plan (Master Plan) for New Bombay was ready.

The position is best understood from a press report in *The Evening News* of 4th May 1973 which said:

> Rashid is an architect and is busy trying to save the nautical institute on Nhava Island. The islet, strangely enough, comes under New Bombay. A grandiose scheme to have a bridge connecting Sewri with Elephanta and then on to Nhava is on the anvil. It will take another 50 years for a plan of this dimension to materialise.
>
> Meanwhile, some stupid government land-grabbers have not spared the charitable institute. Is there anything wrong in allowing a hallowed institution to remain in New Bombay? Or is the 'beauty' of New Bombay going to be spoilt if the quaint, old-time structures housing the Institute, continue to remain?
>
> The trouble with the land requisition order today is (that) it is still largely amorphous and interpreted from Sachivalaya more in political than in judicial terms.

Dr. Leo Barnes Pre-sea Academy, Nhava Campus

> What intrigued this writer when he talked to Rashid was his remarkable social and mental poise, indifferent to the social ruffians around him.

It would have been far better if Rashid Yusuf had lost his poise and reacted strongly against the social ruffians.

The Draft Development Plan (which was published in October 1973) reserved the lands of the charitable institutions and the village as a "Recreational Park". Rashid Yusuf protested, describing this proposal as being nothing short of sacrilege since the institutions were serving a much better and higher public purpose, and their closure would be a tremendous loss to the entire seamen community of Western India. He recalls that he met at least three CIDCO Managing Directors – J.B. D'Souza, (one of the founders of New Bombay, who was later to become Chief Secretary), P. G. Salvi and B.C. Cariappa (later to become Bombay Port Trust Chairman and play another major part in the Nhava Sheva story).

In response to the Draft Development Plan, Rashid Yusuf filed his objections and, as the law requires, was called for a hearing on 23rd July 1974. He wrote that at that hearing, J.B. D'Souza told him that the Institute's objections would be considered sympathetically. However in June 1976 Rashid Yusuf got a shock when he was suddenly informed by P.G. Salvi, J.B. D'Souza's successor, that a decision had finally been taken to acquire the entire land and that the Institute would have to shift since ONGC needed the land on a priority basis for setting up a supply base for their offshore oil and gas fields at Bombay High. B.C.

Firefighting mockup at the firefighting Complex on the Campus at Nhava

Cariappa, who replaced Salvi, confirmed that there was no possibility of the Institute remaining on Nhava Island, and that it would be in their own interest to select an alternative site.

Rashid Yusuf wrote that petitions to the Maharashtra Chief Minister and various authorities, together with numerous visits to the State Government officers met with "sullen hostility". He recalls that B.C. Cariappa treated him very roughly and gave him a lecture to the effect that he should be proud to surrender the land free of cost since paramount national interests were involved. Rashid Yusuf could not ask Cariappa whether the latter had ever surrendered anything free of cost. Cariappa went on to say that, in any case, there was no record whatsoever of the existence of the Nautical Institute on their plans. Reportedly, at that time, CIDCO was using survey maps of the 1870s. The destruction of fine old heritage buildings, of dense wooded areas and sites of great beauty were not even discussed.

All pleas were ignored, and a series of acquisition notices for the entire island, including the entire campus, were received right up to December 1978, and the bulk of the island was acquired.

Nhava was not the only green area across the harbour. There was the sandy Nagaon beach at Karanja and other areas in Uran which, at that time, I knew even better than Nhava. As part of the IIT civil engineering course, at the end of our third year, six weeks had to be spent on practical training. Being very fond of the sea, I approached Maneck Hiranandani, an old family friend whom I had known since childhood.

Captain O.J. D'Souza Survival and Safety Centre on the Nhava Campus

He arranged a training assignment for me in May and June 1962 with Hochtief Modern, the Indian affiliate of Hochtief of Germany, who were then building the naval base at Karanja in Uran. It was a long daily commute from home, with the best part being the hour-long motor-launch ride from Bhau Cha Dhaka (New Ferry Wharf) to Mora Pier and the return journey, especially when the sea started getting fresh with the approach of the monsoons. From Mora Pier, it was a 45-minute walk through an attractive semi-rural area to the construction site. I enjoyed this walk, though the return walk could sometimes be a trudge. I saw the Military Engineering Service (MES) in operation at first hand.

My eyes were opened to the other side of the harbour, especially to Mora Pier, and its pleasant surroundings. In subsequent years, I used to take the ferry to Mora Pier, then a horse-drawn tonga to the quaint town of Uran with its heritage buildings, and the then lovely areas around it. I used to hike in the surrounding areas, which were then still green. I had also sailed several times both to Mora Pier and to Nagaon Beach, which is south of the naval base. Along with other sailors, I had camped overnight on Nagaon beach, which, appropriately, was known to sailors as 'Sandy Cove'. Later, I saw the lovely Bhiwandiwalla Gardens. From Bhau Cha Dhaka, there was also another ferry to Rewas in Alibag taluka where I occasionally used to go for solitary walks. We tried very hard for many years to protect these areas.

ONGC

HOW ONGC GOT ONTO NHAVA was best explained in Debjani Sinha's article entitled 'The battle for Nhava' in the issue of *Business India* dated 26th November 1979. The article said:

The history of ONGC's acquisition of 50 hectares which it now occupies on the offshore island of Nhava is shrouded in mystery.

According to spokesmen of the environmental groups, initially the commission had planned to build an integrated repair and maintenance-cum-supply base and to locate its administrative complex with provision for 350 personnel at Nhava. In pursuance of these plans the commission had requested the state administration to make the entire island, except the 152 hectares which were already earmarked for the Bombay Port Trust for the development of its satellite port Nhava Sheva, available to it for setting up a supply and maintenance base.

Though this request flew directly in the face of the City and Industrial Development Corporation (CIDCO) resolution made in 1970 to preserve the entire northern half of the island as a 'recreational green belt area', which received the state government's official approval in May 1976, during the Emergency when the star of N.B. Prasad, chairman of the commission, was riding high, the CIDCO resolution was superseded and with the stroke of a pen, the Maharashtra government permitted the commission to grab a major portion of the island without any scientific assessment of its land requirements.

Spanish Dagger, one of the rare plant species that grows on Nhava

Initially, ONGC had planned to acquire 700 acres, including the entire island, for locating a supply base for their Bombay High Offshore Project along with a crude oil and natural gas terminal, including a processing unit and a tank farm. Many facilities were sought to be provided, including a helicopter base, an airstrip, a railway siding, a pipe-coating plant, warehouses, an administrative complex and a full-fledged housing colony of 3,500 building units, comprising houses, shops, offices, hospitals, etc. for a population of 15,000.

In July 1976, ONGC commissioned Peter Fraenkel & Partners of London and Glasgow to prepare a master plan for the Nhava Base. The consultants' report of January 1977 discussed a whole range of features such as the wind conditions, rainfall, temperature, visibility, possibility of cyclonic storms, wave characteristics, currents, hydrography, tides, topography of Nhava, details of the vegetation, etc. The plan involved obtaining 32 hectares of flat land by blasting, excavating, quarrying, flattening, terracing and levelling the hills. In addition, 23 hectares were to be reclaimed in the first phase, with another 15 hectares being reclaimed subsequently. The consultants said that in the event that the development proceeded, the village would have to be removed, with the villagers having to be resettled on the mainland, and that CIDCO would need one year to organise the evacuation. There was only one sentence which mentioned the existence of the Nautical Institute and the Marine Museum, but no mention of the fact that these institutions would also be severely affected, if not displaced. As Yusuf recalls, this was despite the fact that he had met Peter Fraenkel himself and shown him around the Institute. The latter had apparently said that he was very impressed and would do what he could to see that the Institute was not dislocated. However, there was no mention of this in the consultants' report.

The site of the oil and gas terminal was moved to Nagaon in Uran, not for environmental reasons, but because the delays involved in the reclamation and site preparation at Nhava were deemed unacceptable and the extensive quarrying required would make the whole operation uneconomic. The fact that **two** beautiful, environmentally sensitive waterfront areas would now be despoiled instead of one did not cross anyone's mind. Similarly, the helicopter base site was moved away from the island, not for environmental reasons, but because large, unobstructed level areas were required, as the site recommended by the consultants was a low-lying area, east of Nhava Island. Much later, the housing colony was shifted away to Panvel, either because of our strong opposition backed by the Maharashtra Government and the Protection Committee constituted by them, or for other reasons. The second tranche of reclamation of 15 hectares, which would have added greatly to the environmental damage, was also dropped, again not for environmental reasons, but because of our furious opposition which led to Prime Minister Indira Gandhi's directive of 1980.

For many years, Rashid Yusuf ran helter-skelter trying to get an alternative site for the Institute. That a nautical training institute needed to be on the waterfront did not seem to be understood by CIDCO. Yusuf's team studied the entire harbour area to find a location which had sufficient depth of water at all states of the tide and concluded that the only suitable site was the twin islands in front of the Panvel Creek Bridge. The authorities rejected this site outright saying that it had been reserved for a "recreational area". Various alternative sites were offered to the Institute, but all turned out to be unsuitable. Yusuf again asked for the islands in front of the Panvel Creek Bridge but was told that these were now required for a railway bridge. In mid-1977, he was offered a site two kilometres away from Nhava Island, but this site was only one kilometre away from the low tide line, in addition to which it was fronted by dense mangroves. Unless CIDCO were prepared to build a long pier, the site was completely unsuitable.

In 1977, as a grim forerunner of what was to follow, one of the dams (*bunds*) was used by CIDCO to build a road connecting the island to the mainland. This was done to make it possible to set up the ONGC base. Thereafter, Yusuf received a notice dated 7th June 1977, saying that the Institute's land would be taken over on 15th June for laying a road which would cut through the heart of the campus. He objected strongly and the land acquisition was temporarily held up. He made a desperate plea that the road be realigned, especially since he had been assured by CIDCO that the Institute would not be disturbed for a year. At a meeting held on 29th September 1977, under the chairmanship of the Law and Judiciary Minister Hussein Dalwai, it was agreed that the road alignment would be shifted. Dalwai also suggested a joint inspection of alternative sites for the campus, which was agreed to by Chief Secretary S.V. Bhave. One of those who attended the meeting was Deputy Secretary Shankar Menon who was to play a key role 20 months later. What was astonishing was that, then and later, till the arrival of the Bombay Environmental Action Group (BEAG) on the scene, there was no mention of preserving the Nautical Institute because of its inherent beauty, environment or heritage on the existing site.

The position worsened with the physical arrival on the scene of ONGC. As a first step, in July 1977, about 54 hectares of land was handed

View from the northern side of Nhava overlooking the mangroves

over to them, with other lands, including 14 hectares of mangroves, scheduled for being handed over thereafter. In April 1978, the *Evening News of India* reported that "most of the picturesque island" had been taken over by ONGC; though the campus itself had been left out for the moment, ONGC was now reported to be "keen" on taking it over, for constructing residential quarters for their staff. The newspaper commented that some alternative plot could surely have been found for the housing colony with the Institute being left undisturbed.

Within the land handed over to ONGC were five charming, quaint, pre-1930 period cottages which had originally formed the Arogya Bhavan (sanatorium) for TB patients and others who needed a change of air. After the CIDCO threat and the suspension of *machhwa* boat services to the island, the cottages had been let out to others, which helped generate a little portion of the much needed income for the Institute. Though the amount was only Rs. 20,000 to 25,000 per year, the loss of this income after the ONGC takeover had dealt a severe blow to the Institute which therefore found it difficult to maintain its buildings. Yusuf repeatedly requested that these cottages be returned to the Trust, but ONGC categorically refused, saying that they would be demolishing these structures. Mercifully, these heritage buildings with their minarets and other period features, though still with ONGC, have not yet been demolished.

ONGC had planned an alignment for their road which would have passed through the Nautical Institute's main campus and cut through a corner of the Museum. I was told much later that appeals had been made to ONGC to make at least a minor shift in the road alignment to avoid cutting through the Museum. ONGC's answer reportedly had been that they were cutting through only a portion of the Museum, and that as the alignment had been fixed by their foreign consultants, their prior consent would be necessary before any changes could be made. As a civil engineer, I did not believe that any engineer could have made such an absurd statement, but I was assured that that was indeed the case. This was confirmed by a letter of November 1978, which I stumbled across while writing the last draft of the Nhava Sheva chapter for my earlier book *Heritage and Environment: An Indian Diary*.

One would have expected a strong protest from the Ministry of Shipping & Transport and the Directorate- General of Shipping, the regulatory bodies of the Nautical Institute. On 30th March 1978, the Deputy Director-General of Shipping did write to the "Managing Directors ONGC/ CIDCO". The letter said that they were not officially aware of ONGC's proposal to acquire the Institute's lands and buildings. The training given by the Institute had been found to be of a high standard and had been recognised by the Government of India for the purpose of employment of the boys in the Deck and Saloon departments of the Merchant Navy. It was strongly felt that the Institute's premises be excluded from acquisition because of the special requirement for seamen's training, the inability to obtain alternative land with a water-frontage, the fact that the Institute was a charitable body and finally because it was situated on a historical location.

This was a pro forma letter, the type that is generally ignored. In addition there were other flaws: it was sent by a relatively low level officer; it was a combined letter to two institutions; it was addressed to the wrong person since ONGC has no managing director; and, finally, it should have been a semi-official letter from the Director-General of Shipping or the Shipping Secretary to the Petroleum Secretary and the ONGC Chairman. Not surprisingly, this mild protest had no impact, especially since there was no follow-up. Both the Shipping Ministry and the Director-General of Shipping abdicated their responsibilities and did hardly anything to preserve an institution under their administrative charge which they were duty bound to protect. The letter did however serve the purpose of establishing the Institute's credentials and was a useful weapon when we started to drum up support for its preservation.

The inflexibility of the authorities on the question of the Nautical Institute and the road was in sharp contrast to another incident beautifully described by J.B. D'Souza in his autobiography, *No Trumpets or Bugles*. When he was Urban Development Secretary, Chief Minister Vasantrao Naik and Urban Development Minister Govindrao Sarnayak were both pressing for the width of a planned 60-foot wide road in Thana to be reduced to 40 feet so as to avoid a plot which contained a nursing home owned by a close relative of the Chief Minister. This was foiled only after J.B. D'Souza was able to provoke the mayor to threaten to lead a satyagraha opposing the reduction. Sadly, he did not deem the Nautical Institute and its surroundings as being worthy of such action.

ONGC was not the only agency which had its eyes on Nhava – Mazagon Docks Ltd. (MDL), the public sector undertaking which is India's leading warship builder, needed a fabrication yard to build offshore platforms for ONGC; the recently formed Coast Guard wanted to set up a base on Nhava; the Indian Air Force contemplated a base to service their operations in the Bombay region; and Bombay Port Trust (BPT) had earmarked roughly the southern half of the island for their proposed Nhava Sheva Port, which was a sacred cow as far as the Maharashtra Government was concerned. All through, CIDCO behaved not as the statutory planning authority for New Bombay whose job it is to plan a new city to decongest Bombay, but almost like a private developer seeking to maximise financial returns with no concern for the environment or heritage.

CIDCO behaved in a similar cavalier and destructive fashion in the case of Nagaon beach on Karanja Island (Uran) where ONGC has set up an oil and gas processing unit. I was told that the Maharashtra Government Chief Secretary had asked ONGC to choose any site they liked, and they plumped for New Bombay's only sandy beach, the sailors' "Sandy Cove", which is right across the harbour from the Gateway of India. When I took up the issue in December 1978, I was told by a senior CIDCO director that this site had been allotted for the ONGC terminal without CIDCO's knowledge. He added that ONGC's Chairman Prasad had said that had he been approached earlier, the location could have been altered but that now it was too late since international tenders had been issued. However, Prasad had said that the pipelines would be underground and no beach areas would be touched. To make matters worse, a few years later, overriding strong environmental objections, ONGC, aided by CIDCO and its managing director, pushed through a huge expansion of the terminal – this involved the takeover of a large additional area immediately next to the beach, even though it had been designated as a "regional park" in CIDCO's own master plan. The Gateway of India therefore now "enjoys" the view of smoke emissions and a gas flare rather than a green hill. In Gujarat, the landfall point is at Umbharat, on an even finer beach, but the processing unit is at Hazira, some distance away, a far less sensitive site. The same could have been done at Uran with just a minimum of forethought by CIDCO. Almost simultaneously with the battle for Nhava, we had another fierce one with ONGC about Nagaon. However, this is not the place for that story.

In the years to come, vast areas were devastated by ONGC in both the locations–large numbers of trees were cut, hills quarried and flattened, and mangrove areas reclaimed.

The Maharashtra Government behaved in a similar fashion when allotting land for a giant chemical complex (which included two huge fertiliser plants, a massive petrochemical complex and a heavy water plant, together with other allied facilities) at Rewas-Mandwa which is just across the harbour from Bombay, and is the maritime entry for visitors to Alibag Taluka of Raigad district. We fought a bitter battle opposing this location and in fact that was how the Bombay Bachao Committee, the forerunner of the Bombay Environmental Action Group, was formed. This story had a partially happy ending since we were able to get the fertiliser plants moved 10 kilometres further away from Bombay to Thal Vaishet and the petrochemical complex was shifted even further away to Nagothna.

In the Nick of Time

In May 1978, I was taken to Nhava on a picnic by Maharashtra Government Urban Development Secretary Govind Lalvani, who had become a good friend. With its stone quay it was still a quiet charming piece of rural Maharashtra, with the added attraction of being an island. I was upset and outraged when I heard that the island was being taken over by ONGC, an organisation I had barely heard of. At that time, I had no clue as to how powerful they were (especially because India was desperately short of oil and the import prices had skyrocketed after the 1973 oil crisis). I was confident that, except for the harbour facilities, we could persuade the authorities to push the warehouses and other ONGC facilities inland.

There are several reasons why Nhava is important, which are even more valid now than they were then.

1. Nhava is virtually the only remaining green scenic area in New

Bombay located on the sea front. The bulk of the other areas on the sea front have been needlessly destroyed or taken over by other agencies, including a brewery and the ONGC terminal at Nagaon in Uran, which do not need a water-frontage. The whole of Sheva has been taken over by the Jawaharlal Nehru Port including the area which had earlier been designated as a regional park. As New Bombay grows, its citizens will want access to the sea front and Nhava is the prime such remaining area.

2. For the citizens of Greater Bombay, Nhava is the only accessible green belt across and within Bombay harbour.

3. Then there is the question of Elephanta, which gets a large number of visitors. Most of them go to Elephanta not to see the caves but mainly to have an outing, with a sea-trip thrown in. This puts undue pressure on the caves and is threatening the remaining archaeological artefacts, both the ones which are excavated and those below the ground. Hence it is vital to develop other green areas across the harbour so as to divert the excessive number of tourists going to Elephanta.

4. The fact that Nhava is the site of India's first Nautical Training Institute and the site of India's first Marine Museum (both of which are still functioning) is very important.

5. Finally, quite apart from the above, with the exception of the area taken over by ONGC and CIDCO, the rest of Nhava is a thickly wooded area and on that ground alone, warrants preservation.

My initial action was very swift. I took up the issue with the Save Bombay Committee (forerunner of BEAG), of which I was the Honorary Secretary. In the meeting of the Executive Committee of 24th May 1978, it was agreed that I should contact various agencies of the Maharashtra Government, including the Department of Tourism, to request them to ensure that the sea frontages across the harbour were maintained as green belts and, if possible, developed for local tourists.

While taking up the issue I did not dare suggest "environment" and "heritage conservation" as being the only reasons for preservation. With none of the decision-makers, whether politicians or bureaucrats, being sailors or otherwise connected with the sea, the concept of trans-harbour green belts was difficult, if not impossible, to sell. Against ONGC, one of the most powerful organisations in the country, green belts would get short shrift. Much more hard-headed arguments were needed and I had to invoke the benefits from tourism.

I also stressed, again and again, the dire need to pay attention to the great burden that tens of thousands of visitors were imposing on Elephanta and its monuments. Nhava was an idyllic spot, ideally suited as a place to divert excess visitors and picnickers from Elephanta, and relieve the pressure on the archaeological sites. I also made similar pleas that, in addition to Nhava, at least part of the waterfront lands at Sheva and the sandy beach at Nagaon on Karanja Island in Uran be preserved.

On 4th September, I wrote to Maharashtra Government Tourism Secretary Malati Tambay-Vaidya and to Lalvani saying that there was an urgent need to develop Nhava and Sheva as green belts or tourism spots for the citizens of Bombay and others. These areas were easily accessible by motor launch, with the journey taking only three-quarters of an hour from the Gateway of India and, if other landing places in north Bombay were developed, the journey time could be further reduced. These areas were just behind and extremely close to Elephanta Island which had been popularised and was very largely patronised by citizens of low and medium income groups. The visitors to Elephanta, then as now, included not just those who came to visit the caves, but also those who came to enjoy the unique experience of being in a green spot surrounded by the sea. On certain days the island was so crowded that the visitors did not find it possible to enjoy the amenities in the manner in which they should.

I suggested that Nhava and Sheva could be developed as green spots so that, with Elephanta, they could form a large green belt complex. I pointed out that Nhava was the site of the Nautical Institute which was situated in extremely aesthetic surroundings, in addition to which there was the Marine Museum. The Museum and the island were currently extremely popular with the few people who had the facilities to visit Nhava, and if these facilities could be expanded, the island would prove to be a very popular tourist spot. As regards the ONGC facilities, I suggested that the industries be moved a distance of two to three kilometres inland and the islands themselves be kept green and developed.

I requested Cyrus Guzder, a friend and colleague on the Save Bombay Committee and a leading professional in the travel and tourism industry, to arrange a meeting with Tambay-Vaidya to discuss the possibility of getting the Nhava Sheva green belt and tourism development plans included in the Sixth Five Year Plan. After some follow-up, we finally met her on 9th October. After that I did not do very much for a couple of months, except for getting Guzder to send her a reminder. However, there did not appear to be any progress.

In early December 1978, I suddenly realised that Lalvani was retiring

Overlooking Nhava Resevoir (tank) from Samander Mahal

at the end of the month and so I started moving frantically. Till 19th December, I had never met Yusuf and hence I did not know that in addition to Lalvani's pending retirement, there was another reason for urgency. Following a site visit by a CIDCO surveyor in early November 1978, the Special Land Acquisition Officer at Panvel had sent a notice on 20th December saying that on 2nd January 1979 land would be acquired for a road. The alignments of the road varied, but in all the alignments the road would come from the south through mangroves, and then run right through the heart of the Nautical Institute, cutting it into two halves. Earlier alignments passed through the parade ground, the tennis courts, the badminton courts, the Founders Memorial and the hospital/dispensary. The latest alignment would slice through a corner of the Marine Museum, pass through the school well, the officers' quarters, one of the staff quarters, one of the dormitories, and the cadets' canteen. In short it would split the Institute into two and make its functioning impossible.

Lalvani was sympathetic but needed a reason to act, which I had to give him very quickly. Nearly 30 years later, while writing this book, it occurred to me that, as Urban Development Secretary, responsible for town and country planning, he could himself have directed that lands be earmarked as green belts. However, he obviously either did not see it that way or it did not occur to him. Being completely ignorant of governmental functioning, it did not occur to me either.

Lalvani was, however, a good friend, and very co-operative. I was able to have a meeting with him on the evening of 7th December. The Under Secretary of the Urban Development Department B.M. Ambhaikar, who was to be very friendly and helpful over the years, was also present. The next day, Lalvani held another meeting, which Tambay-Vaidya attended along with Under Secretary L.K. Gupte of the Social Welfare Department (which was under her), Kulkarni of CIDCO and Ambhaikar. I met her again a couple of hours later and gave her a map of the area.

A few days later, on 13th December, I again wrote to Tambay-Vaidya and Lalvani. I said that about 20 acres of sea frontage on a hill, including the best sea front area and the jetty, had already been handed over to ONGC, yet ONGC also wanted additional land. Since the sea frontage and the hill were of special aesthetic value and would greatly enhance the attraction of the proposed tourist complex, I suggested that ONGC could perhaps be persuaded to return this land to the State Government and in exchange, some other land in the vicinity could be handed over to them. Any additional land to be given to ONGC should also be away from the waterfront. This alternative land would be only a short distance away and would not greatly inconvenience them. As regards the Nautical Institute, it should not be acquired for ONGC or for any other purpose. The Institute, the Museum and the green cover would themselves be prime tourist attractions. The Institute could also furnish the basic initial infrastructure such as water, rest areas, shops, etc. for the tourist complex, thereby keeping the initial expense to a minimum. More development could take place as and when funds became available. I added that Nhava was very suitable for water sports such as sailing, swimming, rowing and so on.

I suggested that Sheva could also similarly be reserved for a tourist/recreation complex.

I also took up the issue of Nagaon beach. I said that while Nhava and Sheva were very suitable for water sports, there was no sandy beach in those areas. However, slightly to the south at Karanja was a beautiful beach often used by yachtsmen and others. A portion of this beach had been taken over by ONGC, but a substantial amount still remained between the ONGC facility and the Naval establishment. The beach is of special value since it is directly across the harbour from the Gateway of India, at a distance of barely four miles. The beach would be of special interest to tourists since it is easily accessible by shallow-draft speedboats in 20 minutes, whereas going to the other beaches in Bombay involved lengthy road journeys. (This point is even more relevant today since road journeys, especially from South Bombay, take huge amounts of time and have become extremely tedious whereas, by contrast, the sea journey to Nagaon is very pleasant.) In addition, a facility already existed in the form of a beach restaurant which was upto international standards. I suggested the beach be earmarked for tourist development and also, that if ONGC wished to expand, they could easily do it one or two kilometres inland.

I added that while funds might not be currently available to develop the above areas in Nhava, Sheva and Nagaon, immediate action was needed to at least earmark the areas before it was too late. A couple of days later, in another note, I stressed the urgency for reservation of these areas, since this was the last chance to keep some of the trans-harbour areas green and open for the citizens of Bombay.

Both Tambay-Vaidya and Lalvani acted fast. The day after I wrote to the former, I called on Under Secretary Gupte who told me that their officer had gone to the CIDCO office in Vashi to collect details. The day after that, I called on Under Secretary Ambhaikar of the Urban Development Department who said that he would forward my note to CIDCO for comments. When I met him a day later, he said that my note had gone to CIDCO.

Since there were barely two weeks before Lalvani retired, I had to keep up the pressure. On 16th December, I met Gupte, who said that B.R. Sawant, who held dual charge as Chief Executive of the Maharashtra Tourism Development Corporation (MTDC) and Joint Director, Department of Tourism, had been asked to prepare a scheme. I immediately went to the MTDC office at Express Towers at Nariman Point, called on Sawant and handed him my note. He too was co-operative. He said that he would like to visit Nhava, but that the Tourism Department note to the Urban Development Department did not need to wait for the visit. A couple of days later he said that he would be meeting Tambay-Vaidya the next day and that the note would be sent a day or two thereafter.

Prasanna Chunekar of MTDC was quick to appreciate the logic. Based on his report, and accepting my arguments, on 20th December 1978, Sawant noted on file that it was necessary to divert visitors from Elephanta where they were straining the facilities. He said that Nhava and the adjacent area of Sheva were suitable for water sports and had the necessary greenery to attract picnickers from Bombay. He added that the Nautical Institute had already been an attraction for visitors in spite of the fact that no publicity had been given to it. With proper publicity, both the Institute and the Marine Museum could be "a certain attraction for tourists". He suggested that further acquisition of land from the Nautical Institute should be avoided, and that in fact, waterfront lands which had been taken over, be exchanged for other land. The MTDC asked for 13 hectares of the land which had been handed over to ONGC.

Regarding Sheva, Sawant noted that it had the same advantages of proximity and greenery as Nhava and could be developed as a tourist spot. Hence the coastal lands on Sheva should also be transferred to the Tourism Department. MTDC asked for 15 hectares of these lands.

Coming to Nagaon, Sawant noted that the beach there was well known. However, though a portion of the beach had been handed over to ONGC, between the ONGC establishment and the naval base there was still a fairly good beach which needed to be preserved and developed. This beach could be handed over to the Tourism Department for future development. He went on to describe Nhava, Sheva, and Nagaon beach as "potential sea resorts", which have "definite scope for development as they are within easy reach of Bombay". The Tourism Department could develop these through MTDC as well as private agencies. He suggested that the Tourism Department move the Urban Development Department for transfer of these lands for development as sea resorts.

Time was running out and I requested Guzder to speak to Tambay-Vaidya and inform her that Lalvani would be holding office only till the subsequent week. I did not know that Tambay-Vaidya had already acted. On 21st December, the very day after Sawant's note, she had noted that "tourism is a subject full of potential and we have got to plan with an eye on the future". With this in view, she could "confidently predict fruitful development of the Elephanta-Nhava-Sheva triangle in the cause of Tourism both foreign and domestic". She endorsed the proposals and requested the Urban Development Department to agree to them. She and Sawant had both kept their word, and that too in double quick time.

In addition to Lalvani and Tambay-Vaidya, I had taken up the issue with several other people. These included Urban Development Minister Hashu Advani, who belonged to the Jana Sangh, which later became the Bharatiya Janata Party (BJP), and Professor S.S. ("Anu") Varde who was a member of the Executive Committee of the Save Bombay Committee, but who was now, by a quirk of politics, Minister for Education, Youth Services and Sports. Both were members, though belonging to different political parties, of the Progressive Democratic Front coalition government (which was incidentally the first non-Congress Government in Maharashtra). I also approached Charles Correa, the famous architect who was a member of BMRDA's Executive Committee and also a director of CIDCO.

My uncle, Hotchand Advani, to whom I was very close, was a well-known leading barrister and educationist who was active in other social causes as well. He was the chairman of many Sindhi institutions, including the Hyderabad (Sind) National Collegiate Board (which runs over a dozen colleges), the Sind Educationists Association (which runs the famous Jai Hind College), the Sindhu Resettlement Corporation and so on. His was a respected name in the Sindhi community. He knew a couple of the Sindhi Jana Sangh leaders very well, and I gave him a copy of my note.

I also requested Guzder to try and get the Travel Agents Association of India to take up the matter with Tambay-Vaidya, Lalvani, Correa and Bombay Metropolitan Commissioner M.S. Palnitkar, the last three of whom were CIDCO directors. After much follow-up, on 30th December, Mahendra Sanghi of the Travel Agents Association finally wrote to Lalvani and Tambay-Vaidya about Nhava, Sheva and Nagaon, but by that time, it was too late to affect the initial decisions. However, this was useful later in reinforcing the case for the preservation of Nhava.

At my request on the lines of a draft which I prepared, on 19th December, Kekoo Gandhy of the Bombay Civic Trust wrote to Professor Varde who was an old friend of his. On 20th December Professor Varde forwarded this letter to Lalvani. He requested Lalvani to talk to Tambay-Vaidya since he was certain that she would be interested, and then take up the matter with ONGC. He added that he was sure that the Tourism Minister would be happy if this idea materialised and went on to say that he would also talk to him.

Lalvani acted immediately. On the very same day, he minuted on the Tourism Department note that specific plots on the beach zone of these places be reserved for tourism and that CIDCO be requested to indicate plots, both in the possession of ONGC and others, which could be so reserved. He added that the matter should be processed at the next CIDCO board meeting which was to be held in a week's time. The next day, the Urban Development Department stayed the acquisition of further lands and buildings from the Nautical Institute.

On 26th December 1978, just five days before he retired and exactly one week before the land was to be acquired, Lalvani had a meeting with ONGC General Manager (Offshore) H.S. Cheema, somebody who

I was to get to know very well indeed over the next few years. I was not present and hence cannot give a firsthand account of what transpired but it turned out to be a crucial meeting. The minutes of the meeting record that Lalvani explained the Tourism Department's proposals to ONGC and pointed out that the buildings of the Nautical Institute, including the Marine Museum, were of interest to tourists. He said that in addition to the Tourism Department's representations, the BMRDA (whom we had also approached in this regard), were keen to preserve Nhava as a green belt. He must have been either very forceful or very persuasive, since Cheema agreed, without too much fuss, to shift the road alignment not just to avoid the Museum, but also "that the road alignment should not cut through the premises of the Institute which should be left undisturbed". There was no mention of having to seek the concurrence of ONGC's foreign consultants.

The minutes further record: "Shri Cheema agreed with the Spl. Secy. and observed that the Nhava Island had a beautiful natural environment with wooded areas and a good water front. Shri Cheema assured that relocation of the activities and operations of the ONGC so as to make available to the Tourism Depart. (the) waterfront areas for development, would be examined and proposals would be submitted to Government". Critically, Cheema said that "the ONGC have agreed to avoid acquisition of the premises of the Institute" and also that ONGC would be willing to restore the lands and buildings taken over from the Nautical Institute.

Cheema perhaps agreed to all this since he wanted 50 hectares of land at Nagaon, to which Lalvani agreed. Here too, Lalvani observed that the need for preservation of the waterfront and adjacent areas at Nagaon was obvious in the light of the Tourism Department's representations. As in the case of Nhava, Cheema agreed to leave out such areas, a promise that was belied.

Like so many other commitments made by ONGC, the commitment to hand back waterfront lands and to restore lands and buildings to the Nautical Institute was never implemented by them. However, at least the key structures and areas of Nhava had been saved by the skin of our teeth, at way past the eleventh hour. It was a very close call. For once, my inertia had had no major permanent ill effects. I used to wonder whether, if I had moved earlier and more energetically, I could have reduced the amount of land taken over by ONGC. However, the land had already been allotted to ONGC in July 1977, ten months before my May 1978 visit to Nhava with Lalvani, and even Maharashtra Government

Sagaresh Suites (formerly Fatima Banu Hospital)

agencies had failed in their efforts to get a review of the land requirements of ONGC.

Concurrent with the above developments, on 18th December 1978, Correa wrote to CIDCO Managing Director B.S. Dhavle about the "beach waterfront near Nagaon Village (Uran)" and "Waterfront of Nhava Island". He said that he would like these discussed at the next CIDCO Board meeting since "both these areas have a great deal of natural beauty and as such will be of considerable importance to the population of New Bombay as it develops".

One immediate outcome of the 26th December meeting was that Rashid Yusuf could now take a tougher line; he wrote to CIDCO and also to ONGC that he had earlier agreed to the road alignment running through the Institute's campus only because they were to be shifted from their existing premises. Now that they were not being shifted, they could not accept the road going through the campus. The diversion of the road also prevented the fencing in of the Institute from the sea and incidentally stopped the handing over of 14 hectares of Khajan land to ONGC and the consequent destruction of the mangroves.

On 31st January 1979 the CIDCO Board resolved "that lands fronting the seashore of the site for New Bombay with a depth of 600 metres be reserved for disposal wholly and exclusively for purposes of tourism, sports and cultural activities and be not offered for industrial or other purposes".

This was a great resolution. If CIDCO had only adhered to it in the years to come, over and above saving Nhava and Nagaon, the whole of New Bombay would have been a wonderful city on the sea. Twenty years later, as described in my first book, *Heritage and Environment: An Indian Diary*, Samir Mehta (one of our activists) and I were locked in a grim battle – one of the severest of my life – with CIDCO, and specially with Managing Director Anil Lakhina, who both seemed to have forgotten or were perhaps unaware of their own Board Resolution. They grossly violated the stipulations of even the reduced distances laid down in the Coastal Regulation Zone (CRZ) Regulations.

Apart from the environment, heritage and tourism, there were other major reasons for the preservation of Nhava, such as the Nautical Institute and the promotion of water sports and youth activities. On 27th December I met Professor Varde, in his capacity as Minister for Education, Youth Services and Sports. I gave him a letter regarding the educational role of the Institute and the development of youth activities on Nhava, Sheva and Nagaon. I pointed out that the Nautical Institute had been running since 1910 and that it had been the first establishment to train Indians as masters (captains) for the Mercantile Marine, well before the *Dufferin*. It was the only private institution recognised by the Government of India, with the selection of students being done by a Joint Selection Board consisting of equal numbers of representatives from the Government and the Institute.

I added that the Institute was living on borrowed time, since 65 hectares (actually 54 hectares) of land had already been acquired by ONGC with the balance being under acquisition. I requested that the Institute premises be left out of the purview of any acquisition. In support, I mentioned and annexed the letter written in March of that year by the Deputy Director-General of Shipping to both ONGC and CIDCO requesting that the Institute's premises be excluded from acquisition. I added that quite apart from the training activities, the campus would be an essential nucleus of the tourist complex proposed by the MTDC. A firm decision was needed since the properties were fast deteriorating. I reiterated that the road alignment should be such that it would not cut through the campus. Furthermore, ONGC needed to be requested to hand back 35 hectares to the Maharashtra Government. This would comprise the five bungalows with their adjoining areas, the coconut plantation, part of the hill and foreshore lands. I said that the above facilities could be used in conjunction with the Tourism Department to set up facilities for youth activities such as hiking, rock climbing, camping, etc. together with water sports like rowing, canoeing, sailing, swimming, water skiing and so on. It would be tragic to lose all this, particularly since it was the only place where a nucleus established for over three-quarters of a century, existed.

Regarding Sheva, apart from land used for defence purposes, the rest was still green and could be reserved and maintained as a green belt for the above youth and sport activities. Where Nagaon was concerned, I said that the beach was ideal (and had been used) for boating, hiking, camping, and rock-climbing expeditions since adjacent to it are green and rocky hills. This was a unique combination and hence these lands should be reserved for the above activities.

Professor Varde immediately sent my letter to Lalvani saying that he agreed with the suggestions and asked him to take up the matter with the ONGC authorities. He also asked that CIDCO should undertake a thorough enquiry into ONGC's land requirements. He added that suggestions should be invited from the Save Bombay Committee and that Department of Tourism also be consulted.

A couple of days later, I met Education Secretary D.M. Sukthankar. He said that he was not concerned with the Nautical Institute, since there was a separate department, namely Technical Education, with a separate Secretary, dealing with vocational training.

I immediately went across to meet Technical Education Secretary S.S. Tinaikar. He began by asking how the Save Bombay Committee was concerned, since Nhava was outside Bombay. He asked whether the Nautical Institute was recognised by the Maharashtra Government and whether the latter had any role to play. He added that he was only concerned with preservation of the Nautical Institute and that other matters like sports and environment did not concern him. He suggested that we should meet the Director of Technical Education who would determine the genuine land requirements of the Nautical Institute. He went on to say that the Government could even think of giving funds to the Institute for its future development. As regards acquisition of land, it was the Revenue Department who was the final deciding authority, and we should contact them.

On 7th February 1979, referring to our meeting and my 27th December letter to Prof. Varde, Tinaikar wrote to me saying that "your property is now excluded from acquisition". This was a huge step forward since it meant that the Institute was now safe, thus ending at least seven years of uncertainty and the Sword of Damocles which had been hanging over the Institute. In his letter, Tinaikar added that he had received a report from the Directorate of Technical Education to the effect that there was scope for starting both a diploma and degree course in marine engineering. He suggested that I get in touch with the Directorate.

In April 1979 I was able to persuade Technical Education Minister Nihal Ahmed to visit Nhava. On 15th April Prof. A. Ghosh, Joint Director of Technical Education and C. Jayavidyacharya, Chairman of the Board of Technical Examinations, visited the Nautical Institute.

On 1st May Tinaikar came with me to Nhava and remarked: "I visited the Institute in the context of our search for a place where we can develop training facilities for trades connected with shipping and water transport. The infrastructural facilities provided here over the labour of decades by [the] Sir Mohamed Yusuf Foundation can provide a base for a much larger training programme in a variety of trades for which there is demand in [the] employment market.

"I hope it would soon be possible to work out a joint venture in expansion of this institute."

On 7th May I wrote to the Directorate requesting their assistance in obtaining firm assurances from the government regarding the preservation of the Institute. On 21st May Rashid Yusuf, Captain Ayappan from the Nautical Institute, and I met Tinaikar, who had with him some of his officers including C. Jayavidyacharya. Tinaikar was most supportive and made several suggestions about the future development of the Institute. However, an unexpected situation arose. Tinaikar asked Yusuf how many of the trainees were Maharashtrian. The answer was that if all those born in Maharashtra were considered to be Maharashtrians, the number would be very high. This was not well received. When I said that even the proportion of locally born Maharashtrians was high, Jayavidyacharya, echoing his boss, replied: "They just happen to be Maharashtrians" (i.e. there was no specific reservation for them). Notwithstanding this, the Department supported the Nautical Institute.

The next day Rashid Yusuf and I met Professor Ghosh and Jayavidyacharya in their office in the beautiful stone Indo-Gothic building near St. Xavier's College. I took with me a letter mentioning additional activities and courses proposed at the Nautical Institute. Professor Ghosh immediately gave me a reply asking for a project report to enable him to submit a proposal to the government to reserve a suitable piece of land on Nhava for the Nautical Institute. There and then I dictated and handed over a letter saying that this would take a substantial amount of time. I said that the land requirement of the Nautical Institute would

Shankar and Sunita Menon

be 61.60 hectares. I pointed out that according to our information, the Marine Academy being set up by the Shipping Corporation of India had been sanctioned roughly 50 to 60 acres of land by the state government. I requested that the land required by the Institute for their present (proposed) and future activities be reserved, so that no other agency could acquire that land. Professor Ghosh agreed to write to the Employment Secretary saying that the land should be reserved and not given for any other use.

Professor Ghosh moved fast, and just three days later on 25th May, he wrote to the Employment Secretary. He mentioned that the Institute planned to include other training courses such as post-sea training for shipping company employees, an officers' training academy, diploma and degree courses in marine engineering and so on, within the location of a portion of the National Maritime Museum. He said that the Institute could not make any detailed plans for their developmental activities since they were not sure about their future existence because of ONGC's demand for their lands. He recommended that 50 hectares of land be reserved for the Institute, so that they could go ahead with their plans.

Another official with whom I discussed the Nhava issue was Shankar Menon, Joint Secretary, Department of Technical Education. Though he was a civil servant, Menon is much better known as a press columnist and was a personal friend. On 13th May 1979, a Sunday, I met him at his home and gave him a set of papers. The next day I left some more papers for him at his office, and the day after that I met him again. On 15th May 1979 without consulting Tinaikar, who was his superior, he sent off a letter to ONGC Member (Offshore) Dr. G. Ramaswamy enclosing a map of Nhava and the minutes of the 26th December meeting between Cheema and Lalvani.

Coincidentally, in reply to my letter of 19th April to ONGC Chairman P.T. Venugopal, Dr. Ramaswamy sent me an acknowledgement after which he agreed to meet me on 22nd May. However in the oil world the stakes are very high and matters sometimes take strange turns. My appointment was cancelled at the last minute since Dr. Ramaswamy was suddenly dismissed by the Government of India, without being given the option to resign. This was because he had reportedly written to the American oil giant Exxon and U.S. Treasury Secretary Blumenthal saying that it was not necessary for the World Bank to give loans to ONGC for oil exploration. However, in spite of Dr. Ramaswamy's dismissal, on 25th May ONGC General Manager Cheema replied to Shankar Menon saying: "We confirm that ONGC is not interested in taking more than the 68 hectares of land already taken over by ONGC." This was critically important since it meant that not just the Nautical Institute but also the remaining areas of Nhava were now safe from acquisition (and destruction) by ONGC.

Incidentally Cheema also agreed that 14 hectares of *khajan* (mangrove) lands, no longer needed for the road, would be handed back. The road would also be realigned to run south of the Nautical Institute and charitable trust properties.

During the discussions and meetings, I got quite friendly with Jayavidyacharya. Once while watching a parade of the Nautical Institute trainees, I mentioned to him that I was sorry that I not taken up the Nhava issue earlier. He reassured me, saying that I had started "when the call came".

In the midst of all the excitement and tension about Nhava, for some months I neglected to seriously follow up the issues of Sheva and Nagaon. I was unaware of what was required, including changes to the Development Plan (Master Plan) of New Bombay. I had no experience of dealing with Development Plans. However, Urban Development Minister Hashu Advani and Professor Varde would surely have supported us, at least for Nagaon where, though I did not know it, the waterfront lands had been designated as a "Regional Park" in the Development

Plan. Was a golden opportunity missed? Would we have been able to counteract ONGC's pressures? Three years later, we were unable to stop them being given an additional 100 acres of Regional Park land.

Malati Tambay-Vaidya was a keen badminton player and used to play at the Bombay Gymkhana, of which I am a member. I am no athlete, and my outdoor recreations were confined to walking, swimming and sailing. However, in those days I used to make it a point to go especially to the Bombay Gymkhana, hoping to bump into her and thereby strike up a relationship. I thought it very strange and sad that a badminton tournament – the name of the Colville Cup still rings a bell – was taking priority over saving a lovely, green island.

Till I went through the file almost 30 years after the event, I did not remember how many times I had met B.R. Sawant. At the end of December 1978 he was promoted and transferred from MTDC to Dhulia. I wrote to him to congratulate him and thank him for his efforts. Five years later, when he was Collector of Satara district, he behaved high-handedly in Mahabaleshwar. Subsequently, when he was Vice Chairman of the Mahabaleshwar-Panchgani Regional Planning Board, I had a minor crossing of swords with him. Rather than going into the substance of my suggestions, he was irritated at my having seen Board documents. Malati Tambay-Vaidya was reportedly convinced by ONGC not to continue her support. The worst was a major difference of opinion with Govind Lalvani over Nhava, which ruptured our friendship. However, I have never forgotten that it was the three of them, together with Prasanna Chunekar, who were instrumental in the initial saving of the Nautical Institute and the Marine Museum.

A couple of years later, at an official meeting in 1980 where Nhava was a key item of discussion, I met one of the Peter Fraenkel engineers. He obviously knew India since, during the Second World War, he had served in the Indian Army in the famous Queen Victoria's Own Madras Sappers and Miners, the oldest regiment of the Royal Indian Engineers and one of the oldest of the Indian army. Thereafter he had been to Cambridge, though to a different college and fourteen years before me. We had a long, cordial chat and he seemed a civilised person. How could he have been a party to such wanton destruction?

For that matter, how could the Maharashtra Government, CIDCO and ONGC officers, planners and engineers have conceived and executed this sort of destruction? How could they have been so obdurate in persisting with it, even when the environmental destruction was pointed out to them and it was right before their eyes? In her article appropriately entitled "Yusuf's idyllic dream – Nhava in turmoil", Heta Pandit gave an answer by asking: "Is it because our government authorities do not have a personal stake in the project they are assigned to supervise? Or that our engineering colleges leave our students to equate 'development' with denuding and concreting the surface of the earth; then air-conditioning the atmosphere in their office cubicles? Must vertically progressive projects be executed regardless of the ethnic habitat or the inhabitants they support?"

Quite different had been the reaction in another island about three decades earlier. During the first few months of 1944, the Second World War was reaching its climax for the British who, along with the Americans, were engrossed with the forthcoming invasion of France across the English Channel – a colossal, make-or-break undertaking. In Italy, they were heavily engaged in battle, and in addition they were concerned about Greece and the possibility of having to send British troops there. London itself was threatened by the first pilotless planes. In addition, the Chiefs of Staff of the three Armed Services were in violent disagreement with Winston Churchill about the strategies to be followed against Japan and were seriously considering resignation. The British forces were spread out from the easternmost part of India to Ceylon (now Sri Lanka), Syria, Iraq, Palestine, Egypt, Libya and other parts of Africa. During this period, Field Marshal Alan Brooke was Chief of the Imperial General Staff and also Chairman of the Chiefs of Staff Committee, who were responsible for the overall direction of Britain's worldwide campaigns. In the midst of all this, he was informed by Dr. David Bannerman, an eminent ornithologist friend of his, that the Royal Air Force were about to use Scotts Head Island, off the eastern coast of England, as a bombing range. Bannerman explained that unless there was careful control and timing, this would disturb the nesting season of the rare roseate tern. Brooke was shocked, spoke to the Chief of Air Staff immediately, and an alternative was found.

Petroleum Secretary

Saad Ali, nephew of the world-renowned ornithologist Salim Ali, was one of the founders of BEAG and its Vice President. He had supported Petroleum Secretary B.B. Vohra (who had a good reputation) when he had been arrested almost immediately after the Janata Government had taken over in 1977. In July 1978, Saad Ali telephoned B.B. Vohra in Delhi, but was unable to meet him. However, at that time, as mentioned earlier, S.K. Das and I had met B.B Vohra. In December 1978 at my request,

Saad Ali wrote to him about Nhava and Nagaon, stressing the urgency since these were the last green areas left across the harbour. He also said that one of us could fly to Delhi and explain the whole situation to him. I should have gone anyway, but I was inexperienced in the ways of Delhi and in any case, the state of our funds did not permit anyone going to Delhi "on spec".

In April 1979 I went to Delhi and met several key officials including Defence Secretary, Sushital Banerjee on a completely different issue, namely the reclamation and construction proposed by service officers and others at Pilot Bunder. I asked for and obtained, without difficulty, an appointment with B.B. Vohra, and we met on 3rd April. He was sympathetic and because of his reputation, I was hopeful. A few days later, on 7th April when I telephoned him, he said that he was flying to Bombay on Monday, and he would visit Nhava. He agreed that I could accompany him. I accordingly cut my holiday short, dipped into my pocket for the airfare and flew to Bombay with him. Landing at Santa Cruz Airport, we were taken to Juhu Airport, from where we were taken by helicopter to Nhava and then to Nagaon. This was exciting, since these were my first helicopter flights.

On Nhava, the ONGC engineers, and Shashi Ruia of Essar Constructions Ltd., the contractor, must have been surprised to see me accompanying B.B. Vohra and were hostile. I was alone and on the defensive. Shashi Ruia was holding a paperback titled (I still remember) *Year of the Golden Ape* by Colin Forbes. In an attempt to diminish the hostility, I said that it was a good book, and received a noncommittal reply. The hostility increased when I showed B.B. Vohra a sketch map of Nhava on which I marked out the areas which should be left alone. The ONGC engineers commented that it was not very accurate, to which I replied that had I been given a map, I would have marked it more accurately. Again, in order to diminish the hostility, I apologised almost ingratiatingly for the inaccuracy to a senior ONGC Superintending Engineer whose name (Bhanu Prakash) I remember even now. The sketch must have upset him since he replied in a minatory tone, as if speaking to a subordinate: "Why did you show it to the Secretary?"

B.B. Vohra said that he would try and help. I believed him but the Maharashtra civil servants smiled cynically when I reported this to them and said that that was the standard response. They were right, since B.B. Vohra did not live up to his promise. With ONGC being a powerful organisation, there was, of course, a limit to what he could do. However, expenditure approval had not yet been issued by the Pe-

troleum Ministry, which would have given B.B. Vohra enough leeway to insist on re-siting, or at least trimming and adjusting the project, so as to minimise the damage. This, together with the official letter to him from the Maharashtra Government, along with several letters from Minister S.S. Varde, would have been enough to give him a lever to reopen the case had he wished to. He did not do that and, at one of our meetings, was frank enough to tell me so. The Petroleum Ministry's expenditure approval was issued only on 1st August 1979, months after B.B. Vohra had promised to do what he could, while the final work order was awarded only in March 1980.

On 30th October 1979 Saad Ali telephoned me from Delhi and said that he and S.P. Godrej (Chairman of the highly reputed Godrej Group of Companies and a keen environmentalist) had met B.B. Vohra regarding Nhava. Saad Ali added that S.P. Godrej had been very convincing and that B.B. Vohra had agreed to reconsider the position and talk to

Sir Yusuf reviewing the cadets of the Marine College in 1935 at the silver jubilee celebrations

the ONGC officials in Bombay. However, either Saad Ali had misunderstood, or B.B. Vohra had not been entirely frank. In fact, instead of just playing a passive role, B.B. Vohra had gone on to repeatedly defend ONGC's actions. Less than a couple of weeks later, in his reply of 12th November 1979 to Prof. Varde, B.B. Vohra requested Prof. Varde to "bless the project". Subsequently he made similar arguments to the Prime Minister.

In Delhi, on 26th December 1979 along with Ajay Balram, an old sailing friend whom I had taken along, I was able to meet B.B. Vohra, though briefly. Cheema and Petroleum Ministry Deputy Secretary Rajinder Singh were also present. B.B. Vohra said that we should proceed on the basis that the ONGC base had to be at Nhava. However, they gave various assurances, for instance that ONGC's land requirements at Nhava would be reassessed; the bulk of ONGC's inventory would be stored on the mainland rather than at Nhava; the pipe-coating plant would be relocated away from Nhava to the mainland and so on. A similar assurance was given regarding Nagaon beach, namely that ONGC would move their facilities away from the beach. None of these assurances were kept, not even that of reviewing the land requirements.

Environmental Atmosphere

Fighting for Nhava was very tough especially at that time when the atmosphere was quite different from today. It is difficult to convey the flavour of those days, the earliest of the activist environmental movements, at least in Bombay. We in the Bombay Bachao Committee were in a head-on confrontation with the Maharashtra Government regarding the Rewas-Mandwa fertiliser plants, whose feedstock was to be the associate gas from the Bombay High oil and gas fields. The Maharashtra Government's response, from the Chief Minister downwards, was ferocious and vituperative. We were branded as being anti-development, anti-Maharashtrian and pro-Gujarat. It was said that several in our group were Gujaratis and names such as Kisan Mehta, who was President of the Save Bombay Committee (which is quite a separate NGO), were bandied about. It was alleged that we wished to have the fertiliser plants relocated within Gujarat, or failing that, at Tarapur. Though within Maharashtra, Tarapur is close to the Gujarat border and the allegation was that we wanted this location so that the ancillary and downstream units would be located in Gujarat. We were further accused of having vested interests in the form of large bungalows in the area. It would not be too far-fetched to say that to the Maharashtra Government, we were public enemy number one. I was the Honorary Secretary of the Bombay Bachao Committee, which was often confused with the Save Bombay Committee of which I was also the Honorary Secretary. My dual role probably added to the confusion. (This campaign, together with the political manoeuvrings, the various twists and turns and the drama, has been briefly recorded by Darryl D'Monte in his *Temples or Tombs?*).

We had taken up several issues simultaneously, and a journalist friend of mine once said to me reprovingly that if we took so many issues to the Government, they would never listen to us. When the Save Bombay Committee proposed a radically new traffic management plan to Chief Minister Vasantdada Patil, I was told by this friend that the Chief Minister, greatly upset as he was with our campaign against the proposed Mandwa fertiliser plants, had said that we had now come up with another crazy plan. On another occasion, one of the Save Bombay

Committee members said that we should be careful otherwise we would be dubbed "old nannies". My cousin Kumar Advani, though a founding member of both the Save Bombay Committee and BEAG, used to tease me and call us the "moanies", saying that we were always moaning about something. A colleague in Tatas told me that we should not oppose the location of the fertiliser plants since the managers would deliberately delay the projects just to prove a point.

At that time, we met Sharad Pawar, then not a national figure but a young Industries Minister of Maharashtra, who said: "We don't care for beaches." Today, more than 30 years down the line, it is unlikely that he would make a similar statement. At the very least, lip service would be paid to beaches and the environment, and at least minimal adjustments to projects would be made, of which Dabhol (discussed later) is just one example.

In 1978 we were in the thick of our campaign against the location of the fertiliser plants at Thal Vaishet. When I took up the case of Nhava and Nagaon, I had to do so with great care and almost apologetically, for fear of being dubbed anti-petroleum, anti-development and anti-Maharashtrian. Subsequently, when I took up the issue of the destruction by ONGC at Nagaon in Uran, Govind Lalvani told me that the politicians would ask: "How many green belts do you want? First Mandwa, then Nhava, now Uran?" I felt like a famished Oliver Twist asking for more. I replied that unless we acted now, these seaside green belts would be destroyed for all time and there would be none left for the future citizens of New Bombay. Govind Lalvani said that the politicians' answer would be *baguyaa*, "We will see later". In direct contrast, in 1980, we were furiously attacked by Kannan Srinivasan in the *Economic and Political Weekly* for fighting only selected issues and ignoring other environmental problems.

There was another statement that made me really angry, but which was probably a reflection of at least some people's attitudes. I once complained about the behaviour of ONGC General Manager H.S. Cheema to Maneck Hiranandani, who also knew Cheema very well. I was hurt and angry when he said that producing 20 million tons of oil was more important than the environment. He added that Cheema had "achieved more than you ever will in a hundred lifetimes". About 20 years later, he repeated the latter statement. This time I pointed out that the same oil could have been produced with far less environmental damage.

Grim battle

AT A PARTY, DURING A CASUAL CONVERSATION with retired Maharashtra Government Chief Secretary D.D Sathe, I complained about the way CIDCO's statutory land use plan had been casually modified to permit such huge destruction. He replied that Government was always accused of being inflexible, and now when they showed flexibility we still attacked them. I pointed out that this flexibility only operated to destroy greenery and heritage, never the other way around. I mentioned the Nautical Institute, to which he replied that all it trained were a few *serangs* and kept repeating that it was an insult to call it a Nautical Institute. A similar statement was made by Kannan Srinivasan in his article of 3rd May 1980 in the *Economic & Political Weekly*, in which he criticised us severely for our action on Nhava. He sarcastically referred to the Nautical Institute as a "second Dartmouth" (the site of the famous Royal Naval College in England). If Kannan Srinivasan and D.D. Sathe were to see the Institute today, they would have to eat their words.

This was one instance where I made an absolute nuisance of myself with everybody whom I thought might be of help. I approached two successive Director-Generals of Shipping, P.G. Gavai and Ram Pradhan. The latter became Maharashtra Chief Secretary in which capacity, too, he gave his support regarding Nhava. In 1979, I made two dozen trips to Nhava, trying to garner support from politicians, bureaucrats, the press, conservationists and others; and over the next few years, I carried on frequently making trips. Saving Nhava had become almost a

Shield at Marine Museum

Shyam at Marine Museum along with Nihal Ahmed, Minister, Government of Maharashtra

personal crusade, if not an obsession. What made it tolerable was that the journeys to and from Nhava were by motor boat, through waters in which I loved to sail. The boat journey and the walk through Nhava, even in the heat, gave the whole exercise a picnic-like feeling.

This campaign was perhaps the most bitter one in which I have been engaged. ONGC officials repeatedly said: "What is this environment you are talking of? We are producing oil for the nation." One ONGC official muttered: "See how they [North Sea Oil] have ruined Aberdeen" – implying that we should not fuss too much about Nhava. The fact that the same oil could be produced with far less environmental damage was brushed aside. ONGC kept saying: "First clean up Bombay and then talk of Nhava." They were obviously aware of the fact that by the time the environment of Bombay could be improved, the whole of Nhava would have been flattened. Many, including some non-government people, were reluctant to act. A common statement was that this was "a national project" and hence should not be opposed. The fact that re-siting of projects, even by a few kilometres, would prevent the destruction of vital green belts and precious waterfront areas was not even considered. Even protests against indiscriminate tree-cutting and massive destruction of the landscape were ignored.

I took press representatives to Nhava on innumerable occasions. Many articles appeared in different newspapers and publications. Then and in subsequent years, we had strong support from the press who were virtually unanimous in supporting our campaign. The titles of some of the press and magazine items are revealing. They included: "The battle for Nhava", "Battling for a Green Belt", "Oldest Nautical School Faces Extinction", "State Protest Going Unheeded?", "Rape of Nhava", " ONGC: Flouting the PM's orders", " ONGC: A Muddy Record", "Slow Destruction of Nhava Island Following Violation of Commitments by ONGC?", "5.7-crore Fine for Eco-crime", " ONGC Vandalism" and "An Isle Deflowered". The only exceptions were an article by Kumar Ketkar in *The Economic Times* and a strong and vituperative attack by Kannan Srinivasan, in the *Economic and Political Weekly*.

Rajiv Shankar, in a front page news item in *The Economic Times* of Sunday 7th October 1979 wrote:

> **Even from a distance, the lush vegetation on Nhava stands out in sharp contrast to the adjoining islands.** However, once ONGC starts clearing the land, the island will become as barren as its neighbour, the island of Sheva. ONGC proposes to chop down over 2,000 trees, and entirely level two hills to clear the way for its supply base. One result of this clearance drive will be to drive away over 50 varieties of birds – mainly migratory – which inhabit this island.
>
> But the most serious loss if ONGC's plans go through will not be the destruction of what exists at present, but what could have come up in the future.
>
> As congestion has rapidly overtaken the open spaces, the need for lungs for the city is being felt more and more acutely. One by one, all the open spaces, the gardens, the parks and playgrounds, which once made Bombay one of the most spacious cities in India, have succumbed to the builders' piledriver. Consequently, more and more people in search of a touch of greenery and a whiff of fresh air are travelling longer distances.
>
> The rapid linear expansion of the city towards the north and the north-east has steadily choked off access to recreation grounds in these directions. Juhu, a weekend resort till only a decade ago, has already fallen a victim to the real estate developers. Industries have proliferated in the entire belt between Sion and Thana, and beyond.
>
> Even Marve, Manori and Gorai, 35 miles north of Bombay, have been declared parts of Urban Bombay, and now wait with bated breath for the building blight to strike them. Only the far side of the harbour remains untouched so far, and even here, the construction of the fertiliser project at Thal, and the petro-chemicals complex at Usar, will dangerously narrow the

> available options.
>
> Nhava, therefore, has tremendous potential as a tourist and recreational centre and provides an excellent location for a marine sports complex. There is an urgent need to preserve the island for this purpose; otherwise it will be impossible to ease significantly the pressure that is building upon Elephanta. In fact the Archaeological Survey of India has written repeatedly to the Tourism Development Corporation to develop an alternative picnic spot, since reckless holiday-makers have damaged many of the unexplored sites on the island. A recreation centre at Nhava would draw away casual picnickers and save Elephanta for serious-minded sightseers.
>
> However, this option is being rapidly pre-empted by the central government authorities intent on serving their immediate requirements.

It was not just Bombay-based publications which sounded the alarm. I took up the issue with the *Hindustan Times* of Delhi, one of India's leading newspapers. In their issue of 27th April 1980, they carried an editorial entitled, "An Island called Nhava: Ruining a Paradise". This said (emphasis added):

> Not everyone would recognise the lush tropical island silhouetted against the glistening ocean and the clear sky in our front-page photograph. **It is Nhava, a small tropical paradise only about six nautical miles from the Gateway of India in Bombay. Amidst the hubbub of the harbour it stands green with as yet undisturbed mangrove forest and palm trees, an ecological 'lung' between the mainland of Bombay and the fast-developing city of Greater Bombay.** Only a mile away from the famous Elephanta Island, it is attractive for picnickers who want a day away from the bustle of Bombay.
>
> Nhava has a history which has gone unregarded for a long time. For instance, on it is located the oldest Maritime Museum in the country. The Museum was founded in 1910, exactly ten years before the famous Prince of Wales Museum was thrown open to the public.
>
> The island of Nhava has a unique role to play in the preservation of the monuments and archaeological sites of Elephanta. The archaeological importance of Elephanta is not confined to the existing world-famous complex of the seventh and eighth century cave monuments and the Maheshmurthy frieze. There are six other caves, two ancient landing points, and an old Buddhist Stupa that is yet to be fully excavated. Elephanta still has tremendous archaeological potential and needs to be carefully

> handled. It is too small to absorb the urge of the Bombay dweller for greenery and fresh air. **Nhava provides a good overflow point for the millions that want to hear birds of which it has still about 50 different varieties.** It is ideal for holidays for people who cannot afford long-distance transport and yet have as great a need as any to get away from their sixth-storey flat, for parents who want their children to feel fresh grass under their feet at least once in the year. As Elephanta becomes more and more the focal point for the specialist, and is less and less able to absorb the nature lover, Nhava comes to the mind of all Bombayites as a good place to go to. The overflow from Elephanta to Nhava would be welcomed by the serious archaeologists who view with dismay the overcrowding of Elephanta that impedes their digging and endangers their sites.
>
> Careful and farsighted planning of the Bombay harbour region is important for the preservation of Elephanta and also for the sanity and health of the city dwellers. Unfortunately no lesson seems to have been learnt in composite and forward planning from the conservation and pollution problems of the more developed countries."

Raising a wider issue, the editorial went on to say:

> **As in the case of the Taj, so with Nhava, the magic word 'oil' has wiped off all major and long-term considerations of ecology and conservation.** It appears that this small island, hardly two square miles in area, is to be the base of a supply depot for the ONGC despite land being easily available in Sheva on the mainland. **The word 'oil' has caused such grievous imbalances in the rest of the world that one should be actively conscious of surrendering to it one's natural preserves and archaeological wonders.** Yes, oil by all means but why one item at the cost of others that are irreparable?" (Emphasis mine).

Expressing the feelings of many non-Delhiites, the editorial added: "The twin islands of Elephanta and Nhava, playing complementary roles to each other, are far away from Delhi. But that is no reason why their relationships should be allowed to be disturbed on highly dubious grounds."

The atmosphere was well summed up and described by *This Fortnight* which said in June 1980: "Like the proverbial Texan cowboy, who was driven to extinction by oil, the ONGC looms large and menacingly over Nhava."

In addition to the Departments of Urban Development, Tourism and

L C Gupta, Managing Director, CIDCO and Rashid Yusuf

Technical Education, I took up the Nhava matter with several departments of the State Government, including Archaeology and Museums, Sports and Education. In Delhi, I brought up the issue with the Department of Petroleum, the Ministry of Shipping and, after its formation, with the Department of Environment.

I sought and received a great deal of support from many individuals. They included Cyrus Guzder and of course, years later, my colleagues Debi Goenka and Heta Pandit. An important role was played by Admiral Jal Cursetji, retired Chief of Naval Staff, whom I knew from the Yachting Association of India and who readily agreed to help. In many circles, representations from a retired Naval Chief, especially on nautical matters, carried far more weight than mine. The one person who was ever willing to take up this issue (as he did so many others) with decision makers at all levels, including Prime Minister Indira Gandhi, was S.P. Godrej. It was not just those outside Government who helped; there were several Government officers whose assistance was crucial. The roles of Govind Lalvani, Malati Tambay-Vaidya, B.R. Sawant, Prasanna Chunekar and Shankar Menon, have already been discussed. Others included Maharashtra Government Director of Archaeology and Museums A.P. Jamkhedkar, and Urban Development Deputy Secretary R.B. Donald. A high degree of moral courage was shown by Vice Admiral M.P. Awati, who took up the issue even though he was a serving officer, and the subject had nothing to do with his official portfolio. He wrote to Hashu Advani and met B.B. Vohra and ONGC Chairman P.T. Venugopal. In over three decades of environmental campaigning, I can remember only one other similar action. This was in the early 1990s, when Louis Menezes, a senior serving IAS officer, opposed the alignment of the Konkan Railway in Goa, a subject way outside his portfolio.

In May 1979 a businessman with interests in publishing and the print media suddenly became interested in our work. He readily agreed, on more than one occasion, to come to Nhava, but that did not work out. However, in August he agreed to write to Union Petroleum and Chemicals Minister T.A. Pai and Union Defence Minister C. Subramaniam on a range of issues including Nhava. In October, he also agreed to speak to Chief Minister Sharad Pawar about Nhava.

He put me in touch with an industrialist whom I knew slightly and who was very friendly with Sharad Pawar. I met the industrialist in his Ballard Estate office on the evening of 6th September. It was a very cordial meeting. I briefed him about the activities of BEAG and of the environmental movement. I gave him the details of the proposed expansion of the fishing harbour at Sassoon Dock in South Colaba, regarding which I handed him a note to give to Sharad Pawar. I was also to send him a note on the high-rise building being planned by Gokak Patel Volkart in South Colaba. I also briefly explained the Nhava issue and it was agreed that I would send him a note to hand to Sharad Pawar. Other than these specific issues, he said that I could write to him suggesting that the Bombay Chamber of Commerce and Industry should form an Environmental Sub Committee. In addition he agreed to pay for the cost of a typist, and said that his businessman friend would do likewise, though to a lesser extent, by paying for the cost of a peon. These were welcome reliefs to our finances.

A month later I spoke to the industrialist who said that he would speak to the Chief Minister in a couple of days, about which I reminded him a few days later. A couple of weeks later, I spoke to him and informed him about the Maharashtra Government Protection Committee (more of which later) whose Chairman was Ram Batra, a business associate of his whom he knew very well. The Committee had been asked by Urban Development Minister Hashu Advani to prepare a report on Nhava. He said that he would speak to Ram Batra, that we would meet after the Committee's report, after which he would take up the matter with Sharad Pawar. The next day the industrialist telephoned me, and I went along to his office. After an hour, I was called in and with him was Ram Batra. It was agreed that we would get a resolution passed by the Protection Committee and that ONGC must be made to move to Sheva.

On 10th November 1979 I took Salim Ali to Nhava. Though he was the BEAG President, his was a non-executive role, and I hardly knew him. He was not an environmental activist, but about three decades earlier, he had intervened decisively to help save the Bharatpur Bird Sanctuary. He described the crisis, which occurred immediately after Independence, relating to what became the Keoladeo Ghana National Park at Bharatpur. Apparently, at the time of accession of the princely states to the Union of India, the Bharatpur Maharaja had insisted on inserting a clause retaining for himself the exclusive shooting rights on the Ghana. While the Government of India agreed to it, this was deeply resented by the anti-Maharaja party in Bharatpur, which was in any case very agitated about his alleged past misdeeds and injustices. They protested strongly and alleged that he was selfishly holding on to the Ghana for the pleasure of his influential Delhi friends and himself, thereby depriving poor farmers of good cultivable land and badly needed water. Salim Ali wrote: "With the backing of crooked politicians, complete physical devastation of the Ghana was plotted, and indeed was imminent, when quite by chance I got wind of the plot." He was at Bharatpur with two Englishmen, Horace Alexander and General Sir Harold Williams (Engineer in Chief of the Indian Army). Jawaharlal Nehru was by then Prime Minister and all of them knew him quite well and also of his deep personal love for nature. They approached him, and through Rafi Ahmed Kidwai, the Union Minister for Agriculture and Irrigation, the matter was settled and the Maharaja pressurised to give up his shooting rights. "Thus was the Ghana saved from certain annihilation, and it stands today as one of the world's most fabulous waterfowl resorts."

Salim Ali got a shock when he saw what was happening on Nhava, described it as "vandalism", and asked me to draft a letter to B.B. Vohra whom he knew very well. This was a golden opportunity to make a powerful statement, which I missed. I did not know of Salim Ali's intervention regarding Bharatpur till about 25 years later when I read his autobiography. I did not know of his stature nor did I realise the great regard which Indira Gandhi had for him or otherwise, as soon as she became Prime Minister, I would have requested him to write to her. This would have had a great impact, as it did nine months later. Salim Ali did however write to B. B. Vohra, but it could not have had the same effect as writing to Indira Gandhi.

Political Action

Most people, especially in the developing world, have a deep suspicion of politicians. I have dealt with them relatively infrequently, preferring to deal with the civil servants who are almost always far better informed, generally much easier to deal with, and usually far more honest. In any case, it is the civil servants who move the files. Yet the politicians are sometimes a welcome corrective to the bureaucracy. So it was in the case of Nhava. We were able to persuade several of them to help us.

I have earlier mentioned my attempts to reach the BJP leaders, my contact with Technical Education Minister Nihal Ahmed, and the effort with Chief Minister Sharad Pawar. I now approached Rajni Patel, the Bombay boss and one of the chief fund-raisers of the Congress-I (Indira Gandhi's party), who had been especially powerful in the days of the Emergency. Although now in Delhi there was a government strongly opposed to the Congress-I, and though in August 1978 Sharad Pawar along with his bunch of MLAs had left the Congress-I, thereby toppling the Maharashtra Government, Rajni Patel still knew Sharad Pawar very well. I had approached him in the past on other issues. This time his reaction was quite different. I noted in my diary of 11th October 1979: "Met Rajni Patel at his office, Cuffe Castle, Cuffe Parade re: fishing harbour, Nhava – got a brush-off – I should write to the CM on these and he will take up."

At the end of November 1979, I gave sets of the Nhava papers to my first cousin Ashok Advani, a barrister who had founded and become publisher of the *Business India* group of magazines. I asked him to take up the issue with Viren Shah, the industrialist and Jana Sangh MP who had been arrested during the Emergency, and with Romesh Thapar, publisher of *Seminar*, an influential Delhi magazine, who had also strongly opposed the Emergency. Both of them were well connected with the top echelons of the Government of India. I also asked him to take up the issue with Rajni Patel. My suggestion was that Viren Shah, Romesh Thapar and Rajni Patel be asked to take up the issue with B.B. Vohra.

The person who gave his strong and continuous personal support was Professor Varde. This was not just on the issue of the historical structures (which was within his portfolio), but also on the whole subject of the preservation of Nhava. He visited Nhava and he wrote to his Cabinet colleagues – Urban Development Minister Hashu Advani, Technical Education Minister Nihal Ahmed, and Tourism Minister Sushil Kumar Shinde (later to become Chief Minister). He also wrote to CIDCO Chairman Ram Kapse and others. In a departure from proto-

Hashu Advani reviewing the Guard of Honour of the cadets at *T.S. Rahaman*

col, Professor Varde wrote several times to B.B. Vohra and took care to diligently answer all the latter's replies. I had my work cut out preparing the answers for Professor Varde to send out. His initiative went a long way in saving Nhava. I was told that the Petroleum Ministry or ONGC eventually complained to Chief Minister Sharad Pawar about a minister in his Government writing repeatedly to the Centre. Reportedly, instructions were issued that such communications to the Centre should, in future, be routed through the Chief Secretary.

Among those I approached was Madhu Deolekar, an MLC (Member of the Legislative Council), who was a friend of Sadashiv Gorakshkar, Director of the Prince of Wales Museum of Western India, whom I knew. Both of them belonged to the erstwhile Jana Sangh (a right wing Hindu nationalist party) which, after the Janata government split in 1979, became the Bharatiya Janata Party (BJP). It was one of the constituents of the Progressive Democratic Front. Deolekar and Gorakshkar accompanied me on 16th June 1979 when I took Professor Varde to Nhava. At the end of the visit, they said that they would give me their full support. I asked if they had seen the names on the boards of the institution; they asked what I meant. I said that the names were Rahaman and Mohamed Yusuf. Since I knew them well, I added, tongue in cheek, that they and their party were all Hindu hardliners and that the institutions had been set up by Muslims. They appeared surprised and said, almost as if I was a naive innocent, that while I had been showing Professor Varde and others around the Nautical Institute, they had gone into the village to check if there was illicit distillation of liquor and activities connected with smuggling. They were now satisfied that the island was clean and they would give their full support. They were as good as their word, and gave me the staunchest possible support. Their backing was crucial since they were very well acquainted with Urban Development Minister Hashu Advani who was also from the Jana Sangh; the question of allotment of lands was in his portfolio.

My father had been an officer of the elite and famous Indian Civil Service, often ironically called the "twice born". He became the second Indian (and till now the only Sindhi) Chief Justice of the Bombay High Court. He had been High Court judge for seventeen years, of which, for the last seven, he had been Chief Justice – a very long time by today's standards – till he was killed in November 1965 by a car while walking across the road. Amongst legal circles, and not only in Bombay, he is still remembered. For Sindhis, his is still a specially respected and remembered name. Forty-five years after his death, I am still sometimes introduced as "Justice Chainani's son". To Hashu Advani, this together with my family relationship with Hotchand Advani, was perhaps a certificate of my credibility, leading to cordiality and support. In fact he had me appointed as a Special Executive Magistrate (the replacement title for Justice of Peace or JP).

Of all the political parties, it was the Jana Sangh members whose support was the most effective.

The situation was aptly described by Rajiv Shankar in *The Economic Times* of 7th October 1979. He wrote: "Even members of the state cabinet belonging to the various constituents – the Socialists, Janata and the parallel Congress – have come out strongly in favour of saving the island."

Trade Union Support

Among those whose assistance I sought was Leo Barnes, the formidable General Secretary of the National Union of Seafarers of India. When I first called on him on 22nd June 1979, he was a bit curt. An environmental activist must accept this sort of treatment, but this time the boot was on the other foot. I told him that I had not come to seek a favour but to try to save an Institute in which his Union was, or should be, interested. He changed his tone and promised his support.

This he gave, and submitted to my frequent prodding with good grace and humour. He took up the issue with several agencies. The flip side was that I had to draft his letters.

He wrote: "The Sword of Damocles has been hanging over the Institute which has consequently been undergoing a sad and steady deterioration." This was because first, the Institute was going to be appropriated by CIDCO as a part of its green belt, and was now being taken over by ONGC which had already got hold of a large part of the Island and the campus, including the sea wall. He added that a Seamen's Training Institute needed access to the sea without which it was useless. No institution could function under such uncertain conditions. For this purpose it was essential that those activities of ONGC which were being carried out on the lands of the Nautical Institute should be shifted away from Nhava.

Leo Barnes also took up the issue with the National Shipping Board which discussed it on 6th July 1979. Completely belying what D.D. Sathe and Kannan Srinivasan said, they minuted that "the training imparted was of a high standard and recognised by the Government for employment on board ships". In addition, "its location had assumed historic significance and therefore the move of the ONGC and CIDCO to acquire the premises occupied by the Institute had to be effectively arrested", [and the Institute lands should be excluded from acquisition, so that] "the valuable work being done by the Institute for nearly 60 years now was not allowed to be hampered". The Director-General of Shipping said that the matter had already been taken up with ONGC and CIDCO and he would also take it up with the Petroleum Ministry at the highest level.

Though always cordial, during one of our visits to Nhava, Leo Barnes had a dig at environmentalists and me. He asked if I had read Arthur Hailey's *Overload*, a fictional account of power breakdowns in California, allegedly partly caused by environmental action. I had not read it at that time and could not reply. Were he alive today, I would refer him to the breakdowns of 2000 and 2001 in California, caused not by environmentalists but by poor deregulatory laws and self-seeking action by ruthless electricity traders, of which Enron was just one example.

Years later, the Seafarers Union gave an interest-free loan of Rs. 4.5 crores to the Sir Mohamed Yusuf Seamen's Welfare Foundation, as a result of which the Dr. Leo Barnes Pre-sea Academy was set up at Nhava.

Maharashtra Government Action

When I approached Hashu Advani, he first asked me (referring to the proposed Nhava Sheva Port): "What will happen to my port?" I informed him that the area of the Nautical Institute fell outside the port boundaries and hence it would not interfere with the port.

The Urban Development Department gave us strong support. An important development was the high-level inter-departmental meeting convened and held under the Chairmanship of Minister Hashu Advani in July 1979. Prior to the meeting, I had approached different departmental secretaries to canvas their support. I was especially keen that ONGC not be invited to the meeting, so that the many reasons given by the different Government departments and non-government organisations for the preservation of Nhava could be assembled and a consolidated Maharashtra Government view be taken. If ONGC were to come and present their grandiose plans, this could be thrown out of gear. In this last attempt, I was successful and ONGC was not invited to the meeting.

After the meeting, on 5th September 1979, Urban Development Secretary K.G. Paranjpe wrote to B.B. Vohra saying that the State Government had received a number of representations from several Government departments and other agencies for the preservation of Nhava, Sheva and Nagaon:

1. The Department of Tourism wanted to develop the waterfront and adjacent areas of Nhava for tourism.
2. The Department of Sports wanted to develop a yachting and marine sports centre at Nhava.
3. The Yachting Association of India wanted to set up a national yachting academy and a zonal yachting academy.
4. The Department of Archaeology wanted Nhava developed expeditiously as a tourist/picnic spot to take the spillover of tourists from Elephanta.
5. The Prince of Wales Museum had made a similar representation.
6. The Department of Museums wanted the Nhava Marine Museum to be developed since it was the oldest marine museum in India.
7. The National Maritime Museum wanted the Marine Museum developed as a part of the National Maritime Museum.
8. The National Union of Seafarers of India wanted the Nautical Institute preserved and developed since it was the oldest nautical institute in India and all the trainees get guaranteed lucrative jobs.

9. The Directorate of Technical Education recommended that the Nautical Institute be greatly expanded to include a range of other courses.

10. Environmental groups, including the Save Bombay Committee and Bombay Bachao Committee (the forerunner of BEAG) had requested that Nhava be preserved as a green belt for the citizens of Bombay and for the developing city of New Bombay.

The Maharashtra Government therefore recommended that ONGC be requested to hand back all lands of the Nautical Institute and adjacent areas. They also recommended that an independent review be conducted as to whether the ONGC base necessarily had to be at Nhava or whether it could be sited at an alternative adjacent location such as Sheva. If it was found that the base necessarily had to be at Nhava, the minimum land requirements needed to be determined and it needed to be seen whether part of such lands could be provided at Sheva.

Regarding **Nagaon**, the Maharashtra Government said that ONGC had been given about 80 hectares of land adjacent to the waterfront. It was felt that the waterfront land, together with all the adjacent land, should be kept free and developed for purposes of tourism, a green belt, yachting and so on. They added that the CIDCO Board had passed a resolution to this effect. Mentioning the obvious point that it would not be possible to develop these activities with a major industrial chemical complex just behind it, they asked that a review be taken up on how the ONGC area of 80 hectares could be reduced. If necessary, additional land could be provided to ONGC in lieu of the waterfront areas.

The operative part of the letter was the request that while these reviews were being conducted, "no further work be carried out at Nhava, and in particular there should be no tree cutting or quarrying or any other activities which would change the landscape of Nhava".

A high-level meeting to be held in Hashu Advani's chamber was scheduled for 16th October 1979. The day before the meeting, Cheema telephoned me saying that he would like to meet me regarding Nhava. He said he had heard a lot about me from mutual friends and mentioned the name of Brigadier Gill. He added that he would like to come and meet me but it would be better if I went there, "so that we can show you what we are doing with our oil". I was unsure whether I could resist his blandishments and answered that I was in a meeting and unwell and would meet him in a day or so. He replied saying that "that will be very late". The next day, when I saw him entering Hashu Advani's chamber, I felt a sense of dread.

Among those who attended the meeting were Urban Development Secretary Vinod Nair, CIDCO Chairman Ram Kapse, CIDCO Managing Director L.C. Gupta, Bombay Port Trust Chief Engineer S.S. Kanvinde and Cheema.

At that time I did not know Ram Kapse (also of the BJP who, more than 20 years later, became Lieutenant Governor of the Andaman and Nicobar Islands); I got to know him in subsequent years and I am sure that had I approached him he would have been sympathetic and helpful. From our side was Sadashiv Gorakshkar, Bakul Khote and myself. The meeting lasted for one hour and the discussions were very heated. I was relatively new to environmental activism, and though I received good support from Bakul Khote, I did not handle matters as well as I should have. Cheema asked why the questions of Nhava and Nagaon were being raised at this late stage after the land had been allotted to ONGC in 1975. I replied that this was because the public had not been aware of the development schemes earlier and that as soon as we had learnt of the schemes for the takeover of Nhava and Nagaon, we had taken up the matter in the middle of 1978 itself. Hashu Advani pointed out that regardless of what had happened in the past, if any errors had been committed, surely the idea should be not to perpetuate them.

After some discussion, Cheema agreed that ONGC would build at their cost a new deep-water jetty for the Institute and in addition, continue to allow public access from the main jetty which they had acquired. He also agreed that when they built their new pier, they would allow public access from that as well. In addition, an area of 14 hectares behind the existing sea wall would be kept completely green and developed as a nursery, to which, along with the sea wall, the public would be allowed access. Most importantly, Cheema agreed that ONGC would consider the possibility of reducing the land occupied by them at Nhava and the land required by them at Nagaon and would submit a proposal on this to the Maharashtra Government. Actually, far from reducing their Nagaon lands, they sought to double them.

These are among the promises ONGC did not keep. Though the sea wall and the 14 hectares behind it have not been used by ONGC and are still green, for over 30 years ONGC has obstinately not made either of them open to the public and denied people the use of a beautiful green habitat. Apart from that, non-access to the sea wall has prevented the Institute and visitors of making use of a lovely high water landing place, a facility which they had used for decades. ONGC has also not built the deep-water jetty for the Nautical Institute as they had prom-

Boards put up by M/s Essar Constructions Ltd. at Nhava earlier and at commencement of work

ised – thereby hindering the training, as well as denying the *mucchwas* (country craft) of the local villagers a landing area which they had promised to Nhava Village.

A few days after the meeting, on 21st October, a major breakthrough occurred when, at our instance, Hashu Advani visited the Nautical Institute. He had probably been to an engagement the previous evening and appeared drowsy but in the launch, en route to Nhava, he showed a keen interest in the naval ships we passed. I was advised by Madhu Deolekar to get a report carried in the press so that ONGC would get to know of his support for the Institute. We were able to do this, and the *Evening News* of 29th October 1979 carried a photograph of Hashu Advani inspecting the trainees at the inauguration of the 69th Seamen's Training Course.

Deforestation and Destruction

In those days, I read the newspapers, even the advertisements, much more carefully than I do today. In July and August 1979, two extremely alarming press advertisements appeared. ONGC's contractor, Essar Constructions Ltd., advertised for a sub-contractor for quarrying approximately 500,000 cubic metres on Nhava. This would totally destroy the landscape and devastate the environment. The other one was a notice issued by ONGC saying that an auction would take place on 10th August for "cutting and taking away about 2000 numbers of trees mainly of Amba, Athrun, Bore, Sawar, Ranjon, Pongora, Gulmohar, Oomber, Sabul, Kaaju and Seewon at Nhava".

The fact of the existence of 2,000 trees on Nhava gave the lie to the statements repeatedly made by ONGC, then and later, including to the Prime Minister, that they had taken over only the barren portions of Nhava.

Urgent action was necessary since the auction was to take place in a matter of days. I rushed to Mantralaya and was taken (as I remember, by Madhu Deolekar) to the concerned minister. There appeared to be some confusion in the minister's mind. He appeared to think that I had come to plead to be permitted to cut the trees!

On 14th August, the Urban Development Department wrote to me saying that at their request ONGC had agreed to postpone the tree-cutting auction. When queried later, ONGC said that the tender notice had been issued through an error and that the auction had been cancelled. However, in spite of all our efforts and all of ONGC's promises, cutting the trees went on, and reportedly the entire area was cleared within two days.

This tree felling almost resulted in a major embarrassment. Even in an NGO, and even when people are working for a common cause, differences of temperament, personality and approaches to problems arise. Tensions had surfaced between one of the Save Bombay Committee (SBC) members and me and I was spending more and more time on BEAG's work which was demanding in itself. This led to a communication gap. Regarding the proposed massive tree felling, the SBC had correctly written to ONGC. In response, Cheema telephoned an SBC office bearer to confirm that he had stayed the tree felling and would like to meet the SBC office bearer to explain ONGC's project. This meeting, about which I knew nothing, took place on 13th August. It was agreed that there would be a joint check of the area so as to decide whether the trees should be shifted or cut. Cheema also agreed that no trees would be cut till the SBC horticulturists advised ONGC in the matter. In addition, Cheema desired SBC's co-operation for the Nhava project. The SBC office bearer conveyed SBC's anxiety "to play its constructive part in the development of the whole area". This last statement was probably made without knowledge of the Nhava campaign. Our whole stand (including Maharashtra Government's request made very shortly thereafter) was that ONGC relocate its project away from Nhava. What part was there for SBC to play in the project? Fortunately nothing came of this. Needless to say, in spite of Cheema's promises, apart from tree cutting a large amount of quarrying was subsequently carried out.

The position was well described in the *Hindustan Times* editorial of April 1980 which said:

> It is time, therefore, to give serious thought to the distressing fact that there is deforestation below the north-easterly headland spur of Nhava, visible from the island of Elephanta. The tree line has been perceptibly denuded and a stretch of characteristic and valuable mangrove forest along the foreshore is similarly threatened.
>
> Today, Nhava stands under the threat of bulldozers that will ruin its forests and greenery. As yet it is a relatively undisturbed haven – an 'emerald isle' in the highly developed and active harbour region of Bombay. But if the authorities are not careful, tomorrow it will be a mass of buildings and hot concrete roads. Instead of playing a sister role to the Elephanta island, it will then be providing its own rush of visitors to the Caves and this will result in further over-crowding of Elephanta which will be hazardous to its monuments. This will be disastrous and has to be stopped.

This Fortnight, in an article of June 1980 entitled "Rape of Nhava" said: "What was once a densely wooded hill where the chatter of birds was predominant is now a mauled mound with the whine of the bulldozer in the background." They went on to say, "Despite outraged representations by individuals, groups and the State Government the ONGC have bulldozed their way through and developments read like a Mickey Spillane thriller."

The Maharashtra Government Protection Committee

Hashu Advani had appointed a Committee called the Maharashtra Government Committee for Protection, Preservation and Beautification of Greater Bombay and its Environs (Maharashtra Government Protection Committee). It consisted of representatives of the State Government, the Bombay Municipal Corporation, and other official agencies along with representatives of NGOs and private individuals. It was chaired by Bombay Sheriff Ram Batra, a Jana Sangh activist. Other non-government members were S.P. Godrej, Sadashiv Gorakshkar, Madhu Deolekar, Foy Nissen, Mrs. Shantu Chatterjee and me. The terms of reference were "to advise Government and other concerned bodies with special reference to measures aimed at the protection, preservation, development and beautification of areas such as green belts, promenades, historical and aesthetical buildings and precincts, areas of public recreation, beaches, parks, playgrounds etc".

Till it was dissolved in December 1988 by Chief Secretary D.M. Sukthankar, the Committee served a very useful purpose by enabling an NGO-Government dialogue on a variety of civic and environmental issues.

At the meeting of 16th October 1979 with ONGC, Hashu Advani requested this Committee to visit Nhava and submit a report. The first meeting of the Committee was held on 23rd October 1979, when several items including the ONGC terminal at Nagaon were placed on the agenda. Several members wanted the Maharashtra Government to issue an order staying further work by ONGC on Nhava. Ram Batra suggested that that be done after the Committee's visit to Nhava, but Madhu Deolekar insisted that it be done immediately. The Joint Director of Tourism opposed this, saying that oil was important, but a resolution asking for a stay was passed. After the meeting, Ram Batra, Gorakshkar, Deolekar, Deputy Secretary R.B. Donald and I went to Hashu Advani and told him of the resolution. Hashu Advani agreed to telephone Cheema but asked us to complete the Committee's report quickly, since even a day's delay would cause a loss to the Government.

The Committee visited Nhava on 29th October and held several discussions with ONGC. ONGC promised the Committee that they would locate no additional projects at Nhava and reiterated their earlier commitment that they had abandoned their earlier plans to claim any more of the Nautical Institute's land. This was very critical for the Institute and for the environment of Nhava and was the third crucial step forward. Also very vital was ONGC's commitment not to build any residential quarters on Nhava.

When the Committee's draft report was discussed, it was agreed that it needed strengthening. No one wants to buck a powerful organisation and ONGC is indeed very powerful. On 28th November when I saw the modified draft I got a shock, since far from being strengthened, the report had been greatly weakened and most of the recommendations had been omitted. The Committee's observations on Nhava were very damaging to ONGC and, right to the end, kept being deleted from the report. A big argument took place. Madhu Deolekar and I wrote to Ram Batra saying that the report needed strengthening. Some other members were also of the same view. Eventually, after more discussions and after eight drafts were prepared, a consensus was arrived at.

ONGC were clearly worried about the Committee's recommendations since on 4th December, when I was with Deputy Secretary R.B. Donald finalising the report, S.G. Kulkarni, their liaison officer, called on Donald trying to find out the latest position. He asked as to when the Maharashtra Government would pass the orders. He added that the issue had become 'hot' and that S.P. Godrej had written to B.B. Vohra and ONGC Chairman P.T. Venugopal.

Contrary to Cheema's assertion that ONGC had not felled more than 10 trees, the Committee Report of December 1979 observed "that truck loads of trees were being cut down from the thickly wooded areas". In addition, "there were extensive operations for excavating and quarrying the hillside". To this ONGC replied that the tree cutting had been done not by them but by outsiders. They did not explain how outsiders had entered the ONGC premises. The Committee noted that it was ONGC's responsibility to protect the trees in its area.

The Committee noted that it had "examined the situation and has come to the conclusion that the position in the Nhava Island with reference to the activities of the ONGC is not a desirable situation and not in the interest of this Island or the citizens of Greater Bombay and New Bombay, as this Island is already within a designated green belt and has natural scenic advantages and a location conveniently close to Bombay which should be developed as a lung for the city. Considerable damage has already been done to the environment and ecology, etc. due to the ONGC setting up their base on the island and it is imperative to curtail further deterioration. The Committee strongly feels that in the overall context and in the interest of the citizens of Greater Bombay and New Bombay and environs, it would be desirable if the ONGC shifts its activities completely to a new site."

The Committee strongly recommended that **"even at this late stage the entire scheme of operation of the ONGC on the Nhava Island should be shifted to any other location (e.g. somewhere along the coast of Ratnagiri)** not only for the reasons already given but also in the interest of the development of the nearby historic Elephanta caves which would necessarily feel the impact of the operation on Nhava Island. This would also be in the interest of the development by Government of the otherwise backward Ratnagiri District." (Emphasis mine.)

The Committee made three key recommendations. The first was that the proposed port should be confined to Sheva, leaving Nhava alone. The second was that no other agency should be permitted to operate a base on Nhava or its vicinity. The third was that no land on Nhava should be allotted to any other agency for any purpose whatsoever.

In addition, the Committee made a number of detailed recommendations, some of which are mentioned below.

1. In case it was not possible to relocate the ONGC base away from Bombay, they should be asked to locate it at Sheva where the ecological damage would be much less.

2. If this was not possible, then a "realistic objective assessment of their land requirement" should be made, and till this was done, ONGC should "be refrained from awarding new contracts".

3. As agreed by ONGC, the activities of the Nautical Institute should not be hindered any more by the threat of acquisition of any of its properties.

4. No quarrying should be permitted on the island.

5. As confirmed by ONGC, no residential quarters should be permitted on Nhava. This must be properly recorded and the State Government should ensure that this decision is not changed at any future date.

6. An area of 14 hectares between the ONGC operational area and the Nautical Institute should be developed as a nursery, kept open to the public and the land taken back from ONGC.

7. The railway siding contemplated by ONGC should be dropped.

8. The road alignment should be altered so that it does not run through green areas, but runs along the southern boundary of the ONGC land, so that both ONGC and the proposed port could use a common road.

9. ONGC be directed to halt all further reclamation at Stage V of its project and even the existing reclamation should be carefully reviewed by Government.

The Committee's Report on Nhava, along with the reports on Mahim Fort, Bandra Fort and the Sassoon Fish Harbour were formally presented to Hashu Advani on 7th December 1979. Sadly, no report was prepared on Nagaon, with its lovely sandy beach and the beautiful Bhiwandiwalla Gardens close by. The subject was not taken up at all by the Committee, either then or later. It was a grievous lapse on all our parts, especially mine.

Ram Batra must have been irritated by my performance in the Committee and by his having been forced to strengthen the report. At a party on the evening of the same day on which the report was presented to Hashu Advani, I met one of the industrialists who was supporting BEAG, and who had in fact agreed to take up the Nhava matter with Chief Minister Sharad Pawar. He said that he would stop helping us

Environmental destruction on the hill slopes, Nhava

because I overstated my case; he refused to listen to any explanations. However, his financial assistance continued for some more time, after which it was abruptly cut off. His businessman friend said the same thing, but agreed to listen, said we should talk later, and continued his assistance for almost 30 years.

The host at the party had business dealings with ONGC and among the guests were Cheema and his wife, to whom I spoke for half an hour. I was disconcerted when my host said I had been rude to them. A few days later, my host telephoned me saying that he wanted to talk to me privately regarding ONGC at Nhava. Was it to discuss a compromise after the Protection Committee's report? I do not remember what happened after that.

Review

ONGC kept repeating that Nhava was the only suitable location for their base and that no other locations were possible. Yet, four years later, they tried very hard to locate another base at Dighi in the Janjira Creek 77 kilometres south of Bombay; this entailed yet another bitter battle.

In the arguments with ONGC, I kept pointing out that even if their jetties had to be on Nhava, at least their storage facilities did not need to be located close to the waterfront and could easily be located on the mainland which is just a few kilometres away. I consulted a few friends connected with shipping and maritime affairs. These included Ajay Balram, Ravi Katari, Commander Lalit Sharma, a retired naval officer, Raj Kadan, and Commander (later Captain) Vijay Shivdasani, then a serving naval officer. They agreed with me. They were also unanimous that the land requirement could be whittled down to a few acres, as against the 54 hectares (133 acres) taken over by ONGC, in addition to the land being reclaimed by them.

Ajay Balram prepared a detailed note based on approximate figures. Firstly, he said that there was no need for the ONGC base to be at Nhava, and that other alternatives were possible. He then pointed out that ONGC was currently operating from a very small area in Victoria Dock in the Bombay Port where the depth of water available is about 17-18 feet. Hence ONGC's insistence that they needed a minimum draft of 9 metres (29.5 feet) appeared excessive, especially for the type of craft that normally ply as support services.

Regarding the area demanded by ONGC, Ajay Balram said that they currently occupied probably not more than 1.5 acres on the Victoria Dock harbour wall. ONGC's requirement of items such as diesel, water, cement, etc. was stated to be about 250,000 tons. Even assuming that the total annual requirement was to be stored (which was unusual), the maximum area required for this would be 15 acres at the outside. What he did not specifically say was that if the comparison was done berth-wise, and even if the five berths sought by ONGC were to be treated the same way as the 50 berths in the Bombay Port which catered for ocean-going vessels, the land required by ONGC would be only one-tenth that of Bombay Port, namely 41 acres. Storage facilities for the material required by them did not have to be on the island and could easily be created on the mainland, which was close by.

As opposed to the above figures, ONGC had acquired over 130 acres on Nhava. This needed to be compared with the Bombay Port which handled about 13-14million tons of cargo annually from an operational area of about 410 acres. This was land grab on a large scale, and of prime wooded and forested areas, at that. Ajay Balram added: "All in all it would seem that the area demanded by them has been on the basis of 'you never know we may need it someday' and also they have not seriously considered locating non-essential facilities on the mainland or for that matter the possibility of arranging regular supplies from Bombay City by water (cheap launches or barges on a charter basis)."

The Maharashtra Government Protection Committee observed in their Report: "The ONGC was not able to mention the specific projects which have necessitated the total land requirement."

Sadly, in spite of repeated urgings by the Maharashtra Government and by us, no review of ONGC's land requirements was ever carried out.

Whatever else needs, or does not need, to be on the waterfront, nobody, not even ONGC, can claim that an oil and gas terminal, tank farm, helicopter base, office complex and housing colony require proximity to the water. The helicopter base, the oil and gas terminal and the tank farm were relocated away from Nhava not for environmental but technical reasons. It is not clear what made ONGC re-site the office complex away from Nhava – our pressure, or their own compulsions.

Their housing colony was very much on the cards when we started our campaign and, as mentioned above, was initially contemplated as a large colony for 15,000 people. As mentioned earlier, as late as April 1978, the *Evening News* had reported that ONGC had been "keen" on taking over the Institute's premises for their staff housing. It was only after sustained pressure from us and from the Maharashtra Government Protection Committee, that ONGC finally made commitments to locate their housing colony away from Nhava. We probably did ONGC a favour since they developed an integrated housing colony for their various facilities at Panvel on the mainland.

Sustained pressure also compelled ONGC to commit that an area of 14 hectares (34 acres) between the Nautical Institute and the ONGC operational area would be greened and developed as a nursery and kept open to the public. The greening was done initially but neglected thereafter. Public access was never given.

Sail boat at the school entrance

The Shipping Ministry

THE ADMINISTRATIVE MINISTRY that should have been concerned about the Nautical Institute was the Ministry of Shipping & Transport. Though the Petroleum Ministry or ONGC could not just ride roughshod over them, the Shipping Ministry had not lifted a finger to save the Institute.

In July 1979, while in Delhi, I met P.G. Gavai who had earlier been the Director-General of Shipping and was subsequently to become Chief Secretary of Maharashtra and Lieutenant Governor of Delhi. He had written to B.B. Vohra a few days earlier referring to a representation he had received from Leo Barnes, asking whether it would be possible for ONGC to let the Nautical Institute remain at the present site. As Gavai pointed out to me, this was a departure from normal protocol, since he was no longer in the shipping chair, and was in a different job in a completely different ministry. He suggested that I get in touch with Shipping Ministry Joint Secretary, Padmanabhan.

Though the notice was short, Padmanabhan agreed to meet me. I gave him a representation along with many letters written by several admirals, Professor Varde, S.S. Tinaikar and Sadashiv Gorakshkar. I pointed out to him that the Nautical Institute was something that his Ministry should be concerned about and requested him to take up the matter with the Petroleum Ministry. A few days later, the Shipping Ministry wrote to the Directorate-General of Shipping.

On my return to Bombay, I suggested to Admiral Cursetji and Leo Barnes that maybe they should also write to Padmanabhan, which both of them did. Clearly Admiral Cursetji had a status that both Leo Barnes and I lacked, since in September he received an acknowledgement from the Ministry saying that they had already taken up examination of the issue based on my letter.

In December 1979 I wrote to Padmanabhan pointing out that ONGC had commenced building their Nhava base without clearance from the Bombay Port Trust, and that this posed a threat to the proposed Nhava Sheva Port. A few days later, when I went to Delhi, Padmanabhan was busy but I was able to meet Under Secretary Krishan Lall and his assistant, Section Officer K.K. Gupta. They told me that Padmanabhan had written to B.B. Vohra a few days earlier, on 20th December, regarding the need to preserve the Nautical Institute. When I referred to ONGC's action, I was told that their section was concerned only with "Shipping" (which covered the Nautical Institute), whereas my latest letter referred to "Ports", which would be referred to Joint Secretary (Ports) D.K. Jain.

The Shipping Ministry had shown no sign of urgency and had taken five months to act. In the meantime, ONGC's destructive action on Nhava had been going on at full blast. However, at least the Shipping Ministry had officially acknowledged the Nautical Institute's problem, probably for the first time.

In April 1980 when I again visited the Shipping Ministry, I ran into a problem, since none of the officers I had met in December was there. Padmanabhan was going out of Delhi, Krishan Lall was out of India and K.K. Gupta had handed over charge. It is the personal assistants who can grant or deny access to senior officers and I was lucky that Swami, Padmanabhan's personal assistant, was helpful. He referred me to Under Secretary Sital Singh who had taken over from Krishan Lall. Sital Singh knew nothing of the matter. The next day when I met him again, he could not trace the file and sent me along to his assistant, Section Officer Krishnan who had recently taken over from K.K. Gupta. Krishnan was not available then but when I was finally able to contact him the next day he turned out to be most diligent. Though he had taken over this assignment only recently and though the file was still untraceable, he was finally able to locate it. It was entitled "Preservation of Nautical Training Institution in Nhava Island in Bombay". He told me that after the letter of 20th December 1979, a reminder should have gone out but it had not. What was worse, the file had been "recorded" i.e. closed. Had we not followed up, no further action would have been taken by the Shipping Ministry. Krishnan promised that the reminder would be sent, but at the level of a Director, which is a lower level. The reminder was sent a few days later. I was very pleasantly surprised that a government officer, especially one I had never met before, was so polite and helpful.

After a number of reminders and a great deal of follow up, the Shipping Ministry eventually replied, first to Admiral Cursetji in October 1980 and then to Leo Barnes. The Shipping Ministry's replies to both of them were virtually identical. Perhaps considering me to be of a lower status than an admiral and a powerful trade union leader, they did not care to reply to me. However, I received a letter on the same lines from the Deputy Director-General of Shipping B.K. Pawar. The Shipping Ministry said:

> This had been examined in consultation with the Department of Petroleum, who informed that if the ONGC's original plan had been implemented, the occupants of about 500 Houses at Nhava village and Yusuf would have been disturbed. But the ONGC have revised their plan and decided to take the barest minimum area in the Nhava Island and they would like to stress that the area taken by them is mostly hilly and they are reclaiming, at a great cost, about 25 hectares of land in the sea. Except for 5 small Yusuf Trust Cottages inside the premises they have not touched any Yusuf Trust Complex.

After all the damage ONGC had caused, what added insult to severe injury was the following statement:

> The ONGC have also taken care to see that the activities of the Nautical College are not hampered in any way. On the contrary, the college will have the benefit of the ONGC's water supply facility, approach roads and any other improvements they make. The ONGC has also decided to make a special small jetty for use for their training purposes. Besides, the area adjoining the complex has been earmarked for the development of a nursery and a garden, while retaining the existing mangroves. **This will enhance the beauty of the area, which the public may use.** (Emphasis mine.)

Two Prime Ministers

One of those who agreed to come to Nhava was Prem Shankar Jha, then Editor of *The Economic Times*. On 6th October 1979 just before we were scheduled to go, Jha said he would like to cry off. He thought his visit would be superfluous since his colleague Rajiv Shankar had written a long piece which would be carried on the front page the next day. However, I was insistent that he come and see for himself; he reluctantly agreed which was very fortunate. When he saw the destruction on Nhava, he was infuriated. Those who have seen Prem Jha's rage will understand the full import of this. Nhava was the direct beneficiary of his anger.

Prem Jha had written a number of articles about agriculture and the difficulties of farmers and this had brought him to the favourable notice of Prime Minister Charan Singh. The day after our Nhava visit, Rajiv Shankar's large front-page item appeared. A couple of weeks later, Prem Jha telephoned me from Delhi and said that he had met Charan Singh and was to give him a note. He later told me that he had had a seven-or-eight-minute discussion on Nhava with Charan Singh, who had heard of the issue and had promised to stop the destruction. Prem Jha had also tried to meet Petroleum Secretary B.B. Vohra but the latter had been busy with the Indian Oil Corporation officers' strike. Prem Jha asked me to send the press item to Prime Minister Charan Singh and also (what I heard him as saying) to his Private Secretary, Krishnaswamy Rao. I telephoned the latter and sent him the papers; it was only when I received an acknowledgement that I realised that the person I had written to was among the most powerful civil servants in India – C.R. Krishnaswamy Rao Sahib, Secretary to the Prime Minister. Prem Jha's intervention had significantly "upped the ante".

At my request, S.P. Godrej met Krishnaswamy Rao Sahib in Delhi. The news he brought back, in the last week of November, was good. Krishnaswamy Rao Sahib knew of the issue and had been sympathetic. He had said that ONGC had been told that merely because money had been spent, that was no reason for them to stay on Nhava.

I followed up the matter and on 2nd December, I telephoned my cousin Ashok Advani who was on a trip to Delhi, and asked him to write to Krishnaswamy Rao Sahib. More important, at that time, Dr. Vasant Bawa was staying with me. He was an IAS (Indian Administrative Service) officer, who had been the first Vice Chairman of the Hyderabad Urban Development Authority, but had taken premature retirement and had become a scholar and activist. He had belonged to the Andhra Pradesh cadre of the IAS, the same cadre to which Krishnaswamy Rao Sahib belonged, and hence knew the latter. I briefed Bawa about Nhava and he wrote to Krishnaswamy Rao Sahib.

I went to Delhi twice in December 1979 hoping to meet the Prime Minister. On my first trip, late in the evening of 13th December, at

Bombay airport, I met S.P. Godrej and prepared draft letters for him to send to B.B. Vohra, Krishnaswamy Rao Sahib and the Prime Minister. I also gave him two copies of the Protection Committee report, one of them being for Krishnaswamy Rao Sahib.

Going along the beautiful green roads of Lutyens' Delhi, in the champagne-like north Indian winter, was so beguiling that I had to force myself to focus on the critical meetings ahead. There was need for haste since the general elections were due very shortly and Charan Singh's government was expected to lose. I raised the question of Nhava with Commander Sureshwar ('Willie') Sinha, an old sailing friend who was an informal security advisor to Charan Singh's Lok Dal party. I requested him to arrange an appointment with the Prime Minister and also to ask for the intervention of Raj Narain – a prominent Lok Dal MP who had decisively defeated Indira Gandhi in the 1977 elections – whom Willie Sinha knew well. Ajay Balram was very helpful in this whole process. Unfortunately, because of the imminence of the general elections, none of these meetings took place. During my second trip to Delhi ten days later, I was told that a meeting could possibly be arranged with J.P. Singh, the Prime Minister's son-in-law. The only concrete response from all these political approaches was a message asking if I could obtain contributions for the party's campaign funds.

However, officers of the Prime Minister's Office (PMO) were friendly. During my first trip, I was able, after waiting for nearly two hours, to have a ten-minute meeting on 15th December evening together with Krishnaswamy Rao Sahib and Joint Secretary Hasmukh Shah. I showed Krishnaswamy Rao Sahib the photographs of the destruction on Nhava. He said that he had received letters from S.P. Godrej and Prof. S.S. Varde and was aware of the report of the Maharashtra Government Committee on Nhava. Perhaps S.P. Godrej had already given or sent him a copy. He added that it was not their intention to destroy Nhava. A couple of days later, I again met Hasmukh Shah and dropped in on Keki Daruwalla, Deputy Secretary in the PMO. Keki Daruwalla said that unfortunately it was election time, otherwise he would have tried to arrange a meeting for me with the Prime Minister. (Incidentally, apart from having been an officer in one of the intelligence services, retiring as Chairman of the Joint Intelligence Committee, Keki Daruwalla is also a well known poet.)

On 27th December Saad Ali and I met Keki Daruwalla. He said that nothing was expected to happen during the next month. While he would be happy to help us on environmental matters, he would not

Destruction of mangroves on Nhava (foreground)

be able to do anything especially at this stage when no important decisions were being taken unless the Prime Minister issued specific instructions.

We then met Hasmukh Shah. He had gone through all the papers I had left earlier. I gave him a letter rebutting the points made by ONGC in their note. He also reiterated that no decisions could be expected at that stage. He had been trying to get hold of B.B. Vohra, but had been unsuccessful since the latter had had an illness in his family. Now B.B. Vohra was going abroad to get oil, and matters would have to wait till his return since oil was more important than birds. At my request, Hasmukh Shah agreed to look into the matter of asking the Petroleum Ministry for a review of their land requirements. I gave him a handwritten aide memoire regarding the above and also requested that it should be checked as to how ONGC had started work without the clearance of the Bombay Port Trust. I reiterated that the best course would be if ONGC relocated the entire Nhava operation as demanded by the Maharashtra Government. Regarding Nagaon, I requested that the Petroleum Ministry be asked to relocate all their fresh facilities two or three miles away from the waterfront behind the hill range.

It was perhaps unrealistic to expect decisions on Nhava at that time. The Russians had just gone into Afghanistan and the Government was not even responding adequately to that. However, what was the harm in trying?

I did not know that the PMO had already started the process by writing to the Petroleum Ministry under whose jurisdiction ONGC falls. Their action must have been very quick, since replies were received from the Ministry of Tourism and Civil Aviation on 29th November and from the Petroleum Secretary in December. The PMO's promptness must have been due to Prem Jha's intercession with the Prime Minister.

Charan Singh was decisively defeated in the elections and was succeeded by Indira Gandhi. Unlike in the USA, in India, when a government changes, it is only the ministers who change; the civil servants remain. It is the strength of our system, that even though the process had started during the tenure of Charan Singh to whom Indira Gandhi was strongly opposed, the PMO under Indira Gandhi continued their follow up – in fact more vigorously than the earlier regime which had initiated the action.

On 2nd February 1980 R. Rajamani, Joint Secretary in the PMO, wrote to the Petroleum Secretary asking for clarifications on the Ministry's note of December 1979. The note said inter alia:

> PM has observed that she would like to have the details of the exact location proposed in the entire ONGC project. She would also like to know whether complaints have been received that the location proposed would lead to environmental damage or pollution. The Ministry of Tourism and Civil Aviation have informed us in their UO note No.2-CT(24)/75-Vol.II dated 29.11.1979 (copy enclosed) that they are of the view that it would be desirable to shift the ONGC installations elsewhere in the Bombay harbour. PM would like to have a note very early dealing with all these points.

What was interesting was the Tourism Ministry's view that the ONGC installations be moved away. Some of our efforts on the tourism front had obviously paid off.

C.P.N. Singh

On 3rd April 1980 I was all set to sail to Mandwa for a long weekend. However, this plan, like so many others, had to be cancelled at the last minute, since at 4.15 p.m. Bombay Port Trust (BPT) Chief Engineer A.V. D'Souza telephoned me asking what our objections to the proposed Nhava Sheva Port were. He wanted to know since the Union Shipping Minister and/or Union Minister of State for Defence, C.P.N. Singh were coming to Bombay. An hour later Commander Sawhney of Mazagon Docks Ltd. (MDL) telephoned me to say that C.P.N. Singh was coming to

Bombay at the request of the Prime Minister to look into the question of the massive expansion scheme of the Sassoon Fish Harbour at Colaba in south Bombay (about which there had been massive citizens' protests led by us) and the ONGC base at Nhava. What I did not then know was that the Prime Minister had issued stop work orders on the Nhava Sheva Port and on the Fish Harbour expansion.

C.P.N. Singh was one of the Sanjay Gandhi brigade (those who had been brought into prominence by the Prime Minister's younger son). Dapper and polished, he spoke with a public school English accent. Sending him was odd, since Mazagon Docks came under his department and this would be a clear conflict of interests, making it difficult for him to make an impartial assessment.

The next few days were a flurry of preparing memoranda and assembling activists and others to meet C.P.N. Singh. When I told Commander Sawhney that we would like to accompany the minister to Nhava, he said that we should make our own way there – he probably felt that he could prevent us from seeing the minister. Perhaps realising that this sounded too brusque, the next night his deputy, Captain Agarwala, telephoned me to say that since the launch was very small, none of us could be accommodated in it. I suggested that the minister be taken to the Nautical Institute.

In my letter of 7th April to C.P.N. Singh, I spelt out the reasons for the preservation of Nhava. I pointed out that as opposed to the 130 acres occupied by ONGC on Nhava, their actual land requirement would only be between 8 to15 acres and added that the Maharashtra Government had asked for a review. I also raised the issue of Nagaon beach in Uran where, as opposed to their own stated requirements of 30 hectares, ONGC had taken 70 hectares. I pleaded that any facilities which had yet to come up, should be located a couple of miles behind the beach so as to preserve as much as possible of the beach and adjacent areas.

Cyrus Guzder, writing both from an archaeological point of view and as a tourism and travel professional, gave a detailed note stressing the importance of Elephanta and pointing out that it was one of India's most important archaeological sites. He added that it was abundantly clear that the only way to save Elephanta from the thousands of picnickers who visited it every weekend was to develop an alternative spot in the harbour. Failing that, Elephanta Island would be doomed and cease being a tranquil spot. In this regard he stressed the beauty and lush greenery of Nhava.

C.P.N. Singh obviously took his mission seriously. Accompanying him were K.P.A. Menon and Dr. D.N. Prasad, Secretary and Joint Secretary respectively of the Department of Defence Production, both of whom, like C.P.N. Singh, also had conflicts of interest, since it was their department which was the controlling department for Mazagon Docks Ltd. Also in the team were Joint Secretary (Navy) S.N. Bajpe and Dr. N.L. Ramanathan, Director of the very small Environment Division of the Department of Science & Technology (DST), which later became the Department of Environment (DOE) – the parent of today's Ministry of Environment & Forests.

We had a busy day ahead. On 8th April 1980 we first visited the Sassoon Fish Harbour, and then went to Nhava. What could the minister have absorbed in this brief period, especially at Nhava? Though some of us were eventually taken by launch to Nhava, the minister went ahead with the MDL top brass, who gave him a one-sided briefing.

That same afternoon, at 2.30 and 3.30 p.m., meetings were convened by the minister regarding Nhava and the Sassoon Fish Harbour. Along with the high-powered Delhi team, there was a phalanx of the Maharashtra Government's top brass, including Chief Secretary P.G. Gavai, Urban Development Secretary Vinod Nair, Revenue Secretary K.K. Uppal, CIDCO Managing Director L.C. Gupta, Planning Secretary V. Venkatesan and Bombay Metropolitan Commissioner M.S. Palnitkar. With them were Bombay Port Trust Chairman B.C. Cariappa, Bombay Port Trust Chief Engineer A.V. D'Souza, Mazagon Docks Ltd. Chairman and Managing Director Vice Admiral N.P. Datta, Ram Batra and of course, Cheema. Amazingly, Shashi Ruia of Essar, ONGC's contractors for Nhava, was also allowed to be present. Thus the conservation lobby comprising S.P. Godrej, Sadashiv Gorakshkar, Cyrus Guzder, Foy Nissen, Navroz Mody, Rashid Yusuf and me were outnumbered and under-powered.

ONGC

The discussions regarding Nhava dealt with two quite separate issues – ONGC's base together with the MDL fabrication yard, and the Nhava Sheva Port. The discussion began with S.P. Godrej, Sadashiv Gorakshkar and me making the case for the preservation of Nhava as a green belt. I pointed out that there were only two islands which were easily accessible to picnickers and visitors from Bombay – Elephanta and Nhava. Both the jetties at Elephanta were in heavy use and there was severe overcrowding, especially on holidays. The visitors to Elephanta fell into two categories – those who wished to see the caves and those

Denuded of trees the landscape presents a picture of devastation

who came just for picnics. It was the second category that needed to be diverted from Elephanta.

S.P. Godrej complained that a large number of trees had been cut in Nhava and pleaded that they be replaced. He added that a long-term view needed to be taken and that since Nhava was a good forested area, it should be preserved as a green lung for Bombay's citizens. Between Nhava and Sheva as a location for the ONGC base, he advised that the choice should be Sheva.

Cheema said that the only suitable site for the ONGC base was Nhava, since it had adequate draft and was sheltered, thus allowing round-the-year operations. In addition, it was close to the Bombay High oil and gas fields and most of the imported materials were received at Bombay. He added that without the Nhava base, it would not be possible to operate the Bombay High installations, leave alone step up oil production. What he did not say was that the draft he was insisting on was required by ocean-going ships and not small offshore vessels. Navroz Mody countered that there was no need for ONGC to concentrate its activities in and around Bombay.

The minutes of the meeting quote K.K. Uppal as saying that a Working Group of the Planning Commission had considered all the sites on the West Coast, had concluded its deliberations on 3rd March 1980 and had concluded that Nhava was the only suitable site. MDL Chairman Admiral Datta said that there were always economic imperatives and supported their stand. One or more of these gentlemen was either not telling the truth or were not aware of the facts, since a few years later ONGC pressed just as hard for a base at Janjira on the west coast, barely 43 nautical miles (about 80 kilometres) south of Nhava. ONGC gave the same justification for establishing a base at Janjira as they had given for Nhava.

Regarding environmental damage, Defence Production Secretary K.P.A. Menon (who was an interested party since Mazagon Docks came under his department) said that ONGC's programme was not anti environment, and that the only trees they were removing were those which were in an eroded condition. To add insult to injury he added that their operations would improve the local conditions. Admiral Datta, another even more interested party, said that the ecology of Nhava would be maintained and even improved. K.K. Uppal said that there were always imperatives and that a thermal power station had been set up in Chandrapur (in the Vidarbha area of Maharashtra) even though it is a forested area. He added that in any case no damage had been done to Nhava. Reading the minutes of the meeting after 30 years, I wonder whether these gentlemen were just naive, had not been correctly briefed or were just prevaricating.

Cheema added that Nhava had been barren when it had been taken over by ONGC. There are dozens of photographs that prove the reverse. He said that no large tree would be removed, though he knew that this was a totally incorrect statement. He kept promising that ONGC would plant two trees for each one that they cut. The bureaucrats all latched onto that, forgetting or conveniently ignoring the fact that replacing forests that had mature, century-old trees with new saplings could hardly compensate.

Many discussions took place about Elephanta and the need to divert visitors from there. S.P. Godrej mentioned a Japanese archaeological team which had surveyed Elephanta. Sadashiv Gorakshkar said that a survey had been done, and apart from the main caves which were publicly known, a Buddhist stupa had been found. From an archaeological point of view, Elephanta could not take any further "development" load. Cyrus Guzder stressed the above along with the ecological importance of Elephanta. Shashi Ruia of Essar asked sarcastically whether Elephanta should be preserved only for the affluent. Dr. D.N. Prasad suggested that transistor radios could be eliminated at the entry point to the caves. However, banning of transistors would not reduce the pressure on the archaeological site.

Coming to the trans-harbour green belts, C.P.N. Singh inquired whether any study had been done regarding the setting up of open spaces in Bombay. Bombay Metropolitan Commissioner M.S. Palnitkar said that the Maharashtra Government had constituted a committee seven or eight months before and that an area of 85 acres near Belapur had been identified for a tree park. That the area was in New Bombay, away from the waterfront and relatively inaccessible to Bombayites, was ignored by him. Cheema suggested that for picnics, etc. other places opposite Bombay such as Mandwa and Dharamtar Creek should be developed. However, Dharamtar is outside the harbour and much further away than Nhava, and both Dharamtar and Mandwa are inaccessible by ferry during the monsoons. In any case, Belapur, Mandwa or Dharamtar would never have served to divert visitors away from Elephanta.

If one has no answer to the criticism, what better than to go for the critic? Shashi Ruia said that in the Nhava area, there had been mosquitoes and mudflats, and nobody had bothered to visit it till October 1979. Now that roads had come up and power provided, the cost of land had gone up and various groups and committees had come up. In the past, the villagers had cut a lot of trees in areas not occupied by ONGC but nobody had bothered to do anything. He added that a large number of tree groves had been cut at the Tata thermal power station "near Vikhroli" but nobody had objected. In an obvious reference to me, he asked whether it was because this was part of the Tata group.

The answers to Shashi Ruia's objections were simple. Firstly, no one had asked for the roads and power about which he talked so proudly. Nhava had been an idyllic spot without these "facilities". As regards the cost of land having gone up, that was hardly relevant since, apart from the land of the Nautical Institute, the rest of the land had been acquired by CIDCO. As to no one having visited Nhava till October 1979, that statement in itself was absurd. We had started our campaign in May 1978 and Shashi Ruia had obviously forgotten that I had met him at Nhava in April 1979 when I had come there with B. B. Vohra. Much more importantly, Nhava had had on it the Marine School since 1912, together with the Marine Museum, and had been a popular visitor destination for more than half a century before Shashi Ruia, ONGC and CIDCO had even heard of it. The Tata thermal power station (which is at Trombay, not Vikhroli), had been set up decades earlier, when both Navroz Mody and I were still in school and when the importance of environmental issues had not been realised. Regarding its expansion, as Navroz Mody pointed out, we had joined with SOCLEEN, another NGO, to protest.

He added that we had also opposed the expansion of the RCF fertiliser plant at Chembur (which is close to the Tata thermal power station), and the setting up of Deepak Nitrite's fertiliser plant at Uran. At least, the Uran plant had not come up. Incidentally, in opposing the various Tata thermal expansions over the years, I almost lost my job. And in any case, what relevance did our actions about the Tata thermal power plant have to do with the ongoing destruction on Nhava?

Shashi Ruia went on to say that a large portion of Elephanta Island was barren and should be developed. Perhaps deliberately, he ignored the whole point that it was essential to divert people away from Elephanta. He then turned to a tiny dot called Panje on the map of New Bombay, and said that we had not done our homework when we said that there were no trans-harbour green belts other than Nhava. I had to point out that the area shown was very small and inaccessible by launch. In any case, that should be an addition to, and not in lieu of Nhava.

Continuing on the same tack as Shashi Ruia, Maharashtra Planning Secretary V. Venkatesan asked if he could say something. On being given permission to do so, he said that it was very costly to acquire urban land for picnickers. However, there were big chunks of vacant land which could be acquired at a fairly reasonable cost. He specifically referred to the "large chunk of land belonging to Shri Godrej". S.P. Godrej replied calmly. He could have said, but did not, that much of the land was in the "no development zone" and that it did not belong to him, but to charitable trusts. About 3,000 acres were, in the years to come, converted into a mangrove park.

K.P.A. Menon observed that it appeared that all the islands were being denuded and that no work was being done by anybody to keep them green. C.P.N Singh added that he had noticed erosion on the south side of Elephanta and that this area was barren. He gave us a homily saying that no action had been taken for tree planting in this area by either the Save Bombay Committee or the BEAG. He added that the Save Bombay Committee should rename itself the "Develop Bombay Committee" and take up "concrete" work by planting trees, setting up parks, etc. We hear this sort of statement regularly, generally from those who have never done anything of this nature themselves. It is often made by project promoters to divert attention from their misdeeds. Since C.P.N. Singh was in the chair, we could not say that this would require a complete change in our objectives and activities, rather like asking a heart specialist to become a general practitioner; it would also require huge amounts of funds and a large organisation. Also while this was being done there would be no one to stop the ravaging of existing green areas such as Nhava. Later, in a dig at me, he said, "I fought the *netas* (political leaders)". Even Ram Batra told me later that this was an unreasonable position taken by the minister.

Many statements had been made about Nhava having been barren. To prove the opposite, the day after the meeting I took an old painting of Nhava with me to Raj Bhavan, where C.P.N. Singh was staying, which clearly showed it as being densely wooded. I don't know what impression this made on him.

Ten days later I went to Delhi. At C.P.N. Singh's South Block office, I left a note with his PA asking for an appointment to show him some Nhava photographs. Dr. D.N. Prasad agreed to meet me. Admiral Datta and Commander Sawhney were also there and they were all preoccupied with a forthcoming foreign trip that they were making. At the half-hour meeting, I was able to show D.N. Prasad the photographs. However, he said, "I will do what the minister orders me to do" and hence I do not know what effect this had. A few days later when I telephoned him, he said that he had shown the photographs to C.P.N. Singh. He was going abroad that evening for four weeks, but I was welcome to approach him if I had a problem. He added that we seemed to have no faith, but our point of view had been fully reflected in the report.

Not getting an appointment with C.P.N. Singh, I went before 9 a.m. to his house at 2 Akbar Road in the spacious Lutyens' Bungalow Zone, and waited like any other supplicant. I was able to see him for precisely one minute as he got into his car. He said that he had seen the photographs and had already given his report to the Prime Minister; he refused to meet me.

Nhava Sheva Port

BEING HEAVILY PREOCCUPIED WITH NHAVA and under severe pressure, and anyway thinking it to be a lost cause, we unfortunately did not present the case for the preservation of Sheva. This was a big mistake on my part, one for which we are still paying the price.

Strong arguments were made in favour of the Nhava Sheva Port, especially by the Maharashtra Government civil servants – both in terms of there being no alternative site and in terms of decongesting Bombay. The Metropolitan Commissioner M.S. Palnitkar said that from the users' point of view, a satellite port at Nhava Sheva was essential, since most of the end-users were located within a 60- kilometre radius of the port and sixty percent of the cargo also came from that region. With industrial growth going all the way up to Poona, the development of a satellite port south of Nhava Sheva would be essential.

K.K. Uppal added that there was no suitable site other than Nhava Sheva for a decentralised port, as there was no draft available elsewhere. At Bombay the maximum available draft was 31 feet, at Janjira it was 17 feet, whereas at Nhava Sheva it was 40 feet. Due to draft limitations, ships of more than 14,000 tons could not be handled at Bombay Port. He went on to say that unless the port could handle container traffic, it would lose its business. With the rush of increasing traffic, if a site other than Nhava Sheva was chosen, trade would be lost. In addition, if there was a fire in the port, help would not be possible since there was inadequate space for assistance to enter. If the existing Bombay Port had to survive, this could only be done by shifting across the harbour.

Paradise flycatcher. Nhava is rich in birdlife

Disembarking on the sea wall on the north side of the Campus which was subsequently levelled to the ground

Bombay Port Trust Chairman B.C. Cariappa said that we had almost missed the bus regarding container traffic, which in Bombay Port had gone up from 30,600 in the whole of 1976-77 (i.e. 2,550 per month), to 9,000 per month. For handling container traffic, 55 to 60 acres would be needed, which was impossible to provide in Bombay. In addition, they could, with great difficulty, only handle ships of 94 feet beam width, whereas the requirement was an ability to handle ships of 120 to 130 feet beam width. Hence, it was imperative to go across the harbour to relieve the congestion in Bombay Port.

Coming to the effects on the city of Bombay, several promises were made. B.C. Cariappa said that this would provide definite relief to de-congest Bombay, as the work force would move from the city. Currently more than 9,000 trucks moved daily along P.D'Mello Road, causing the release of a lot of carbon dioxide resulting in a huge amount of pollution. By having a satellite port across the harbour, this would be minimised. In addition, Bombay would get a clean waterfront. In one of our meetings, Cariappa had said that with the coming up of the port at Nhava Sheva, land from within the BPT's extensive holdings in Bombay would become available for parks and gardens.

Speaking as head of the Bombay Metropolitan Region Development Authority, Metropolitan Commissioner M.S. Palnitkar said that with the development of the Bandra Kurla Complex and other measures, it was planned to shift 5,00,000 jobs northwards from the island city.

The wholesale markets had already shifted. The pace of shifting just could not be separated from the satellite harbour.

We were pointedly asked more than once that as we objected to the ONGC base, why did we not object to the port as well? We were in a fix. The port was being touted as a mantra for the ills of Bombay on the grounds that it would divert port traffic away from Bombay, and thereby reduce congestion in the city. Kisan Mehta and others of the Save Bombay Committee strongly supported it. In addition, all the "experts" said, completely incorrectly as it turned out, that the only suitable location on the West Coast, not just for a satellite port but for a new port, was Nhava Sheva.

My own view has always been that instead of the one port then existing in the Bombay Metropolitan Region, there would now be two, thereby adding to, instead of reducing, congestion in the Region. Furthermore, investment of such huge amounts in Nhava Sheva would preempt investments being made in the backward areas of Maharashtra. It would also destroy huge green areas close to Bombay. However, for reasons mentioned later, I did not even dare to raise these concerns. We did however say that though we did not wish to oppose Maharashtra State policies, we were in favour of decentralisation of ports. In a subsequent letter, Navroz Mody and I pleaded that the extremely sparse open spaces around Bombay, specially the trans-harbour waterfront areas, be preserved. Regarding the port, we requested that it be confined to Sheva alone, leaving Nhava untouched; failing this, the port should take the minimum possible land on Nhava, on its southern side.

It was left to C.P.N. Singh to raise this fundamental issue about the port. What is of critical importance now was the statement in his report which said (emphasis added):

> **The rationale for location of a port at Nhava-Sheva...is evidently based on the assumption that Nhava-Sheva will decongest the existing port by diverting part of the existing port traffic to the new location across the harbour...it is inevitable that over a long period, unless port traffic naturally flowing to the Bombay Harbour is diverted to other ports on the west and east coasts of India, it is bound to grow substantially. Any increases in overall traffic will increase the circular flow of goods and services from the eastern end of Bombay harbour across the mainland back to the Bombay Island. Instead of relieving congestion,** depending on the increase in volume of traffic, **we may end up aggravating the problem.**

The Planning Commission's Working Group has only curso-

> rily examined the question of diversion of traffic to some ports on the West Coast, viz. Mormugao, Kandla and Ratnagiri. **A much more detailed study of the potential development of major ports, both on the West and the East coasts is required to be carried out for dealing with the problem of increasing port capacities in India** to cater to the growing requirements of increase in our international trade.

Our fears and C.P.N. Singh's assessment were both well founded. The Jawaharlal Nehru Port at Sheva has been in operation for over a decade and a half. Large green areas have been built upon, but the corresponding benefit to Bombay of parks and decongestion has not come about. In fact, Bombay Port is going ahead with a massive expansion which will worsen congestion in Bombay.

Though we did not know about it till months later, on 4th July 1980 Indira Gandhi issued a Directive which said:

> With regard to the...setting up of off-shore facilities at Mazagon Dock in the Nhava Sheva island and ONGC's supply base, Ministry of Petroleum may be asked to go ahead with the project limiting it to the level now contemplated and they may be informed also that **no further expansion of the activity of any Central agency should be allowed on this island.** Further they should constitute a committee of Central Government, ONGC, State Government and Department of Science & Technology to ensure that the safeguards for planting of trees, etc. are observed. (Emphasis mine.)

Indira Gandhi's action turned Nhava Sheva into a hot political issue and the Union Government came under heavy parliamentary pressure. The Madras edition of *The Indian Express* of 26th July carried a press item entitled "Government discomfiture over Nhava-Sheva scheme". Several MPs had raised the issue in the Rajya Sabha (Upper House of Parliament). The Minister of State for Shipping Buta Singh was reported as having had a difficult time clearing the MPs' doubts and had kept repeating his answers. Even the interventions of Rajya Sabha Chairman Hidayatullah had not helped in getting answers that satisfied the MPs, while Congress-I MP and former Maharashtra Cabinet Minister Rafiq Zakaria was reported as being angry that Buta Singh was giving "evasive" replies and making an important issue a non-issue. He asked what was behind the Government's "obstructionist attitude" and asked them to clarify their stand. Several MPs asked about C.P.N. Singh's report, to which Buta Singh was quoted as saying that the project was

not being held up due to lack of funds, but that the environmentalists had raised objections to the Sassoon Fish Harbour and ONGC's Nhava base. He added that the proposal was under consideration. He went on to say that some statements had been made during the time of the previous Janata Government which had taken a "populistic stand" on Nhava Sheva. However, nothing had been done at that time whereas the processing of the proposal was currently in an advanced stage. After 20 minutes of questioning, it was decided that a further half-hour discussion would be held later.

Photo approaching the Campus from the Sea. Showing Anchorage Bungalow and Marine Museum to the left and sea wall on North of Campus

Dabhol

In the meantime, on 5th July 1980, one B.N. Gore from Poona had written to Indira Gandhi saying that he was a well-experienced retired engineer, that he did not know what objections BEAG had raised regarding the Nhava Sheva proposal, but he had studied the proposal from all angles and, a long time back, had come to the conclusion that this proposal was "atrocious, very costly and time-taking". He added that the Maharashtra Government was strongly pressing the Government of India to accept this proposal in a hurry, was misguiding the people and mounting propaganda, which should be stopped in the interest of a fair decision by the Government of India. He also said he knew the reasons which the State Government was giving in favour of the Nhava Sheva scheme, but he did not mention them in his letter.

Gore went on to say that the British, who used to look 50 years ahead, wanted to effectively curb the growth in the Bombay region and had therefore decided to develop another major port on the West Coast. Their choice had fallen on Dabhol (about 150 kilometres to the south-east of Bombay), which was considered to be on par with Surat but had fallen into disuse for 500 years. They had started taking initial and necessary steps and, in 1914, had asked the MSM Railway to survey a rail line from Karad to Chiplun to Dabhol. This survey had been completed a long time ago.

As long ago as 1970, Gore had suggested Dabhol "as a far better alternative, since it would be much more economical in time and money, in addition to completely avoiding worsening of Bombay Region". Fearing, with cogent reasons, that he "would not be heeded to by that Govt.", he had "suggested the appointment of a small Committee consisting of TOP, RETIRED AND WELL EXPERIENCED GOVT. OFFICERS," and if the report of the Committee had been favourable, to recommend it to the Government of India. Since the report of the Enquiry Committee would be highly dependent on its personnel, he had suggested some unimpeachable names. The State Government did not appoint this Committee, probably fearing that the Central Government would prefer Dabhol to Nhava Sheva. He went on to say that, bent on somehow making the Central Government accept the Nhava-Sheva scheme, the State Government had "resorted to falsehood and cheating". In 1973 the State Government had declared in the Legislative Assembly that the Dabhol Scheme was utterly impracticable, and had also created a false image of it at the Centre. However, in 1978 the Chief Ports Officer, in the presence of the concerned minister, had had to admit that the report was false and misleading.

Gore said that the Karad-Chiplun-Dabhol rail line would cost only about Rs. 50 crores, and be of use to the four Deccan states to divert their trade through Dabhol. He added that the Dabhol scheme could be commissioned satisfactorily within five to seven years and would cost a total of Rs. 100 crores, including the cost of the railway line. According to him, this would result in cost savings of Rs. 1,000 crores to the Central Government and Rs. 500 crores to the Maharashtra Government, which both the Central and Maharashtra Governments would have to spend on the Nhava Sheva scheme. In addition it would help "in the solution of the present pressing Bombay problems".

An international authority on ports had opined that Dabhol would be the best port in India and had expressed the view that in other countries advantage would have been taken of it many years earlier. What was wanted was "a firm policy in consultation with well-experienced national-minded, retired Top Govt. Officers, with the execution alone being left to the bureaucracy".

Dabhol, on the estuary of the Vashishti River, is a picturesque area. It was indeed famous as an ancient port, far older than Bombay, and a great deal has been written about it. In 1508 the Portuguese governor, Dom Francisco d'Almeida, described it as having a very fine fort. It was sacked by Shivaji in 1660 and 1661 and soon thereafter became part of the Maratha kingdom. After a brief occupation by the Siddis, Dabhol came under the control of Tulaji Angre in 1744, then of the Peshwas in 1755 and finally the East India Company in 1818. In spite of all this warfare, a fine mosque, built around 1659 by the Bijapur princess Aisha Bibi, still survives.

It was perhaps fortunate (for the sake of its own beauty and environment) that the port was located at Sheva rather than at Dabhol. Less than 15 years after Gore's letter, Bittu Sahgal (Editor of *Sanctuary*, India's leading wildlife and ecology magazine) and I, as members of the Environment Ministry's Expert Committee on Thermal Power Projects, failed in a grim battle to prevent Enron's controversial power plant from being located there. However, we were at least able to ensure that the power plant and the housing colony would both be located at least 500 metres away from the High Tide Line. With the setting up of a large number of ports with minimal environmental scrutiny, the environment of Dabhol, and our entire coastline, is in grave danger.

Political Pressures

United Nations Development Programme (UNDP) 'Adviser'

Indira Gandhi's stay order and Directive on Nhava also covered Nhava Sheva Port and put us reluctantly on centrestage. On 27th May 1980, I received a telephone call from Dr. F.P. Antia of the Bombay Civic Trust. He said that he was a member of a Government of India Committee on the National Transport Policy and wanted me to speak to one of the other members, who was a UNDP adviser to the Planning Commission in Delhi. I spoke to the "adviser" at length. He was under the impression that we had opposed the Nhava Sheva Port. I pointed out to him, and also a few days later sent him the papers, which said that Bombay Port

Trust had officially recorded that ONGC's Nhava base might interfere with the proposed port.

On 19th June 1980 I received another call from Dr. Antia. He said that the UNDP "adviser" was in Bombay and wanted to meet us regarding the Nhava Sheva Port. This person was very anxious to get a statement from us that we were not against the Nhava Sheva Port Project. I invited him and Dr. Antia to the Yacht Club that evening and had a two-hour-long meeting with them. I took care to be accompanied by Navroz Mody and a friend, Abe Aboody, who had been assisting us in our work. The UNDP "adviser" mentioned that he had been a classmate of Chief Minister Antulay.

He began with a long disquisition on the need to locate the fertiliser plants based on Bombay High gas in the Konkan region, and about the need to build the Konkan Railway. Thereafter he said that the country needed deepwater port facilities and that "except for the little patch between Nhava and Sheva," there was no other suitable site on the entire West Coast. For the country's import-export trade, a port at Nhava Sheva was needed and by 1977 the case had been fully accepted. However, at that moment the Congress government at the Centre had fallen and the new Prime Minister Morarji Desai (who hailed from Gujarat) had asked why Kandla in Gujarat could not be developed. The "adviser" described Kandla as a "disaster" since it has the same hinterland as Karachi, now in Pakistan. Furthermore, the draft available at Kandla was only 28 feet. In any case it was not connected to northern India and its capacity needed to be fully utilised before further capacity was created there. Coming to Salaya in Gujarat, he said that the available draft was not more than 28 to 30 feet. The case for Nhava Sheva had now been well argued, all the relevant ministries were convinced and the Planning Commission had also agreed.

The "Adviser" said that three weeks earlier, the Prime Minister had issued a Directive staying further work on the port. He showed us a letter written by Joint Secretary (Ports) D.K. Jain which said that the PMO had instructed that work on preparation of the Detailed Project Report for the port project be held up till the environmental issues raised by the Save Bombay Committee were sorted out. He informed us that he had given a statement to *The Economic Times* to the effect that BEAG was not against the port project but only against the ONGC base at Nhava. He was very anxious that we issue a similar statement. He put a lot of pressure on us and said that we would be rendering a great service if we issued this statement and added that the Union Shipping and Transport

Minister A.P. Sharma had asked him to obtain this statement from us. However, he evaded our queries on, and soft-pedalled the issue of, the ONGC base interfering with the Nhava Sheva Port, and the Bombay Port Trust recommendation that ONGC not be allowed to develop and operate the Nhava base. Without explaining why, he said that Chief Minister Antulay could not write to A.P. Sharma on this subject. He went on to say that there was a feeling that environmentalists were capitalists. In those days, the heyday of socialism, this was a damning indictment. We said that we had been misquoted so often that we were reluctant to give such a statement. In any case, if the Government had doubts, why did they not write to us directly?

Looking back, all this seems most odd. Why would the Government, either at the Centre or State, use an adviser or an employee of an international agency as an intermediary to approach us when they could do so directly? We were, after all, in regular touch with the Maharashtra Government. I was well known to many senior civil servants and was a member of several official committees. In fact that very afternoon, I had received a letter from the Government appointing me a Special Executive Magistrate.

A few days later I bumped into Govind Lalvani, who had retired from Government service six months earlier but had been appointed Chairman Maharashtra, Prevention of Water Pollution Board and Chairman Maharashtra, Water Supply & Sewerage Board. Over drinks, he told me that he thought that the person who had met me was a fraud, and that whatever else he was, it was improbable that he was a UNDP Adviser. Lalvani said that the UNDP would not send Indian advisers to India, and that the Planning Commission would not accept UNDP advisers for a subject such as transport policy. The same person had earlier met him saying that he was a water supply expert and had asked for information regarding a water supply project in Ratnagiri, which information he had refused to provide. Lalvani said that he had written to the Planning Commission Secretary asking for verification of this gentleman's background. He requested me to send him this gentleman's card and said that he would pursue his enquiries with the Planning Commission.

When I showed the draft of the chapter (on which this book is based) to a couple of my civil servant friends, one of whom had served for ten years in the Planning Commission, they both said that there was no such creature as a UNDP adviser to the Planning Commission. I checked with another friend, who had served as an adviser in the Planning Commission. He endorsed what they said. All this was most mysterious since the gentleman's card and a letter from him, which are both in our files, gave his designation as "UNDP Adviser on Transport Policy". This gentleman clearly had an official or semi-official interaction with the Planning Commission but as what? It was probably in the role of a "consultant" – which is a far cry from being an "adviser". One of my civil servant friends said that he recollected someone of the same name being a "consultant". An article on the internet also described him as a "consultant".

Chief Minister Antulay

The next step came soon after when Chief Minister Antulay requested Salim Ali, who was BEAG President, to meet him. Was Salim Ali invited because of his letter to B.B. Vohra or because he was BEAG President? Salim Ali was treated as a VIP visitor and Urban Development Deputy Secretary R.B. Donald was specially sent to Bandra to fetch him and personally escort him to Mantralaya. Salim Ali apparently told Antulay that he had made a representation only regarding the ONGC Base at Nhava, and that concerning the Nhava Sheva Port the Chief Minister should talk to Navroz Mody and me. On 25th July 1980 Urban Development Secretary S. Ramamoorthi telephoned me to say that as a result of the Chief Minister's meeting with Salim Ali, the Chief Minister wished to meet us informally over dinner at his residence four days later. He wanted to invite Salim Ali, Navroz Mody, me and anyone else we cared to suggest. He had also wanted to invite esteemed conservationist Zafar Fatehally but had been informed that the latter was in Bangalore.

However, like at the time of C.P.N. Singh's visit, we faced a major problem. Opposition to Nhava Sheva Port would have placed us in direct conflict even with other NGOS such as the Save Bombay Committee, from which I had resigned as Honorary Secretary three months earlier. In addition, opposition to the port would have invited even more attacks saying that we were anti-Maharashtrian, anti-development and so on. Rightly or wrongly we did not oppose the port, but instead drew up a list of environmental safeguards.

At my request, my cousin Kumar Advani wrote to Indira Gandhi, C.P.N. Singh, Planning Commission Deputy Chairman Dr. M.S. Swaminathan and others, pointing out that if the port were to come up at Nhava Sheva, it would imply the death knell of all efforts to set up a port in the backward areas of the Konkan which the Maharashtra Government was avowedly keen to develop. He also suggested the preparation of a total environmental plan for the Elephanta-Nhava-

Sheva triangle.

During the next few days, with the help of Navroz Mody, I drew up an aide memoire. This was not that difficult since I had recently prepared the letters which Kumar Advani had written.

The suggested safeguards were:

• That the ONGC base be relocated away from the Nhava Sheva area.

• That the port be confined to Sheva, leaving Nhava alone. This was an important point.

• No other agency should be permitted to come up around Nhava and Sheva.

• Since the purpose of the new port was to decongest Bombay, no other industry – other than essential port-related warehousing facilities – should be allowed in the vicinity of Nhava Sheva.

• In order to prevent ribbon development, the areas adjacent to Nhava and Sheva on the landward side should be earmarked as green belts.

• On Sheva, the green areas which had been marked should be preserved and this point be included in the brief to the consultants.

• Immediate action should be taken by CIDCO, the Tourism Department and other government departments to preserve and develop the whole of Nhava island as green belts and also those parts of Sheva which had been marked as green.

• Most important for Bombay was our suggestion that since the avowed purpose of the port was to decongest Bombay by diverting traffic to the mainland, the development of Sheva port should proceed side by side with the release of land and dock areas from Bombay for the purposes of open space and recreation.

Tuesday 29th July, as I recorded in my diary, was a "crowded and important day". The day began very well with a conversation with my brother-in-law, Indru Shahani. He said that Cyrus Guzder had told him that I was anticipating a major clash with Tatas on environmental matters, and that in such an eventuality, I should not worry, since, should I wish to work full time on environmental matters, his father, Jamshed "Jimmy" Guzder, would find the finances. At noon was a meeting with Begum Ali Yavar Jung (widow of the late Maharashtra Governor Ali Yavar Jung) about the Sassoon Fish Harbour expansion and other issues. In the evening, just before the meeting with Antulay, I had to give a talk to the Bombay Local History Society.

As if all this was not enough, in between, at 3.30 in the afternoon, was a tricky meeting. Damu Malkani, who was functioning as the Honorary Secretary of the Save Bombay Committee, came to my Bombay House office to see me. He said that Sushilabehn Adivarekar (a Member of Parliament who had been instrumental in fixing a meeting with Indira Gandhi regarding the Sassoon Fish Harbour Project) wanted to know our stand on the Nhava Sheva Port. I gave him some papers relating to ONGC at Nhava along with a note spelling out the suggested safeguards, with the proviso (to which he agreed) that these should not be taken as our considered views. He agreed with all the suggested safeguards except that ONGC be asked to move out of Nhava and that the new port confine itself to Sheva. I pointed out that this would violate the earlier stand taken by the Save Bombay Committee, quite apart from embarrassing our friends in the Maharashtra Government who had taken up the issue of ONGC moving out of Nhava. It would also, incidentally, undercut the Protection Committee members, both government and non-government, who had taken the stand, at our instance, that the port be confined to Sheva. I immediately sent an urgent note to Cyrus Guzder informing him about the meeting with Damu Malkani, that Mrs. Adivarekar wanted a statement on Nhava, and that Save Bombay Committee, President, Kisan Mehta wanted to issue one. I requested him to either get the statement delayed, or issued along the lines of our note. The next day, Cyrus Guzder told me that he had written emphatically to Kisan Mehta not to issue a statement without incorporating our safeguards and that he did not think that the latter would now issue a statement contrary to ours. Damu Malkani also agreed not to issue a statement without consulting us. A few days later, Cyrus Guzder asked me to draft a statement which the Save Bombay Committee could adopt. I prepared this draft, based on which Cyrus Guzder prepared a note for Kisan Mehta to finalise. When I told Cyrus Guzder that the Save Bombay Committee may have issued a statement "clearing" the port, he replied that if it was contrary to his letter to Kisan Mehta, he would resign from the Save Bombay Committee. This prevented a huge embarrassment which a difference of opinion between two environmental groups on such a major high-profile issue would have caused. More importantly, it also safeguarded the safeguards.

The dinner meeting with Antulay, who was accompanied by Finance and Urban Development Minister Ramrao Adik, took place at the Sahyadri Government Guest House (a famous heritage building on Ridge Road, now sadly demolished and rebuilt). The civil servants present were Industries Secretary D.M. Sukthankar, S. Ramamoorthi and R.B. Donald. Our side was represented by Salim Ali who brought

Photo taken from the south side of Nhava

with him his close colleague Dilnavaz Variava, Saad Ali, Navroz Mody, and me. Contrary to the overbearing arrogant attitude which Antulay frequently adopted with his civil servants and for which he was notorious, he was the very epitome of a graceful host, though verbose and long-winded. He began by saying he had heard that we were called "environmentalists", that it was too long a word and that we should be called "those knowledgeable in environmental science". There was no point in arguing about that. He then said that he wanted our advice since it was free and that the Finance Minister had agreed to this meeting only on that basis.

Regarding Nhava Sheva Port, Antulay said that it not only had the requisite draft but it was also sheltered from winds, and that there was no other suitable site on the Maharashtra coast. Not to be outdone, Ramamoorthi said that there was no other suitable site on the entire Indian coastline. Both were very clearly wrong since several ports are now being planned in Maharashtra and other points on India's coastline. One of them is a port being planned at Rewas on the Dharamtar Creek, 15 kilometres south of Sheva as the crow flies, which envisages an area of 5,000 hectares, twice that of the Sheva Port. In addition a large number of other ports are being, and have been, built all along the West Coast.

Antulay went on to say that Nhava Sheva should not be a satellite port to Bombay, but the main port, since a lot of land was available behind it. Navroz Mody said that C.P.N. Singh had asked us that if we were opposing the ONGC base on Nhava, how was it that we were not opposing the Nhava Sheva Port? Antulay replied saying that "C.P.N. Singh may be illiterate on this point."

Navroz Mody said that one of our anxieties was that if a new port came up, a whole range of industries would follow, creating congestion and pollution similar to that at Chembur (which was often referred to as 'Gas Chamber'). Antulay replied that the new port would be beneficial from the environmental point of view since it would reduce the existing congestion in Bombay. He added that even without the new port, industry could come up there due to its proximity to Bombay Port. However, he agreed that the new port should not be used as a handle for fresh industry to come up; he would see that a perspective plan was prepared and adhered to. He said that our stand would help him since his district was elsewhere.

I also raised the question of the location of the housing colony of RCF (Rashtriya Chemicals & Fertilisers) Thal Vaishet fertiliser plants, which Antulay had allowed to be set up very close to the beautiful unspoilt Kihim beach, north of Alibag town. Antulay replied that the first thing he had done on becoming Chief Minister was to insist on the fertiliser plant being located at Thal Vaishet since he would have looked foolish if the first thing that happened on his assumption of office was that the fertiliser plant evaporated away. He had allowed the housing colony to come up at Kihim since he wished to give no excuse at all to the RCF officers to shift the plant away from Maharashtra. He said that he could give any amount of green belts and a proper plan could be drawn up. This of course evaded the issue of despoliation of Kihim's environment.

Regarding the subjects of forests and birds which Dilnavaz Variava raised, Antulay said that he would give all possible help for conducting studies and would instruct the Forest Department accordingly. We raised a few other environmental issues, such as developments at Chembur, Uran and the Tata Thermal power plant at Trombay, but Antulay was really interested only in the port.

After the hour-and-a-half-long meeting, I worked till 1 a.m. drafting a letter to Antulay on the Nhava Sheva Port. It had indeed been a crowded day. That was 30 years ago and I would not attempt that today. Over the next couple of days, after consulting Saad Ali, Dilnavaz Variava and Navroz Mody, including getting a revised draft from Navroz Mody, I finalised a letter to Antulay which incorporated the safeguards suggested by us regarding Nhava Sheva.

On 1st August, my birthday, before going off for lunch with friends, I made sure that our letter to Antulay was sent off to him, Ramrao Adik and others. That night, I was relieved when during my annual monsoon birthday party, I received a call from Kekoo Gandhy saying that our letter to Antulay was first class.

The next day, *The Times of India* in Bombay carried a front page news item datelined 1st August from Delhi with the *Hindustan Times*, a Delhi newspaper, carrying a similar item. The news reports said that cutting across party lines, Opposition MPS in the Rajya Sabha had raised the issue and a half-hour discussion had ensued. The *Hindustan Times* reported that, in the discussion J.P. Mathur of the BJP had alleged that preparation of the project report had been held up as a result of an intervention by the Prime Minister's Office. *The Times of India* said: "Mr. A.G. Kulkarni (Cong.-U) read out a telex message of July 25th from the Maharashtra chief minister, Mr. A.R. Antulay, regarding Dr. Salim Ali and other environmentalists having no objection to the project but they wanted a development of the hinterland." The press item said that the MPS had "today urged the government to accept in principle to clear the Nhava-Sheva project now that the environmentalists in the ' Save Bombay Committee' had declared that they had no objection to it". The *Hindustan Times* reported that when A.G. Kulkarni had "confronted" Shipping and Transport Minister A.P. Sharma with Salim Ali's "views", A.P. Sharma had had no answer – quite reasonably, since the information was false.

All this was most odd. How did Antulay and A.G. Kulkarni get the impression that Salim Ali and the environmentalists had no objection to the project? How could Antulay have sent a telex message on 25th July when we had met him only on the night of 29th July, with our letter being sent to him only on 1st August? Donald told me later that no minutes had been kept of the meeting, which had been treated as off the record. He also added that Antulay had sent his telex only after our meeting on 29th July. However, the telex had obviously been sent before the receipt of our letter. Were there two telexes, one before our meeting and one after? The telexes, or at least the reference to them, were incorrect.

A.G. Kulkarni was reported to have read out a news report in a New Delhi daily which talked of a message which Indira Gandhi had purportedly sent to the Stockholm World Environmental Conference. According to him, she had said that the environment problem was of no importance to developing countries. The news report quoted Indira

Gandhi saying that when a large segment of humanity in developing countries was burdened by poverty, any discussion on the protection of wildlife and ecology was meaningless. A.G. Kulkarni was reported to have objected to the Prime Minister adopting one policy on ecology for Indian consumption and a contradictory one for the rest of the world.

According to the UNDP "adviser", A.P. Sharma was in favour of the port. However, presumably because of Indira Gandhi's stand, in spite of all the pressure, he gave no commitment that the project would be implemented. He was quoted as saying that "further steps will be taken after the consideration of a report given by Mr. C.P.N. Singh, Minister of State for Defence Production". He was further reported to have said that after the environmental doubts had been cleared, the Detailed Project Report would be placed before the Public Investment Board.

Had we fully appreciated Indira Gandhi's tough environmental stand, we would perhaps have been much less apologetic and far more forthright in expressing our own concerns. An allegation was made by some MPs that landlords feared acquisition of their properties. Obviously, environmental concerns were beyond their comprehension.

Prime Minister Indira Gandhi

Presumably Indira Gandhi had her doubts about Salim Ali's and the other environmentalists' reported "no objection". On Sunday 3rd August, I had gone to the Willingdon Club, which is especially lovely in the monsoons. I was sorely tempted to spend the whole afternoon there with Govind Lalvani who was my host, but it was fortuitous that I did not. When I reached home, there was a call from Saad Ali saying that V.S. Tripathi, Joint Secretary in the PMO, had telephoned to say that a meeting had been scheduled in Delhi the next day at 5 p.m. to discuss the ONGC base on Nhava and the Nhava Sheva Port, and that notes from Salim Ali giving his views were urgently required. V.S. Tripathi called again at 6 p.m. to say that in addition to the above, notes on the Thal Vaishet fertiliser plant and the Sassoon Fish Harbour expansion were also required. When asked how the notes would reach Delhi in time, V.S. Tripathi said that the Maharashtra Government would have them collected and that an officer would bring them to Delhi. When asked as to how we could get the notes typed on a Sunday, Saad Ali was asked to contact the Chief Minister's office for a typist. Foolishly, on the grounds of confidentiality, we did not use the Chief Minister's staff for typing. This misjudgement cost us a lot.

Though it was a Sunday, I was able to enter and unlock my office in Bombay House and retrieve the papers. Along with Navroz Mody, I rushed to Saad Ali's lovely house in Bandra (now sadly demolished) where Salim Ali used to live. It was 6 p.m. by the time we reached there. Racing against time, we made brief notes giving our views and suggesting the safeguards.

Salim Ali felt that if we opposed the port, people would say we were anti-development. In his letter to Indira Gandhi, he wrote that in principle we had not opposed the port since we had been assured that it would significantly decongest Bombay. He added that at our meeting with Chief Minister Antulay, the latter had broadly agreed about the manner in which the port should develop. He annexed our letter to the Chief Minister and gave a list of suggested safeguards. He added that it was imperative that an agency such as the National Council for Environmental Planning and Coordination (NCEPC) be asked to draw up a master plan for land use and economic activity in the Nhava Sheva region. He stressed the importance of giving environmental NGOs adequate representation on the NCEPC study team and on other bodies concerned with the planning for the project. About the ONGC base, Salim Ali wrote: "It is not at all convincing that the ONGC cannot find any other suitable location along the 1,000- mile West Coast."

There was not enough time to include all the points. The note on Thal Vaishet was especially brief, which was perhaps why no directions were given on this key issue by Indira Gandhi. One of the reasons was that except for Saad Ali's son Rauf Ali, none of us knew how to type. In addition, Salim Ali was beginning to feel drowsy – he was 83 and had been for his early morning bird-watching hike.

One of the Private Secretaries to the Chief Minister, who arrived at 9:30 p.m. to collect the notes, had in fact to type two of them. Everything was ready only by 11:15 p.m. The Private Secretary could not have had much sleep that night since he had to deliver the notes at the airport at 5 a.m. to D.M. Sukthankar, who would carry them to Delhi. Clearly, everyone was in a "flap". We made an error; one of us should have also gone to Delhi to try and present our views to the Prime Minister. However, our lack of professionalism, not to speak of our parlous financial condition, precluded that.

A few days later, in response to Salim Ali's condolence letter on Sanjay Gandhi's death, Indira Gandhi wrote that she was referring all environmental matters to him. Indira Gandhi probably consulted Salim Ali because she had known him a long time. In his autobiography, *The Fall of a Sparrow*, he wrote that after his *Book of Indian Birds* was first published in August 1941, one of its earliest readers was Jawaharlal Nehru, Indira Gandhi's father, who in 1942 got a copy autographed by Salim Ali to present to Indira Gandhi who was herself in Naini jail. Salim Ali quoted Indira Gandhi as saying that like most Indians she took birds for granted till, from Dehra Dun jail, Jawaharlal Nehru sent her Salim Ali's book "and opened my eyes to an entirely new world". On another occasion she added that she didn't know much about birds till she was in Naini jail, where for the first time she paid attention to bird song. On release from prison she was able to identify the birds from Salim Ali's book.

The Prime Minister's Directives

Five weeks later, Dr. Ramanathan told me that Indira Gandhi's meeting on 4th August had lasted for an hour and a quarter and that she had issued Directives on four projects on which we had sought her intervention. The four (actually five) projects were Nhava Sheva Port, the operations of both ONGC and Mazagon Docks Ltd. on Nhava, the Fishing Harbour expansion at Sassoon Docks, and the Rashtriya Chemical & Fertiliser plant's housing colony which had been built very near an exquisite beach at Kihim in Alibag taluka and to whose siting and expansion we had vehemently objected. He was surprised at the "pull" which BEAG had with the Prime Minister. PMO Joint Secretary Rajamani was dealing with such matters and all our letters were being sent by the PMO to him the day after receipt.

In September 1980, as per the Prime Minister's Directive, the Department of Science & Technology (DST) set up a Monitoring Committee to check the adherence to the Prime Minister's Directives. Dr. Ramanathan said that this Committee had been set up as an experiment. The chairman was Dr. A.K. Ganguly of the Bhabha Atomic Research Centre (BARC), who one of the Department of Environment (DOE) scientists called the "Grand Old Man" of the Department of Environment. Most unusually, representatives of two NGOS, Society for Clean Environment (SOCLEEN) and BEAG, were nominated as members. P. Abraham, also of BARC, and I were the SOCLEEN and BEAG representatives respectively.

It was typical of the way that the DST, and later the DOE, functioned that the Prime Minister's Directives were not given to the Committee whose role it was to monitor adherence to the Directives. We had to virtually beg the Department to give them to us. In November, I had to write to Dr. Ganguly saying that we believed that serious violations of the Prime Minister's Directives were taking place and it was therefore urgent that authentic copies of the Directives be obtained. Apparently the concerned officer wanted Joint Secretary Nalni Jayal's approval before sending the Directives to the Committee. It was not till the end of November, more than two months after the Monitoring Committee had been constituted, that copies of the Directives were sent to the members. Even then, for no rhyme or reason, a crucial Directive regarding Elephanta and another regarding the Tata Electric Companies at Trombay, were both excised from the version given to us. Obviously, Right to Information concepts did not feature in the bureaucrats' book.

The Directives regarding Nhava and Sheva were detailed and comprehensive. It was a delight to see these Directives, especially because many of the safeguards suggested by us had been incorporated.

These were, inter alia, as follows:

1. "The Nhava village, picnic spots, Nautical Institute, Museum, etc. should be left untouched and no further area should be taken from any of these activities".

2. Mazagon Docks Ltd. and ONGC were permitted to "go ahead with the project limiting it to the level now contemplated".

3. "No further expansion of the activity of any Central agency should be allowed on this Island".

4. " Bombay Port Trust also should not have any activity on this Island that would endanger the environment or result in any further reclamation".

5. "No other agency (other than the existing military unit at Sheva) should be allowed around Nhava Sheva and areas around Nhava Sheva Port planned as a green belt".

6. Regarding Nhava Sheva Port: "Project feasibility report which is being processed by Ministry of Shipping & Transport should be scrutinised to ensure that it would significantly decongest Bombay".

7. "The feasibility report should provide for the release of land and dock areas in existing Bombay Port area for parks, etc."

The last few conditions were not capricious. There was no reason why ONGC and MDL should expand at Nhava; they had caused immense damage already, and other sites were available. BPT had started no physical work at all on the Nhava Sheva Port and could easily avoid Nhava. Similarly, while there could be some justification for a port being located at Sheva, there was no reason for other activities to be located there. One justification for the new port was that it would decongest Bombay. In fact, BPT Chairman B.C. Cariappa had said, in response to arguments that green areas across the harbour would be destroyed and that lands from the existing port areas in Bombay would be released for parks and gardens. This last was an exciting prospect, but as with so many other commitments, has not been implemented though more than a quarter of a century has elapsed.

The Directives owed a great deal to C.P.N. Singh's report, in the drafting of which Dr. Ramanathan, who had accompanied C.P.N. Singh to Bombay, played a major role. Several of our suggested safeguards found a place in the Directives. Admiral Cursetji told me that he had never seen such a definite Directive on matters such as these. Tragically, after Indira Gandhi, with the exception of her son Rajiv Gandhi, no other Prime Minister has shown anywhere near the same degree of concern for the environment.

Indira Gandhi's Directives were not popular in all quarters. One of the trustees of the Bombay Port Trust (BPT) told me that Shipping Minister Veerendra Patil, at his meeting with the BPT Trustees, had said that in these days anyone calling themselves environmentalists could go to the Prime Minister and stall projects. The Nhava Sheva Port had been held up by the environmentalists for several months for no reason. Also the country was short of oil and the environmentalists were against ONGC's Nhava base. Veerendra Patil had obviously not cared to brief himself about the environmental implications.

One small relief was that several ONGC engineers, who had earlier been very offhand, if not rude, suddenly became polite.

For the next several years, until the Monitoring Committee was dissolved, there were furious, heated arguments with ONGC and with the port authorities. I watched over Nhava like a hawk. The Monitoring Committee tried hard to get the Bombay Port Trust to implement their promises to release land for parks, etc. Dr. Ganguly and P. Abraham also took strong stands, which were crucial.

Department of Environment

On the same occasion that he told me about Indira Gandhi's Directives, Dr. Ramanathan added that the Prime Minister had cleared the constitution of a Department of Environment (DOE) at the Centre. A brief account of the Department of Environment in its early years is necessary to provide a backdrop, to help explain what happened and what did not happen, and also as a matter of historical record before the original actors vanish and documents are weeded out, get misplaced or otherwise disappear. The DOE (later to be called DOEn to prevent it being confused with the Department of Electronics) was eventually constituted on 1st November 1980.

The creation of the new department was not just a whim of Indira Gandhi. In January 1980, she had announced in Parliament the setting up of a high-powered Committee under Planning Commission Deputy Chairman Narain Dutt Tiwari to examine the need for such a department. The Vice Chairman was the famous agricultural scientist Dr. M.S. Swaminathan, the Member Secretary was Agriculture Ministry Joint Secretary Nalni Jayal (later to become Joint Secretary in the DOE), supported by a Technical Secretariat (headed by Thomas Mathew, Senior Scientific Officer of the DST) to provide research support. Members included DST Secretary M.G.K. Menon, a number of Government Secretaries, along with conservationists Duleep Matthai and Zafar Fatehally and eminent naturalist M. Krishnan. There were interesting discussions within the Committee including policy issues such as whether there should be a separate Wildlife Conservation cadre within the Indian Forest Service. More germane was the challenge posed by a senior secretary who said that environmental planning was nothing more than good governance, that there was no Ministry of Good Governance, and so why should there be a Ministry of Environment. However the Committee's report, which resoundingly stressed the need for a Ministry of Environment, was tabled in Parliament and accepted by the Government.

Initially the creation of the DOE was just a paper transfer, with the eleven-man (plus supporting staff) Environment Division of the Department of Science & Technology (DST) being hived off and renamed the Department of Environment (DOE), whose mandate was to look after the subjects of Environment and Ecology. The officers, including those who came from the National Council of Environmental Planning and Coordination (NCEPC), included Dr. N.L. Ramanathan, Dilip Biswas, Dr. S.C. Maudgal, M. Parabrahmam, Dr. B.S. Attri, H.R. Bharadwaj, M.C.K. Swamy, K.K. Jain and Thomas Mathew (though Mathew left for greener pastures and eventually went overseas). Over the years, a couple of them did a great deal for environmental protection, the others less so.

Policy inputs were to be provided by the NCEPC, which was chaired by Dr. B.P. Pal. Distinguished scientist though he was, he has been described by someone who worked with him in DST as "a well known agricultural scientist and an authority on the breeding of roses. He was a courtly gentleman, refined and cultured, but he was 74 and lacking in any drive in moving the environmental agenda forward". To me he appeared old, ineffective and closeted in his ivory tower. Dr. Ramanathan, whom I got to know very well, said that Dr. Pal had been reluctant to meet me but had been persuaded to do so because Dr. Ramanathan had said that it was groups like ours which gave the Department its importance. Especially after the creation of the Department of Environment, the NCEPC and its successor the NCEP (National Committee for Environmental Planning) had very little, if any impact. At least one Environment Secretary spoke contemptuously to me about it.

The first Environment Secretary was DST Secretary, Professor M.G.K. Menon who was said to have opposed the creation of the new Department. The Department was tiny, and he presumably perceived it as being just a small part of his responsibilities, and it is doubtful if he took much interest in it. I was told that he particularly did not wish to get involved in the issue of RCF's housing colony, feeling that the Department could get bogged down in housing colony issues all over India. In principle he was perhaps correct, but this colony had been located in a beautiful, environmentally sensitive area where it should not have been sited. It had been built by a Central Government undertaking and if the Central Government's Department of Environment did not intervene, who else could?

M.G.K. Menon was succeeded by Dr. S.Z. Qasim, Director of the National Institute of Oceanography, who subsequently led the first Indian expedition to Antarctica. The planning and execution of this expedition must have taken a great deal of the attention which he should have given to environmental protection. During its most crucial, nascent stage, this Department was not given anywhere near the consideration it deserved. The third Secretary was Dr. T.N. Khoshoo, a botanist. I was on very cordial terms with both Dr. Qasim and Dr. Khoshoo. However, under these three scientist Secretaries, the Department made little headway. For an activist NGO, in many ways the Department was a hindrance, since the possibilities of approaches to and intervention by the Prime Minister's Office were drastically reduced. After Rajiv Gandhi became Prime Minister, perhaps because of the non-performance of the Department, or because of his reported clashes with the Minister, or for other reasons, Dr. Khoshoo's tenure was abruptly cut short.

A Cambridge contemporary and very good friend, who was Joint Secretary in the Prime Minister's Office under both Indira Gandhi and Rajiv Gandhi, told me later, defending their actions (or inactions), that no advice had been given by the Prime Minister to stop "development" because of environmental concerns. However, Indira Gandhi and Ra-

Photo from Samander Mahal looking towards ONGC area

jiv Gandhi were both strongly supportive of the environment. It was Indira Gandhi who issued the famous '500 metre' directive on beaches (which led to the CRZ Notification) and it was during her tenure that Project Tiger was established, and the Forest (Conservation) Act 1980 was enacted, which has been a huge factor in protecting our forests. It was in Rajiv Gandhi's tenure that The Environment (Protection) Act 1986 (E.P. Act), was enacted. Sadly, the support of both Prime Ministers was subsequently frittered away.

Below the Secretary's level, things were not much better. The Joint Secretary had long been reputed to have an interest in and a concern for the environment. I had heard about him years earlier on one of my holiday trips to Delhi and high hopes were placed on him. However, he kept saying that the issues we were bringing to him were small issues compared to the Himalayas and so on. He reportedly said the same thing to activists who complained to him about large-scale tree-cutting in Delhi. The concerned 'Senior Environmental Officer' who worked under him also kept saying that these were issues to be sorted out at the state level, and that the Department of Environment was to handle only policy issues. I kept pointing out that this Department had been set up at the Centre precisely because the state governments were not doing their job. I added that if the Prime Minister could take the trouble to issue directives, the very least the Environment Department officers could do was to enforce them. All this cut no ice; in fact the reverse. Apparently after a trip to Nhava, the Joint Secretary complained to BEAG Chairman Saad Ali (whom he knew personally), and I was pulled up by the latter. Over tea at the Parisian Restaurant next to Tata group headquarters, Bombay House, where I was working, he said that while I was very dedicated, I should not go on and on about the subject. I complained about the Joint Secretary to Pupul Jayakar (perhaps Indira Gandhi's closest personal friend and an authority on textiles and crafts) and to Arun Singh, then a close friend and aide of Indira Gandhi's son, Rajiv Gandhi. According to former Cabinet Secretary, T.S.R. Subramanian who during that period, was a Joint Secretary in Delhi: "At that time, Rajiv was the rising star and even though he had no official position, his word was law." This made Arun Singh extremely influential. Arun Singh knew or knew of the Joint Secretary, and was surprised at what I said. Whatever the reason, a couple of years later, the Joint Secretary was transferred to the Planning Commission. He was very cut up with me saying: "Who the hell DOES Shyam Chainani think he is?" I was unapologetic. But this was in the future.

The fourth Secretary, who took over in 1985, was J. Kalyanakrishnan, an IAS officer of the Uttar Pradesh cadre, who later became Union Home Secretary. As a seasoned civil servant, he obviously knew how to operate the system. When I met him, he said that a pedigreed dog knew when to bark and did not do so indiscriminately. This obviously implied that the Department would take up only selective issues. I was told that he had been told by P.K. Kaul, the Cabinet Secretary (who plays a vital role in the careers of senior government officers), that he did not want the Environment Department to become a "no" department. Few officers would be bold enough to defy the Cabinet Secretary. In any case, whether he was effective or not, Kalyanakrishnan stayed only for some months before he was transferred. All this was not encouraging at all.

It was not till late 1985, five years after the DOE had been formed, that it became effective. This change occurred after the redoubtable T.N. Seshan became Environment Secretary, used the teeth that the DOE had been given and deployed the Prime Minister's support which it had always had. Though always good to me, Seshan's brusque and bullying nature made him cordially disliked by many, including many of his juniors, and he was nicknamed "Alsatian". He has also been accused by some scientific officers of the Environment Ministry of being dictatorial and of destroying its scientific character. The first criticism was valid, the second one only partially so, since the primary task of the DOE, and the reason for which it had been constituted, was not science but environmental protection. Seshan used to keep saying that in the early years the DOE had been primarily a research department. Unlike his three scientist predecessors, he generally took a firm stand on environmental issues and changed the Department from being little more than a fifth wheel in the coach, to a real defender of the environment. With him, there was no talk of pedigreed dogs; he was ready to bark at, if not bite, almost everybody.

Former Maharashtra Chief Secretary N. Raghunathan who served in senior posts in Delhi at that time, wrote that Seshan "projected himself as uncompromising and tough and proved to be the despair of many a Chief Minister who found many of their State projects, especially those involving deforestation, being rejected. Many projects floundered on environmental grounds. He knew his facts well and had the backing of Prime Minister Rajiv Gandhi, who was also the Minister for Environment."

B.G. Deshmukh, who was Cabinet Secretary at that time, went further and, in his memoirs *A Cabinet Secretary Looks Back,* accused Seshan of "sheer sycophancy" since Seshan, "knowing of the prime minister's passionate commitment to this cause, became over enthusiastic and more loyal than the king and would throw his weight around. Many secretaries in the ministries as well as chief secretaries in the states started complaining about his high-handedness, but Seshan went on regardless as he knew the prime minister's mind."

B.G. Deshmukh felt sufficiently strongly about Seshan to include a separate chapter on him in his earlier book *A Cabinet Secretary Thinks Aloud*. He wrote that his first contact with Seshan was when, as Maharashtra Chief Secretary, he had written to Seshan, who at that time was Union Forests Secretary. When he became Cabinet Secretary and called Seshan to the Cabinet Secretariat, "To my surprise however, he was nothing but sweet reasonableness and readily agreed to re-examine the matter as suggested by me." B.G. Deshmukh was taken aback with his reaction, thinking that Seshan would stick to his decision. "But the secret was out when at the end of the meeting" Seshan said that he would be in the running for the post of Cabinet Secretary, but the U.P. lobby was against him which was why the earlier Cabinet Secretary, P.K. Kaul, had not given him an important ministry. He requested B.G.

Deshmukh to keep his name in mind whenever the Secretary's posts of either the Home Ministry or the Defence Ministry became vacant and to try and place him there.

B.G. Deshmukh added that Seshan "had found out that Rajiv Gandhi was fully committed to the protection of environment and allied matters. Seshan fully exploited this and adopted a highly tough if not arrogant attitude, not because he believed in environment-friendly policies but because he knew that this was the best way to please the Prime Minister. And he ascertained to what extent he could go. When he found that Rajiv Gandhi would not approve going beyond a certain limit, he stopped at it." Deshmukh gave the example of the Tehri Dam where he had the "firm impression that in the last stages of the process of clearance, Seshan was more than willing to give up his so-called tough position when he found out that Rajiv Gandhi had decided to approve the project". Deshmukh went on to say that Seshan's "performance in the case of the Narmada Dam Reservoir was on the surface very tough but all of us could easily see that he had found out the limits to which he could go without displeasing Rajiv Gandhi."

Another picture of Seshan was given by Thomas Mathew who knew Seshan well and described him as being: "a man of formidable intellect with tremendous analytical skills who could bring to bear a vast knowledge base in science, law, administration and development policy. All this was crowned by an arrogant style and monumental ego. He became Rajiv Gandhi's loyal foot soldier, and where appropriate, his 'attack dog'."

Moreover, it was not just arrogance and reading the Prime Minister's mind that characterised Seshan. Seshan's predecessors would also have known their Prime Ministers' minds. More important, according to Thomas Mathew, "Since Seshan had the ear of the PM, he influenced the latter's decisions on key issues." It was also Seshan, whatever his reasons, who used the Prime Minister's backing to the hilt. B.G. Deshmukh said: "Rajiv Gandhi later gave up the Ministry of Environment and Forests and appointed an independent Cabinet Minister in charge of it. Seshan rode roughshod over the next two ministers who had to tolerate him as they knew that he had direct and frequent access to the PM as his Secretary (Security); and that the PM still continued to have a lot of personal interest in environment policies and matters." Why did not his two successor Secretaries during Rajiv Gandhi's tenure do the same?

Seshan is the person who put the Ministry of Environment and Forests on the map. It was he who was responsible for the E.P. Act which, with all its defects, has spawned a whole plethora of environmental regulations, including the famous CRZ notification, stipulations regarding Mandatory Environmental Impact Assessment of Projects, Doon Valley, Murud-Janjira, Dahanu, Aravallis, Matheran, Mahabaleshwar, Panchgani, Mount Abu and others. It is under that Act that some protection has been given and additional protection sought for Nhava and Sheva.

Seshan also made a brilliant choice of an officer to head the key section dealing with environmental assessment of projects – Dr. S.C. Maudgal, a fearless individual of uncompromising integrity, who ultimately paid the price for his candour and courage by being deprived of meaningful responsibilities. Seshan's transfer to the Defence Ministry in 1988 was a severe blow – to me a personal one.

After Seshan became Defence Secretary, I expected him to take a sympathetic view on matters concerning the navy which, as Environment Secretary, he had taken up at my instance. However, as Defence Secretary, he strongly and abrasively took the opposite view and we had a clash. His pro-navy stance continued even when he became Cabinet Secretary. This reversal of stand upset the Environment Ministry officials, affected his credibility with them, and was a severe jolt to me.

However, criticisms of Seshan should not be allowed to obscure his achievements as Environment Secretary. Whatever he did later, while he was Environment Secretary he virtually always consistently took a tough uncompromising pro-environment stand which none of his predecessors and hardly any of his successors did.

After Seshan, in the succeeding two decades, the Environment Ministry has fallen well short of public expectations, having had some reputedly corrupt ministers, several weak and disinterested Secretaries (with honourable exceptions in both categories), and at least one recent incumbent being anti-environment. In spite of that, Indira Gandhi's decision to constitute the Department of Environment (later to become part of the Ministry of Environment and Forests) was hugely important, since there have been many functionaries – ministers, secretaries and other officials – who have fought effectively for the environment. As a hugely welcome relief, the appointment of Jairam Ramesh has brought a new wave to the Ministry.

Personal Pressures

WHILE ALL THESE HIGH-LEVEL CONFABULATIONS were going on, there were other, seemingly mundane distractions, but they were potentially disabling. My typist assistant left without giving any notice since he had obtained a quasi-government job; and getting a replacement took time, which caused a real problem. To worsen the situation, the industrialist who was paying for the cost of the typist, as mentioned earlier, cut off all aid to us. In addition, the NGO in whose office we had kept all our files and where we had our registered office, asked us to leave since they did not agree with our stand on a particular issue, the expansion of Sassoon Fish Harbour. All our files had to be moved out, alternative arrangements had to be made and if Cyrus Guzder had not helped, we would have had a real problem. Worst of all, my closest colleague Navroz Mody, whom I always referred to as the right side of my brain, relocated to Pondicherry in December 1980.

What was more serious for me personally was what was happening to me at Tatas, my employers, where I was a member of the 'elite' Tata Administrative Service (TAS). On 7th May 1980 I was summoned by a senior officer in Tatas and was told that Tata Financial Services, where I was working, was a very small set-up and could not carry a spare person. He added that since my environmental work was very worthwhile, would it not be better if I found a niche in a large department which could afford an extra person so that I could carry on my work? I replied that I would cut down my environmental work and also offered to take

Anchor motifs on Marine Museum staircase

a cut in salary and work half-time. This offer was refused. I also mentioned a tentative idea mooted by Dinshah Malegamvala of the Dorab Tata Trust to form a Tata Environmental Institute.

That evening, I spoke to my cousin Kumar Advani and told him that BEAG must now expedite getting a full-time activist. He agreed to contact Bill Drayton (an American friend and contemporary from his and his brother Ashok's Oxford days) who had formed the Ashoka Foundation and who had agreed to give Rs. 2,000 per month for this purpose. Kumar agreed to co-ordinate with him and Navroz Mody as to the best way to do this.

A few days later I met Dinshah Malegamvala. In addition to running the Dorab Tata Trust and the J.N. Tata Endowment, he was also Member Secretary of the TAS Committee, and my strongest and most consistent supporter in Tatas. He said that my first priority should now be office work since no other Tata company would allow me to spend so much time on environmental work. I suggested that he think of the Tata Trusts paying for a full-time activist for BEAG, which would cost Rs. 2,000 to Rs. 3,000 per month, but he felt that that would be too high. I requested him to keep it in mind.

The whole matter came up again six months later. On 3rd January 1981 I was again told that I must make up my mind regarding my job. Though my work was good, I was spending so much time on environmental conservation that the office work was suffering and some solution needed to be found. I had never dreamt that environment would take over my whole life, and I replied that I was not taking on any more commitments, and was, in fact, phasing out existing ones.

Three-and-a-half weeks later, on 29th January, Dinshah Malegamvala cautioned me, saying that another executive had been hired to join our office in place of or in addition to me and that therefore I should be careful since my job was now at stake. Malegamvala also felt that my being hired by the Tatas for environmental work was unlikely, since it would clash with their interests. He specifically mentioned the Tata Electric Companies thermal power plant at Chembur, Trombay. I said that if the Tata Trusts were to hire me for environmental work, I would be willing to take a drop in salary and even work from home. His response was that even if the Trusts were to set up an environmental cell, I would not be the one to head it. Though he supported me strongly, some people felt that I was too "het up". That night I felt that my days in Tatas were numbered. However six weeks later, because of the generous stand taken by my boss Noshir Soonawala, the clouds vanished, at least for the time being.

However a few days later, another issue arose. On 17th March 1981 I received a telephone call from Adi Katrak, who had been a friend for 20 years and was also a TAS colleague. He was now Chief Public Relations Officer of Tata Services Limited. The background was that, at my request, the wife of one of the very senior directors of Tatas had written to Prime Minister Indira Gandhi on several issues including the RCF plant at Thal Vaishet and the RCF housing colony at Kihim. When I met him, Adi Katrak said that the Union Petroleum Minister had met the director when J.R.D. Tata had been present and had told the director to stop his wife from writing to the Prime Minister. It had been very embarrassing and she would not be able to write such letters in the future. I wondered if J.R.D. Tata would order me too to stop writing to the Prime Minister, especially on petroleum issues, which were "hotting up" and about which I was in bitter conflict with several oil sector companies. If so, what would be my stand and my future in Tatas?

My fears were belied. In the next 20 years, there were other clashes and differences of opinion. However, I recollect only one occasion when two directors asked me to give a letter on the BEAG letterhead saying that I had no objection to one of their key projects. I refused point blank but courteously, and was worried about the comeback, but there was none. Other than that, though I came perilously close to being sacked on several occasions, never once was I asked not to write to the Prime Minister or to anyone else or to refrain from legal action or protests. How many other companies would have behaved like this? I have discussed this in greater detail in my first book.

Broken Promises

ONGC General Manager H.S. Cheema broke many of the promises which he made to the Protection Committee. One of the excuses he gave for this was that the minutes of the earlier 16th October 1979 meeting with Hashu Advani were issued on 4th December, after the meetings with the Protection Committee. This was a novel excuse which I had never heard before nor since.

What happened could be best summed up by the letter written in April 1981 to Union Petroleum Secretary Lavraj Kumar by Ram Batra, in his capacity as Chairman of the Maharashtra Government Protection Committee. Being a businessman and a political worker, and therefore not wanting to unduly annoy anyone, he was reluctant to act. He once pulled me up for replying strongly to ONGC and used to keep saying that

Bare and desolate landscape after large-scal cutting of trees

I was too fiery. However, when the violations were pointed out repeatedly, he had no choice but to say that if even half of what had been reported was correct, the situation was serious. His language was mild. Referring to the several discussions held with ONGC, he pointed out the violations of several assurances given by them. About tree-cutting and quarrying, he noted:

1. "The Committee, during their visit to Nhava, noted that thickly wooded hills (the Eastern Hills) were being cut by the ONGC's contractors. The Committee was repeatedly assured that the hills would not be flattened but only terraced, with the terracing starting at a height of 35 metres and coming down to a height of 20 metres. Furthermore, this terracing was to be confined only to the barren portion of the hills, with trees being planted on the slopes.

2. "The clumps of trees on the top of the hills were not to be touched by the ONGC."

3. The Commitee was told that the façade and view from the north would be left untouched.

4. ONGC further informed the Committee "that as far as possible, they would avoid cutting of trees and that their original tender for cutting of 2,000 trees had been cancelled."

He went on to add that:

1. "The hills have been cut almost vertically and are being fast flattened and destroyed. Planting of trees on such slopes as now remain

would not now be feasible. Furthermore, the hills that have been so destroyed comprise some of the greenest areas on Nhava."

2. "With the type of hill-cutting that has gone on, it would not be possible for the trees to survive.

3. "The façade and view from the north have now been completely devastated.

4. "The areas now occupied by ONGC are being fast denuded of their once thick tree cover."

The NGOs, the Maharashtra Government Protection Committee and the Department of Environment Monitoring Committee were not the only ones to complain about ONGC's violation of their commitments. The Bombay Port Trustees met on 1st December 1979 to consider granting permission to the ONGC's Nhava project. **The agenda note said: "We have advised the government that going by past experience, we will have to be prepared to face unlimited prevarications by the ONGC, once their scheme is completed, without being in a position to enforce anything which the interest of the port may demand.** (Emphasis mine.) In the light of Indira Gandhi's reputation, when C.P.N. Singh had come to Bombay, Ram Batra had assured me that "no one will try any monkey tricks with her". However, he was proved to be completely incorrect as her Directives were flouted with impunity.

Further Directive

I kept complaining repeatedly and stridently to the Prime Minister, to successive Environment Secretaries and at meetings of the Monitoring Committee, that the Prime Minister's Directives were being flagrantly violated. Eventually PMO Joint Secretary R. Rajamani visited Nhava leading to Prime Minister Indira Gandhi issuing a further Directive on 10th August 1982, parts of which said:

> In the light of a recent inspection of the area from our office, Prime Minister has directed that the activities of ONGC should be strictly limited to the present area taken up by them and the Environmental Committee should visit the place once at least in three months to ensure that the safeguards prescribed are being implemented according to the agreed plan. Also the workers' quarters should be dismantled as soon as the work is over.
>
> Prime Minister has further directed that in order to ensure that no further projects are taken up on the Nhava Island, it may be suggested to the Maharashtra Government to take over the rest of the Island and convert it into a park and also ensure

> that the Nautical Institute is not permitted to give up its operations in future to allow buildings to come up. Maharashtra Government should be asked to ensure that on the Nhava and Elephanta Islands no commercial or building activity of any description is allowed and positive steps are taken to green them and if necessary convert them into parks with birds, wildlife, etc.

Petroleum Ministry (in)action

Breaking the virtual monopoly of the IAS Secretary level posts and in a departure from normal practice, in early 1981 the powerful and coveted job of Union Petroleum Secretary was given to a non-IAS technocrat. The new incumbent was Lavraj Kumar who had been a Rhodes Scholar and was a former executive of Burmah Shell (the Indian affiliate of Shell). He was highly regarded and reputed to hold progressive views. Friends knew him; perhaps more importantly we were referred to him by associates of Rajiv Gandhi. Hence getting an appointment with him was not difficult.

We were at that time in a conflict situation not only with ONGC but also with several other very large organisations in the petroleum sector. We were hopeful of a different response from Lavraj Kumar because of his reputation. However, while there was a lot of sweet talk from him, his emphasis in dealing with our objections appeared to be more on giving plausible answers rather than on trying to sort out the problems. When Cyrus Guzder once complained to him about ONGC's gross violations of their commitments, he replied that the problem was that Cheema and I did not get on. Even Ram Batra's letter to him spelling out in detail the large number of violations by ONGC evoked no response.

Lavraj Kumar did, however, set up the Petroleum Ministry Advisory Committee for Environmental Planning and Coordination in June 1981. This Committee included as members Dr. A.K. Ganguly, Chairman of the Monitoring Committee (which had been set up to check the adherence to the Prime Minister's Directives), Dr. T.R. Saranathan of SOCLEEN and me. Malvika Singh of *Seminar* magazine told me that Lavraj Kumar had set up this Committee so that the government servants and environmentalists could get a feel for each other's perceptions. Another reason could have been that at that time "Environment" was a trendy buzzword in some circles, and Indira Gandhi's commitment to it was well known, leading to a great deal of tokenism, including several senior officers hanging large pictures of tigers and other wildlife on their office walls.

Lavraj Kumar took considerable interest in the Committee's functioning and used to chair its meetings personally. However, it appeared that the Committee had been set up with a heavy official bias, so that a claim could be made that matters had been discussed at an environmental committee which included NGOS, and that clearance had been obtained from them. From Lavraj Kumar's personal approach, it seemed that the purpose of the Committee was not so much to find solutions to environmental problems as to give replies to the objections. However, he never tried to stop me from having my full say and Dr. Ramanathan said that he had given me "a lot of lift".

Membership of this Committee was an extremely arduous and demanding task involving ceaseless vigilance and constant arguments. In particular, the minutes needed close attention and I had to keep issuing detailed corrections and supplements, with the modifications often being almost as long as the draft minutes. Nhava was one of the issues battled out at great length. In the case of the ONGC terminal at Nagaon beach in Uran, there was an extremely acrimonious fight and I gave a long dissent note.

I had a very difficult task since it was only the two of us, Dr. Saranathan and me, who were facing the combined onslaught of the petroleum sector companies such as ONGC, Engineers India Limited, Hindustan Petroleum (the successor company to the Indian affiliates of Standard Oil and Caltex), Bharat Petroleum (the successor company of the Indian affiliate of Shell), and so on. Each of them brought a number of executives to the meetings, whereas Saranathan and I were alone. On occasions, discussions got heated and Dr. Ganguly once gently chided me saying, "Don't lose your temper, use your temper".

In all these meetings, I got little if any support from the Department of Environment (DOE) representatives even though on at least one occasion, Environment Secretary Dr. S.Z. Qasim himself attended the meeting. This was in spite of the fact that it was the Prime Minister, Indira Gandhi, who had created the Department of Environment and whose support to environmental issues was well known.

Darryl D'Monte in his *Temples or Tombs?* wrote about this Committee:

> Through the Mandwa-Thal controversy, Mody and Chainani had acquired considerable notoriety in official circles and Lavraj Kumar, when he took over as Petroleum Secretary, sought to win them over by appointing Chainani as a member of the

> newly created environmental advisory committee attached to the Department of Petroleum in 1981. T. Saranathan of SOCLEEN and Dr. Ganguly were also similarly sought to be appeased.
>
> Interestingly, the Petroleum Ministry has even tried to buy the acquiescence of environmentalists by appointing them as directors of public sector corporations for a term. Thus Dr. Ganguly was nominated on the board of Bharat Petroleum, Saranathan on Hindustan Petroleum and Dr. Nilay Chaudhuri on IOC.

After reading this, Lavraj Kumar told me that I had been unfair to him, but I could not forget the many incidents which had happened. However, in spite of all its defects, till it was wound up many years later by Petroleum Minister Ram Naik, this Committee proved to be an excellent forum for the exchange of views. One major outcome was the shift, after a major battle, of the site of the giant petrochemical complex (planned to be located initially at Mandwa, then at Thal and then at Usar near Alibag) to Nagothna across a range of hills, further south-east of Alibag town.

Praise from those on the other side of the fence is doubly welcome. After a meeting at the Digboi oil refinery in Assam, a couple of the junior oil company executives said to me that the environmental issues I had raised, which did not deal with pollution, had never occurred to them.

Chief Secretary's Committee

In November 1982 Maharashtra Chief Secretary Ram Pradhan (who had been Director-General of Shipping and with whom I had repeatedly raised the question of the Nautical Institute) took an important initiative. At his instance a high-level committee with wide-ranging terms of reference was constituted. Among these was overseeing the projects about which the Prime Minister or the Union Department of Environment had issued Directives. Another was to supervise the implementation of state government schemes specifically designed for environmental improvement and beautification in the Bombay Metropolitan Region. The committee was a high-powered one, presided over by Chief Secretary Ram Pradhan, who chaired the meetings personally and took a great deal of interest. The membership comprised the Bombay Municipal Commissioner, the Bombay Metropolitan Commissioner, the CIDCO Managing Director, and the Tourism Secretary with the Urban Development Secretary being Member Secretary. The non-official members were S.P. Godrej and me.

Membership of this committee seemed to be much sought after. On reading of its constitution in the newspapers, a prominent former member of the Maharashtra Pollution Control Board whom I knew well and who was generally supportive, telephoned me saying that he would like to be a member. I had nothing to do with appointing members, but he thought, incorrectly, that I had some influence. I replied that the prime function of the Committee was to oversee the implementation of the Prime Minister's Directives regarding Nhava and Sheva. He answered: "I started Nhava Sheva." When I asked for the Nhava Sheva papers, he replied that he would give them to me when he was nominated to the committee and put the telephone down. I did not suggest his name, nor did anyone else; he was not nominated, and I never did get the papers.

This committee could not be brushed aside by ONGC. Trying to impress the committee, one of the senior ONGC officers said that they were giving several crores of revenue per day to the Central Government and the Cabinet Secretary was personally monitoring the progress daily. Ram Pradhan, a seasoned bureaucrat, was not swayed by this.

While the committee played a very useful role and Pradhan was supportive, he unwittingly caused a serious problem for us. Pradhan did not like the road alignment which passed through Samander Mahal and the Hasham Yusuf reservoir, and thereby cut through the charitable institution's campus. He felt that the road should come from outside the charitable trust premises, from the north, along the sea front. This would be somewhat similar to the earlier, seaside alignment of the road which had been dropped five years ago and would have enclosed the island on the seaward side, blocking its waterfront access and the great sea view. It was an anxious period but, with great persuasion, we were able to get the seaside alignment dropped. Some years ago, the road alignment was changed to the other side of the Hasham water reservoir, thereby avoiding cutting through the institute.

Continuing Destruction

This high-powered committee visited Nhava on 11th December 1982. Following this, the Maharashtra Government wrote to ONGC Member (Offshore) Anil Malhotra laying down several stipulations. These included the directives: "Hill features to be maintained and no more trees to be cut or damaged on any account by ONGC"; and "No more quarrying to be done on the hill, nor should good topsoil be removed or excavated

from any place for earth-filling work by ONGC or Mazagon Docks Ltd."

The rubble from quarrying is used as building

Independently of the above, another action was taking place at the initiative of Raigad District Collector, Arun Bhatia. What happened thereafter was best described by Coomi Kapoor in *India Today* of 30th September 1983. She wrote:

> For over two years, ONGC has been illegally quarrying earth and *muram* (gravel and broken stones) from Nhava island in order to reclaim land for building a wharf and setting up an offshore base which would supply vessels and material for the Bombay offshore drilling. Despite repeated reminders from the Raigad Collectorate that the excavation was in violation of the Maharashtra Land Revenue Act and the Bombay Minor Mineral Extraction Rules unless royalty was paid, ONGC's contractors, Essar Construction Ltd., refused to even fill up the pro forma and explain how much earth and *muram* had been excavated. ONGC itself did nothing to persuade its contractors to comply with the government rules. Finally in December 1982 the collectorate, making its own measurements at the site, computed that 69,875 brass of earth and *muram* had been quarried, amounting to Rs. 56 lakhs worth of royalty due to the Government.
>
> **Indifference:** When no response was forthcoming from either ONGC or its contractors, **they were both served show-cause notices in January 1983 that they were being fined at the maximum rate stipulated in the Act** – three times the value of

> the quarried material, **a whopping Rs. 5.77 crores**. However, the quarrying continued undeterred, night and day, with the contractors ultimately condescending to pay a measly Rs. 46,936 as royalty. (Emphasis mine.)
>
> Following a request from the Government of India's Department of Environment, on 7th May 1983, the Maharashtra Government Urban Development Secretary L.C. Gupta wrote to Anil Malhotra directing ONGC "to stop forthwith quarrying on the island".

The *India Today* article went on to say: "Again the order had no effect. Following a logical sequence of acquisition, the tehsildar and assistant collector of Panvel then registered a case of theft against ONGC's contractors for stealing government earth. The same night Panvel police confiscated a truck and tipper at Nhava."

However, the ground was cut away from beneath the Maharashtra Government's feet by the Department of Environment. On 19th May 1983, DOE's Joint Secretary Nalni Jayal wrote to Maharashtra Chief Secretary Ram Pradhan saying that this issue needed to be looked into carefully by the Environment and Petroleum Secretaries, the ONGC Chairman and the Monitoring Committee Chairman. In the meantime, he suggested that the stop work order be kept in abeyance. This was an amazing directive. Normally when environmental degradation is taking place, a stay order is issued on the activity. Here the stay order was lifted and degradation was allowed to continue. The fine on ONGC was also subsequently reduced.

The situation was described eloquently by Jaya Ramanathan writing in *Celebrity* magazine of April 1984 in an article entitled "Oh Island in the Sun". She wrote:

> NHAVA – a pear-shaped beautiful island at the head of Bombay harbour nestling between Elephanta Island and the mainland coast. The sun-kissed luxuriant habitat of migratory birds and peace-lovers. The island one could escape to in under one hour, far from the madding crowd and man's ignoble strife – now faces extinction. Despite the exorbitant penalty imposed, deforestation and denudation by the ONGC over the last four years have been wreaking havoc on the island and the pity is that the calamity has not been wrought by nature but is entirely the evil design of man. And if our pig-headed bureaucracy does not heed the writing on the wall in time and call a halt to the devastation – Nhava will be lost forever. Time is already running out...

Coconut trees rise from a stark and barren land on an ONGC plantation

Small World

It is often a smaller world than one imagines. My chief opponent in the Nhava battle was ONGC General Manager, H.S. Cheema. A competent engineer, he was tough and extremely aggressive during discussions and meetings. We had several clashes and I repeatedly accused him of going back on his promises and breaking his word. However, something in my mind rang a bell.

During my training with Hochtief Modern at Uran in 1962, both the Germans, the Director, Kurt Ing Vogl and the Site Manager, Hans Kelm, were friendly. But my direct superior and day-to-day contact then had been H.S. Cheema whom I had found soft-spoken, courteous and considerate. We had got on very well together. It was very different 17 years later. I was astounded when I suddenly realised that it was the same person. From 1979, regarding Nhava and Nagaon, he made my life miserable. Equally, we caused him problems. He told one of my friends who had business dealings with ONGC: "*Woh humko bahut satata hai*" ("He is troubling us a great deal"). In June 1981 *The Economic Times* quoted him as saying that ONGC had had to fight every inch of the way. On another occasion when someone complained, he apparently said that that was nothing – he had had to face Indira Gandhi on this issue.

Old Boy Network

When I was at Cambridge, there was much talk about "old boy' networks", about how they functioned and about how powerful they were. I have studied at several institutions; and though my school, the Cathedral & John Connon School is one of the leading ("public" in British and "private" in US terminology) schools in India, the really strong old boys' network is that of IIT Kharagpur.

During the first of my two trips to Delhi in December 1979, I stayed with IIT alumnus Prem Shivdasani and his wife Leetu. I do not now remember, but it must have been from Prem that I learnt that one of his batch mates in IIT, Anil Malhotra, whom he knew well, was probably taking over as Member (Offshore) in ONGC, one of the seniormost positions. Though the latter had, like Prem, been two years my senior, he had, like me, been in the Civil Engineering branch at IIT, and I knew him. A brilliant student, he had got into the coveted Indian Railway Service of Engineers (IRSE), from where he had moved to Engineers India Limited (EIL), a leading public sector consulting firm. He was about 40, very young for such a senior and coveted post.

On my next visit to Delhi just before Christmas, I called on Anil Malhotra at his home. He and his wife were cordial and we had a long chat. He had read in *Business India* about my opposition to the ONGC base on Nhava. We agreed to meet later. In EIL he had been Cheema's superior and since he would again be Cheema's superior in ONGC, I was hopeful.

In April 1980, during a trip to Delhi, I telephoned Anil Malhotra. He said that he had recently taken over his ONGC assignment, that he normally spent three or four days a week in Bombay, and that we should meet. Changing his tone, he said that we "should try to get in on projects before investments are made", since otherwise if objections were raised after money has had been spent, it would be unfair to the party concerned. I did not, at that time, ask how we could raise objections before investments were made, if the plans were shrouded in secrecy and information denied. He asked me not to take legal action till we had a chance to talk; I agreed. However, when we met subsequently in Bombay, he took a hard and aggressive line. It was almost as if he was a different individual from the polite, soft-spoken person whom I had known. He complained that the press gave a great deal of coverage to our activities and asked why they didn't instead highlight "those who do something" (i.e. extract oil and gas).

We met in several fora over the years, including at meetings of the

Petroleum Ministry's Environmental Advisory Committee. We often had brisk clashes. He told me once that we were making an undue fuss about Nhava and asked why ONGC could not replace it with another, artificial, island. After long discussions about the excessive land taken over by ONGC on Nhava, I told him that if he personally wrote to me saying that the land occupied by ONGC at Nhava could not be reduced, I would withdraw my objections. No such letter came. On another occasion, he informed me that he had withdrawn the explosives from Nhava and hence no further quarrying could take place. I was delighted, but my happiness was short-lived. When the Maharashtra Government Committee visited Nhava, quarrying was going on with full vigour. There was little point in continuing with this sort of dialogue.

An IIT batchmate of Anil Malhotra said that I was misdirecting my efforts. I should create a climate of opinion in favour of environmental protection and Anil would then start paying more attention; he would never swim against the tide since "that is the nature of the beast". To add insult to injury, Rahul Singh, a well-known journalist and a good friend of Anil Malhotra, said to me that by attacking ONGC's offshore projects on environmental grounds, I was only giving a handle to a couple of corrupt senior officers in ONGC (whom he named) to attack Anil who, according to Rahul, was honest.

Romesh Thapar, publisher of *Seminar* magazine, had carried an article by me on Nhava. I had told him that I was very hopeful since I would now have a friend in high places in ONGC. He had replied that my friend would be the worst of the lot; he was not far wrong.

Anil Malhotra did however form an Advisory Group on Ecology and Environment for ONGC's Bombay Offshore project. This would have been a useful forum, but nothing much came of it and unlike the Petroleum Ministry Advisory Committee on Environment, it soon fizzled out.

Our antagonistic relationship complicated, though only slightly, my social life. We had many friends in common. In spite of all our clashes, with India being fortunately what it is, on social occasions the courtesies were always preserved. On one occasion he was a guest at a large party thrown by my sister. I treated him, as I have had to do with others in similar circumstances, as any other welcome guest.

Regimental Tie

I tried another personal approach, this time at the highest level in ONGC. On 1st October 1981 Colonel Wahi was appointed as ONGC Chairman. Before his move to the public sector, he had been a career officer in the army's Electrical and Mechanical Engineers (EME). My first cousin, the late Brigadier Gul Chainani, to whom I was very close, had been one of the very first batch of officers commissioned in 1943 directly into what was then called the "Indian Electrical and Mechanical Engineers". At the time of his voluntary premature retirement in 1968, he was among the seniormost serving EME officers. Though without the usual soldierly physique, soft-spoken, a teetotaller, and completely without the normal military swagger, he was very highly regarded within his corps. I experienced this first-hand on many occasions over the years, when I had to deal with EME officers from the rank of captain to three-star general. And this was after his retirement when he could neither help nor harm his juniors. He knew Colonel Wahi who had been much junior to him in service. We met Colonel Wahi together, were cordially received, and several assurances were given, then and later, including that there would be no more quarrying on Nhava. Few, if any of them were implemented, even when violations were pointed out. An officer and gentleman's word was clearly no longer his bond.

The old boy network had not worked; the regimental and college ties had not been tight enough.

Lost Friendship

There was one outcome which was wholly negative. I had become very friendly with a senior Maharashtra civil servant. Everyone was puzzled that we were so friendly, since he was not popular socially and he was more than 20 years older than me. However, we were on the same wavelength (or so I thought); I enjoyed his company; we used to meet for drinks, go to the races together and so on. He was helpful, almost instrumental, in saving Nhava. As he approached retirement, I spoke to my uncle Hotchand Advani, who approached Urban Development Minister Hashu Advani saying that my friend was doing good work and suggesting that his services should be continued. At my request, Kekoo Gandhy wrote in a similar vein to Prof. Varde. Hashu Advani gave my friend a post-retirement assignment in which the latter took strong pro-environment stands. In August 1980, after the Government had changed, my friend was asked to resign. Thereafter he became active with the Bombay Civic Trust, where he again took pro-environment stands.

In 1981, during the conflicts with ONGC, Anil Malhotra said that instead of merely criticising them, we should give them a person who could show them what to do and therefore minimise the conflict. This was a great idea and I suggested my friend, who was promptly hired by ONGC as a consultant with the title of Adviser (Environment). At a meeting of the ONGC Bombay Offshore Project Advisory Group on Ecology and Environment, Anil Malhotra said that the consultant would be judged on the basis of whether the environmental conflicts were reduced.

I was in for a shock since the Environmental Adviser saw it as his role not to reduce the environmental damage caused by ONGC, but to justify their actions on legalistic grounds. This was a complete reversal of his earlier stand and increased, rather than reduced, the environmental conflicts with ONGC.

I considered this as a stab in the back and took it very badly. My uncle Hotchand Advani asked me why I was so upset. He said that my friend had had one master earlier and now he had a new one. I broke off all relations, which seemed to puzzle this friend and also once put me in an embarrassing position. A close relative of his hosted a party at his house, to which I was invited. I was in a quandary since I had no quarrel at all with the relative. My family said that a disagreement was no reason for not going. I saw it differently; I had no problems with disagreement, having often had to sue friends and institutions that I hold dear. However, to me, his behaviour was not disagreement, but dishonourable. My cousin Ashok Advani was the only one who said that if I felt that way, I should not attend. I followed Ashok's advice, which led to queries which I could not answer.

Attacks and Threats

Kannan Srinivasan attacked the BEAG severely in two articles in the *Economic and Political Weekly* in April and May 1980. He said that the points raised by us regarding Nhava were an "afterthought" on our part since we had "enjoyed" this green belt and since "the island was their own" before ONGC took over part of Nhava. This was grossly incorrect. I had been to Nhava only twice before I took up the issue and none of the other environmentalists had ever been there.

Much worse was Kannan Srinivasan's allegation against S.P. Godrej (without mentioning his name) which is best explained in my reply which said: "Srinivasan also refers to a prominent industrialist on the above Committee who 'is a substantial property holder in the

Kulaba District, of which Nhava Island is a part'. Elsewhere, he said that this industrialist owned land in the Alibag area. Alibag is about 30 kilometres as the crow flies from Nhava Island and perhaps double that distance by road. Assuming that his statement about the industrialist's property was correct, it was the equivalent of saying that an environmentalist opposes an industrial unit at Thana because he owns land at Colaba in South Bombay! Was the implication that having ONGC on Nhava would jeopardise his land? If not, what purpose was served by Srinivasan's allegation?" Even this tenuous attack was factually incorrect, since it was not S.P. Godrej who owned the land but his brother, and the property was not "substantial" but a bungalow.

After my reply, Kannan Srinivasan said that the industrialist's residence was not in Alibag town "but at Mandwa in the Alibag taluka just below Nhava". Either he had not looked at the map, or was deliberately prevaricating, since between Nhava and Mandwa, there is Sheva and then the large mass of Karanja in Uran. Even as the crow flies, the distance is 20 kilometres, with the distance by road being several times longer. In fact, Bombay is closer to Nhava than is Mandwa. This would mean that Bombayites who were fighting for Nhava were doing so in order to protect their flats!

Launching an attack on the very basis of our argument, Kannan Srinivasan said that Nhava had never been legally designated as a green belt and gave details of the legal procedure involved in such a declaration. He added that once a Master Plan had been sanctioned, retroactive changes could not be made. He was wrong on both counts since Master Plans are always being changed. If CIDCO, the statutory Planning Authority for New Bombay, could not change the Master Plan, who could?

CIDCO's Board Resolution of 31st January 1979 clearly stated: "RESOLVED FURTHER THAT lands fronting on the seashore of the site for New Bombay with a depth of 600 metres, be, as and when transferred by the State Government to the Corporation, reserved for disposal wholly and exclusively for purposes of tourism, sports and cultural activities and be not offered for industrial or other purposes.

"RESOLVED FURTHER THAT the foregoing policy as to land Disposal be reviewed after five years."

This Resolution was the first step in changing the Master Plan. In any case, even if an area has not been legally designated as a green belt, this does not mean that it is not green and worthy of protection.

Srinivasan did not dismiss the need for a "green belt". However, he

Area cleared of mangroves on the north of Nhava

said that there were other potential green belts much closer to Bombay, with several thousand acres of vacant land in Bombay being held by families and businesses. We have always pressed for such lands to be kept green. He added that one of the prominent environmentalists himself owned 700 acres of land "for a private green belt and future industrial expansions". First of all, none of these green belts was either a trans-harbour green belt or in New Bombay; as regards the industrialist-environmentalist, the mangrove lands have all been turned into a mangrove park.

I replied, giving examples of the environmentalists' battles for green belts over the previous 10 years; the environmental groups had been consistently campaigning against the destruction of green belts and for the protection of whatever green areas that remained. To mention just a few of these campaigns, the earliest campaign (successful) was for the preservation of Bandra Beach as an open space; it was the environmentalists who were responsible for protecting Horniman Circle garden; it was the environmentalists who fought the private builders and ensured the retention of reclaimed land at Warden Road and Nepean Sea Road as public parks; it was the environmentalists who are responsible for the development of the Mahim Creek Nature Park of 400 acres; it was the environmentalists who had agitated for the preservation of Bandra Lands End as a green belt and taken a large private builder to court; it was the environmentalists again, who had been ceaselessly campaigning for the protection and beautification of the city's maidans and in fact, had recently been successful in preventing a row of shops coming up at Oval Maidan.

Kannan Srinivasan launched an attack on the Nautical Institute which he sarcastically called "a second Dartmouth". He said that it trained 97 students per year, of which 27 were seamen, with the rest being cooks. What he chose to ignore was the fact that all trainees at the Institute, including the cooks, were mariners, all of whom require special sea training. It is mandatory that all mariners, regardless of their trade, receive basic sea training including life saving and lifeboat drills (which may save their lives). This is an essential part of all naval and merchant naval training institutes in India and overseas.

Kannan Srinivasan wrote that the Nautical Institute had functioned on two hectares for over 70 years and asked why they needed 50 hectares. His figure was wrong by a factor of more than 400%. Quite apart from that, the Institute had access to the Charitable Foundation's other lands. Far more serious was the fact that the main jetty and the sea wall (where boat landings used to take place) had both been taken over by ONGC. He also did not take into account the expansion plans of the Institute.

Kannan Srinivasan added that due to the shipping recession of the last several years there was no case for expansion of the Institute. However, recessions in shipping, as in other industries, come and go; just because there is a recession, training institutes are never abolished. In fact, just a few years earlier, the training period at Training Ship *Rajendra* (which trained merchant navy officer cadets) was cut in half and the output of cadets doubled to cope with the dearth of marine personnel. Similarly, the output of marine engineers had been increased by taking graduate engineers and putting them through a one-year course instead of the normal four-year course. These shortened training periods were continuing even during the recession. In matters of education and training, it is essential to take a long-term view.

Kannan Srinivasan also contended that the "marine training facilities of the Institute are altogether limited". The best answer to this was in a letter of 2nd July 1979 by Leo Barnes, General Secretary, National Union of Seafarers of India (who could be presumed to know what he was talking about), to Petroleum Secretary B.B. Vohra. He wrote:

> Since the past 10 years, however, the Sword of Damocles has been hanging over the Institute which has consequently been undergoing a sad and steady deterioration. This is because the

> Institute was first supposed to be taken over by CIDCO as a part of its green belt and now is being taken over by the ONGC. The ONGC has already taken over the bulk of Nhava Island and a large part of the campus, including the sea wall and a sanatorium/Arogya Bhavan which was providing a valuable income to the Institute. You will readily appreciate that a Seamen's Training Institute needs access to the sea, without which its training is useless. This access to the sea has now been cut off since the sea wall is in the possession of the ONGC.
>
> During my last visit to Nhava, I saw a portion of a building which was demolished since the ONGC insisted on running a road through the building. Earlier, this road was to run through the dormitories and the parade ground.
>
> You will appreciate that no Institution can function or survive under such uncertain conditions. What is urgently needed is an unequivocal assurance that the Institute, its Campus, the surrounding charitable trust properties will not be disturbed and that no roads or other facilities will be run through the Institute or the trust properties and premises.

Leo Barnes felt strongly enough to add: "It is essential that the activities of the ONGC which have been carried out upon the land and the properties of the Seamen's Training Institute are shifted away from Nhava."

Kannan Srinivasan stated, incorrectly, that the Institute had only "one unmechanised fishing craft, and one lifeboat discarded by a shipping line". He was wrong. The correct position was that the Institute possessed one motor boat, one 'A' class lifeboat (with engine), two 'B' class lifeboats, one sailing dinghy, and other sailing boats. There was another major misconception; it was **not** the **boats** that were discarded, but the **ships** from which these boats came that were discarded. The boats themselves were perfectly functional and had in fact been presented to the Institute by shipping companies in recognition of, and to support the work done by the Institute. The sailing dinghy was in fact built at the Institute, and never discarded, neither by a shipping line, nor by anyone else.

In any case, Srinivasan's arguments were self-contradictory. He asserted that the Institute needed no waterfront. In that case surely they need no boats (in fact they would be unable to operate them). If they needed boats, they needed a waterfront – which ONGC had taken over. Kannan Srinivasan dismissed as irrelevant the fact that Training Ship *Rahaman* was the oldest nautical institute in the country, by saying that "Viscount Nelson's flagship *Victory* is no longer an active member of the Mediterranean squadron". While T.S. *Rahaman* is no HMS Victory, it needs to be noted that the *Victory* is still lovingly and carefully maintained, as is the *Foudroyant*, a ship built by the Bombay Dockyard.

Kannan Srinivasan was more loyal than the king. Two-and-a-half years earlier in 1978, ONGC had committed that they would not ask for more land on Nhava, and, further, that they would not interfere with the Nautical Institute. They had been carrying on on Nhava since then. However, Kannan Srinivasan queried whether preserving the Nautical Institute was a justified competing claim to the ONGC supply base. This was funny logic. It would mean that any public sector organisation could locate itself on beautiful environmentally sensitive areas and displace a venerable institution even when several other alternatives were available. Could not the environment be protected even while "development" was going on?

Regarding the possibility of ONGC moving to Sheva, he argued firstly, that there was not enough space on Sheva, and secondly, that the draft was inadequate as against ONGC's requirement of six to nine metres. In addition, the port at Sheva would be only a tidal port. However, as Srinivasan himself admitted after my reply, there was enough space left on Sheva which had not been earmarked for the port. As regards the draft, if it were adequate for ocean-going vessels, it would surely be more than adequate for ONGC supply vessels which are far smaller and had much shallower drafts – four to five metres (as compared to the six to nine metres claimed by Srinivasan). Even assuming the statement that Sheva would be only a tidal port to be correct, tides change every six hours and the waiting time would be less, which is not a great delay.

As regards the requirements of deep water, ONGC had said that the reason that they were reclaiming over 50 acres of land on Nhava at enormous cost was to enable it to reach deep water. In that case why could this land not be reclaimed at Sheva?

Srinivasan stated that an " ONGC survey team spent five years going up and down the western coastline. It considered in detail Dabhol, Dighi, Madh Island, Daman, Albert-Victor, Porbander and Tarapur. However, all these are tidal ports." Nevertheless, in 1984 ONGC had pressed very hard for a supply base at Dighi, as did Mazagon Docks Ltd. for a base there. How did Dighi suddenly become suitable?

Kannan Srinivasan said that in 1977, the Bombay Bachao Committee had had its hands full with the threat of the fertiliser plant which was scheduled to come up at Mandwa. With the decision taken in 1978 to shift the location to Thal Vaishet, "the environmental lobby turned its attention to Nhava". What he did not add, though he knew it very well (having just written an article about it), was that we had opposed the Thal Vaishet location just as we had opposed Mandwa, and that our opposition was continuing as he was writing his articles. The reason for the late start to our campaign on Nhava was that till May 1978, when I happened to visit Nhava, I was blissfully unaware of ONGC's Nhava plans.

In any case, the Bombay Bachao Committee and the Bombay Environmental Action Group were active on more than one issue. Subsequently our activities over the years have ranged from the northernmost parts of India to the southernmost and the westernmost to the easternmost – from Kashmir to Tamil Nadu and the Andamans to Lakshadweep.

Kannan Srinivasan stated that the island was a private preserve and went on to ask whether launch services were run to Nhava. The fact of the matter was that the island had always been open to the public, and in bygone days there had been regular and frequent launch services to the island. In fact, the Charitable Trust had maintained a jetty, a dharamshala, a canteen and an Arogya Bhavan of five bungalows for the public. It was these very facilities that were taken over by ONGC and it was precisely these facilities which the Maharashtra Government wanted returned. Prior to the takeover, over a period of 60 years, thousands of people had visited the Island and the premises of the Charitable Trust.

Kannan Srinivasan said that the idea to develop tourism in Nhava was clearly an afterthought on the part of the environmentalists, some of whom had "enjoyed this 'green belt' long before they thought of sharing it with common tourists". I replied that none of the environmentalists had any connection with the ownership of Nhava Island, "nor were they frequent visitors to the island". Had we been frequent visitors to Nhava, we would surely have taken action much earlier, rather than two years after ONGC entered the island. Srinivasan countered by saying that "the family of one of them had owned the island since 1883." This was a clear reference to Rashid Yusuf who is not a member of any environmental group.

One major criticism of our campaign by ONGC and journalists Kannan Srinivasan and Kumar Ketkar, was that we laid a lot of emphasis on the need for preserving Nhava for yachting and yachtsmen. Srinivasan said that "till now the entire 'trans-harbour green belt' including Nhava, Sheva, Uran, Karanja, Panje, etc., had been their own backyard. They have always sailed, swum, and boated in these waters; now they find their private environment threatened by a takeover by outsiders" [which they resented]...it is, however, incorrect for them not to have declared their interest in organisations such as Bombay Bachao."

The fact of the matter is that I was the leading environmentalist in the campaign to save Nhava and I had sailed to Nhava only once. I have never gone there by sailboat after that. None of the other environmentalists were sailors. There was a German sailor (Gunther Krueger), who used to rent one of the bungalows of the charitable trust on Nhava. Even that had been stopped by the takeover of ONGC. As regards the other places mentioned by Kannan Srinivasan, none of them were sailing bases, or even sailing destinations, except that people used to occasionally sail to Karanja. In any case, it is surely desirable to protect the few remaining open spaces where environment-friendly watersports can be promoted.

Regarding the Marine Museum, Srinivasan said that it had "fallen into disrepair" and had been renovated over the past year making "one more argument created after the fact of acquisition". He was factually wrong; the Museum had **not** been acquired; it had been saved at the eleventh hour. Before that date, it had not been treated with great attention since a road was to run through it and the whole Institute was to be removed from the premises. Once these threats were eliminated, and with the advice of Sadashiv Gorakshkar of the Prince of Wales Museum, the Marine Museum had been renovated. The Central Government, on the recommendation of the state government, had recently sanctioned a financial grant for this Marine Museum.

Much more could be said about this Marine Museum, but to quote only one authority, the Director of the National Museum in New Delhi, N.R. Banerjee: "It was at once a revealing and refreshing experience. The potential of the Naval Museum as a storehouse of naval history, in all its manifestations, and as an educational institution not merely for the trainees of the Institute but for the general public as well, is enormous, and would call for far greater publicity for the Institute and Museum than there is at the moment, and also greater support, not only for its survival but for its prosperity. Conscious effort on the part of all concerned to maintain the beauty of the island and its ecological balance is the desideration of the hour." Kannan Srinivasan did not even refer to the views of the National Museum Director.

Kannan Srinivasan stated that the governmental decisions were taken "at a time of weak and divided government, both at the Centre and the State and uncertain policy". In 1978 and 1979, both the Centre

Shyam (extreme left) with members of the Batra Maharashtra Government Commitee

and the State were ruled by coalition Governments (as is the case today), which took decisions in the normal way. At the Centre, two Prime Ministers, strongly opposed to each other, both took actions to save Nhava. In 1980, Indira Gandhi became Prime Minister and no one ever called her a weak Prime Minister. Similarly, in Maharashtra the government was headed by the redoubtable Sharad Pawar, who lost power only when his government was dismissed by the Centre in 1980.

Kannan Srinivasan added that we had "sympathisers among ministers of the then Progressive Democratic Front Government in Maharashtra as well as among senior civil servants". Of the Ministers, I knew only Professor Varde and of the civil servants I knew only Govind Lalvani who were both persuaded, as were other ministers and civil servants, by our arguments in favour of the preservation of Nhava. Anyhow, what is wrong with having sympathisers? It means that many diverse people supported our arguments.

Kannan Srinivasan brushed aside the various agencies which had made representations for the preservation of Nhava. The Maharashtra Tourism Development Corporation and the Maharashtra Government Tourism Department had not shown "any evidence of intelligence or responsibility". The Ministry of Urban Development "was misinformed by its environmental friends" and it had not cared to check its facts. Anyone who deals with a government department knows how slowly they proceed especially when powerful Central Government agencies are involved. Regarding the pleas of the Director of the Prince of Wales Museum and the Department of Archaeology to divert visitors to Nhava in order to save Elephanta, these were dismissed as being "clearly an afterthought on the part of the environmentalists". He did not deal with the arguments of the archaeological experts. The violation of solemn promises by ONGC did not bother him nor did the colossal environmental damage caused by them.

The alternative that he did not contemplate was the fact that we were correct and that we had been able to convince the diverse multitude of agencies in different fields, namely Tourism (Department of Tourism, Maharashtra Tourism Development Corporation and others), Sports (Department of Sports, Yachting Association of India and others), Department of Archaeology, Museums (Prince of Wales Museum, Maharashtra Government Department of Museums, National Maritime Museum and the National Museum), Technical Education (namely the National Union of Seafarers of India, and the Department of Technical Education) Shipping (Ministry of Shipping, Director-General of Shipping, National Shipping Board and so on), Department of Urban Development, and CIDCO. It is unlikely that we would have been able to bamboozle all these hard-headed organisations.

The progress made by T.S. *Rahaman*, the Marine Museum and the Charitable Foundation have been mentioned elsewhere in the book. I wonder what Kannan Srinivasan and other critics would say if they went to Nhava today.

It was not only the environmentalists who were unhappy with what was happening at Nhava. Writing in *Times* of 20th June 1981, Kumar Ketkar said that about 25-30 persons, whom he called "hired hooligans", stoned official vehicles and contractors' trucks in a bid to block the road and prevent construction on Nhava. Eventually the State Reserve Police had to be summoned, and the construction resumed.

Kumar Ketkar added that the blockade had been going on for several months and even drinking water was being carried by barges, with staff movement going on by helicopters. It was stated that this was because of the agitation launched by the Peasants and Workers Party (PWP) along with environmentalists. ONGC officials said that the PWP had started the agitation only after the Progressive Democratic Front (of which the PWP had been a constituent) had been dismissed. ONGC officials claimed that having realised that "they had lost the 'game', the environmentalists had therefore joined hands with certain disgruntled political elements to mount the agitation".

Labour camp of M/s Essar Construction in the North of Nhava

Kumar Ketkar said that "many officials in ONGC were convinced that behind the big sounding ecological arguments are certain entrenched 'vested' interests. For instance, members of a yacht club, small property owners and a couple of industrialists. Some of them have realised that their land can now fetch substantially higher prices because the approach road is ready."

ONGC General Manager Cheema was quoted as saying that the modus operandi of the environmentalists was to go to court, bring a stay or an injunction, organise demonstrations, go to ministers and organise press campaigns.

Most of the statements were false. First of all, we had had **no** contact at all with the Peasants and Workers Party and knew only a couple of the people concerned (and that too had been in connection with the Thal Vaishet Fertiliser Plant). Secondly we had **not** gone to court though we had been advised that we had a strong case in law. Thirdly, we had **not** obtained any stays or injunctions from the courts. Fourthly, we had **not** organised any demonstrations; in fact, ours is a very small group with no manpower to organise a demonstration. Fifthly, who were the property owners and industrialists who owned lands on Nhava? Except for the ONGC lands, the Nautical Institute, the Charitable Institute lands and the village, all the land had been acquired by CIDCO. Sixth, there were virtually no yachtsmen sailing to Nhava.

As I pointed out in my reply, once the land is notified for acquisition, the price at which it is to be acquired gets frozen. Hence the property owners would not benefit if the prices were raised. I challenged ONGC to publicly name the property owners and industrialists who allegedly owned land on Nhava. We had also repeatedly said in writing that the available land in Nhava should be handed over to CIDCO, preserved as a green belt and thrown open to the public.

Kumar Ketkar said: "As far as the environmentalists' case of destruction of trees is concerned, ONGC appears to have clearly met it." Even a casual visitor to Nhava, then and now, can see how untrue this statement is. Ketkar was a respected journalist and I wish he had telephoned me to check his facts.

All this was not purely an intellectual exercise. I received a warning from Ravi Katari, a friend and one of those whom I had consulted. The oil business, he said, was big business, and those involved in it were ruthless and would stop at nothing. I should therefore be careful about my safety. I laughed this off; the ONGC managers were engineers, trained the same way as I had been, and would not resort to physical tactics. What I did not realise was that one of ONGC's leading contractors was, indeed, ruthless. Years later, on a totally different issue, he resorted to below-the-belt, though not violent, methods. I understand that the expression in American English for these kinds of tactics is 'playing for keeps'. In the middle of 1996, I was contacted by a reporter from *Loksatta*, a leading Marathi newspaper belonging to the *Indian Express* Group. They told me that representatives of Rupa Investments, a company belonging to the Essar Group, had given them a list of donations totalling Rs. 1.22 crores which had allegedly been given to us by various companies and business houses as inducements to stop us taking action against them. The provocation for this was a stay order obtained by us against the construction of a residential building being built by the Ruias of Essar at Walkeshwar Road on the sea coast of Bombay in violation of the Development Control Regulations and the CRZ Notification.

The list of the alleged paymasters included some of the biggest names in industry and business, such as Reliance Petrochemicals (of the Ambani Group, who were supposed to have given us Rs. 30 lakhs), NOCIL (belonging to the Mafatlal Group, who were supposed to have given us Rs. 10 lakhs), Rahejas (who were supposed to have given us Rs. 10 lakhs), Mahindra and Mahindra (who were supposed to have given us Rs. 10 lakhs) and Larsen and Toubro (who were supposed to have given us Rs. 10 lakhs). I pointed out to the reporter that we had opposed the first two of these groups head on. As regards the Ambanis, we had opposed a higher FSI for their building 'Sea Wind' at Colaba. Much more seriously, we had (unsuccessfully) opposed the location of their giant petrochemical complex at Kawas-Hazira close to Surat in Gujarat. We had also (unsuccessfully) opposed NOCIL's large expansion at New Bombay. As regards Rahejas, who are developers, we had consistently pleaded for lower FSI and tighter controls on building development. Hence it was extremely unlikely that these three business houses would have supported us. Till now I haven't even met the Mafatlals or the Rahejas (nor do I even know what they look like) and only briefly said hello to the Ambanis. None of these five business houses had given us any donations. I also said that the same could be verified from our annual accounts, to which the answer was that the amounts could have been given to me personally.

The paper carried this press item on 7th June 1996. It did not occur to me to sue them for libel. It was enough that no one believed these allegations and that whenever I have mentioned these allegations, even my opponents have laughed them off.

ONGC and the Local Population

ONGC'S PROBLEM WITH THE LOCAL VILLAGERS did not end in 1981. Writing in the *India Today* of 30th September 1983, one of their experienced correspondents, Coomi Kapoor, wrote that when ONGC was planning to set up projects in this area, it was suggested that they move to more barren sites, but they refused.

Residents of Uran had another bone to pick with ONGC. Despite the latter's avowed policy of providing jobs to Project Affected Persons (PAPS), till April that year ONGC's record had been pathetic. Despite repeated reminders from the Collector's Office, ONGC had not given any employment statistics. This led to several agitations and one firing. It had led Raigarh Collector Arun Bhatia to crack the whip. However, he was transferred in June, either because of his action on the employment issue, or for his action in enforcing the Rs. 5.77-crore fine on ONGC for quarrying (as mentioned earlier), or for other reasons.

ONGC claimed that not all the local people had the minimum qualifications required of an unskilled worker. However, the Collectorate proved that out of the 212 PAP families, four individuals were graduates, 40 had passed the SSC examination and 107 had cleared the eighth standard.

A year later in April 1984 Jaya Ramanathan wrote in *Celebrity* magazine that when ONGC took over Nhava, over 1,000 people were rendered homeless and jobless, and these PAPS were agitating.

Balustrade with anchor motif at the Marine museum

As for the PAPS, instead of giving them preference, ONGC was

Quarrying activities being conducted at Nhava

allegedly being partial to people who had connections with MLAs and others who had influence.

There were anonymous letters accusing our counsel, who appear for us entirely pro bono, of living in five-star hotels in Delhi. Though I have never engaged in commerce, there were allegations that I was using my home for commercial purposes. Municipal officers came to my home to check. My colleague Debi Goenka asked me why I was so nervous. According to him, I was doing social work from my home and rather than feeling defensive, I should feel proud. I asked him if he would defend me in the event of press criticism; I was greatly reassured when he said yes.

Since the Nhava campaign, we have taken up many other issues, several of which have involved action against many people who are not renowned either for their respect for the law, or for their adherence to the Gandhian principles of non-violence. Well-meaning friends have cautioned me several times. I was once warned by one of my mentors, Dinshah Malegamvala, Secretary of the Tata Administrative Service (TAS) Committee who had been a member of the panel that had selected me for the TAS. He cautioned me: “You will need a suit of armour.” I replied, “God will be my armour.” This pleased him, but Dr. A.K. Ganguly said: “No bravado.” These may be famous last words, and I may have been exceptionally lucky, but nothing untoward has happened (so far).

Coast Guard Base

ONGC were by no means the only ones who coveted Nhava; another major threat was from the Coast Guard, a relatively new service, which had been created to relieve the Navy of some of its auxiliary tasks and which sought to set up a base on Nhava.

The history of the constitution of the Coast Guard is interesting. In 1974 the Navy suggested the formation of a separate armed force on the lines of the US Coast Guard, stressing also the importance of inter-ministerial coordination in the case of personnel recruitment, setting up of communication networks, use of naval repair facilities and an integrated Navy- Coast Guard development. On 25th August 1976 the Maritime Zones Act was passed, by which India claimed territorial waters up to 12 miles from land, a 24-mile Contiguous Zone, a 200-mile Exclusive Economic Zone (EEZ), and a continental shelf. Even before this Act had been passed, discussions had been going on as to how the EEZ was to be protected. After the Act was passed, a committee was constituted and three options emerged. The first was to give this task to the Maritime Wing of the Ministry of Finance, which also had a number of anti-smuggling vessels. The second option was to set up a Coastal Command as a part of the Navy; this would have the obvious advantage of avoiding the expenditure involved in raising a separate force. It is for this reason that relatively few countries have set up separate coast guard services and this question remains an ongoing item of debate all over the world. However, the External Affairs Ministry felt that a defence force should not be used for protection of the EEZ. The third option was to set up a separate armed force on the lines of the US Coast Guard, and this was the option finally adopted.

The reasons stated included the inadequacy of naval force levels for non-military tasks, and the perceived need not to "waste" high-technology naval vessels and highly trained naval personnel for tasks that were essentially civilian in nature. It was not clear why less sophisticated vessels could not be operated by the Navy themselves for these tasks. An unstated reason was a feeling expressed by many in the Navy, including at least one Chief of Naval Staff, that the Navy should not be corrupted by handling civilian police functions. This decision was to have its impact on Nhava.

An Interim Coast Guard was constituted on 1st February 1977 and functioned under the aegis of the Navy until 1st August 1978. The Interim Coast Guard was placed, not under the Home Ministry as are most other paramilitary organisations, but under the Defence Ministry and when the Coast Guard Act came into force on 19th August 1978 it was constituted as a separate armed force. It takes great care to emphasise that it is not a paramilitary force but that it is (after the Army, Navy and Air Force), the fourth armed service.

When Admiral Cursetji had been Chief of Naval Staff, he had promised full support to the Coast Guard which started with ships which were transferred from the Indian Navy in August 1978 – two outdated *Khukri*-class, anti-submarine frigates (*Kuthar* and *Kirpan*, sister ships of *INS Khukri* which had been sunk by the Pakistani submarine *Hangor* in the 1971 war) and five patrol boats (*Panvel*, *Pamban*, *Panaji*, *Pulicat* and *Puri*). Around 1980, they also imported six small vessels with a shallower draft than the *Pamban*-class patrol boats. The personnel, officers and sailors, were also from the Navy, initially on deputation, but subsequently on re-employment or on permanent absorption. The Coast Guard has for many years been recruiting its own officers and sailors who are trained by the Navy and at the Coast Guard Training Centre at Cochin, but it has obviously taken time for the Coast Guard officers to reach the higher ranks. Till now, the Director-General has always been a naval officer, with the first Director-General being Vice Admiral V.A. Kamath, who had retired as Vice Chief of Naval Staff.

Like any other organisation, the Coast Guard sought to have its own independent facilities. Commodore Amrik Singh, the Deputy Inspector General of the Western Region, had been one of those who had visited Nhava during one of our earlier visits. I was told later that he had liked Nhava and had expressed a desire to set up the Coast Guard base on or near the Nautical Institute. This was cause for concern, since, though nowhere near as powerful as ONGC, the Coast Guard is an armed service, and each armed service has considerable clout. A base by them on Nhava would involve the destruction of either the Nautical Institute, or of the lush green mangroves abutting it, or of both.

After our campaign got under way and had received a great deal of publicity, on 6th December 1979 I received a telephone call from a Coast Guard official asking about an article I had written on Nhava. I said that I had not written anything but referred him to an article which had appeared in *Bombay Magazine* and also told him that many other press items had appeared.

Shortly after that, when in Delhi, I spoke to Admiral Awati. He said that he had met Coast Guard Director-General Kamath. Awati's feeling was that the Coast Guard was really interested not in Nhava but in Sheva, and that they were making only tentative enquiries regarding

Nhava. In fact they wanted to be on the Bombay side of the harbour, but it was the Navy which was pushing them to the other side.

On a chilly December afternoon, I called on Admiral Kamath, who had with him Commander Mallik. I was courteously received and the usual niceties were observed. The officers said that they wanted land on Sheva but added that the port's requirements came first. In addition, they wanted some land on Nhava so as to be able to use ONGC's Nhava facilities and the repair facilities of Mazagon Docks Ltd. In fact, something was said (which sounds unbelievable) about ONGC offering them land on Nhava within their own area. Admiral Kamath and Commander Mallik were both clear that they wanted land on Nhava.

I was shown a map which indicated the location of the proposed base as 12 hectares east of the Institute, on "land" below the high tide line, on the north side of the *bundh* which links Nhava Island to the mainland. The saving grace was that the base avoided the Nautical Institute. However, it was adjacent to it and would hem it in, quite apart from destroying a large area of well grown mangroves. I did not realise till later that this would require a substantial amount of reclamation, both to provide usable land and also because with the water being shallow, reclamation or a long pier would be needed till deeper water was reached. This could have considerably disturbed the water regime, caused silting, and consequently damaged the surviving mangroves, apart from causing other environmental damage.

Admiral Kamath asked whether as a sailor, I would not welcome an activity which would involve movement of boats and consequent support to sailing, especially in terms of rescue facilities and allied assistance. While I love the sound of motor-boat engines and naval whistles, and while rescue facilities are always welcome when one is in danger (or becalmed), Nhava was far more precious. I said that I would certainly not welcome the Coast Guard base at Nhava.

I gave them several documents including the set of press items which showed the environmental damage on Nhava and the objections to the same, together with Professor Varde's and the Maharashtra Government's letters to B.B. Vohra. I drew their special attention to the Protection Committee's recommendations specially the one which said that no other agency should be permitted to operate a base on Nhava or its vicinity, and that no lands be allotted to any other agency for any purposes whatsoever. I added that we had a strong legal case against their locating a base on Nhava, but that we would have much less objection to Sheva.

Devastation of the landscape at the ONGC site

When I asked for a copy of the map, Admiral Kamath said that I could get it from Commodore Amrik Singh. However, when I contacted Commodore Amrik Singh, he refused to give me the map, presumably thinking that he could bulldoze his way through.

On Friday 5th September 1980, after the Prime Minister's Directives had been issued, I received a telephone call from Commodore Amrik Singh. He said that the Coast Guard wanted to set up a base on Nhava in an area which was under water near Nhava village. He had been told that until the Coast Guard "gets a clearance from Shyam Chainani", they could not go ahead. He added that they could not go to Sheva since the Bombay Port Trust would not allow them there till the project report for their port was finalised, which he said would take many years. He wanted to meet me very urgently.

I replied that when I had met Admiral Kamath the previous December, I had understood that the Coast Guard had dropped the idea of Nhava. I reminded him that though the admiral had agreed that I could have a copy of the map, he (Amrik Singh) had refused. I asked him what the rush was now but nevertheless, I invited him for a drink to the Bombay Gymkhana where we could discuss the matter further. On the date fixed for the meeting (10th September), I cancelled an appointment and postponed the meeting of a Malabar & Cumballa Hill Residents Association. However, Commodore Amrik Singh did not show up.

A couple of months later, on the night of 6th November, I bumped into Commodore Amrik Singh at a Regatta party on board the Sea Cadet Corps Training Ship *Jawahar*. He said that the Coast Guard was still interested in Nhava and that if they came there, they would make it green. This is a standard promise, routinely given by many agencies who engage in environmental destruction. Even if these promises are kept, which very often they are not, how can artificial tree plantation compensate for the felling of natural forests, wooded areas and mature century-old trees, destruction of the hills and the rest of the topography and loss of the rustic atmosphere? He added that Commander Mallik had said that we were not interested in the area. He went on to say that I was "the kingpin" and made a gratuitous remark that I was a "politician". I countered by saying that it was he who had not given me the promised map, and that it was he who had not turned up when I had cancelled an appointment to meet him. I should have added that far from my being a "politician", it was he who was playing games. He said that I was "a big man" and suggested that we go to Nhava together by road, but evaded any discussion about giving me the map.

Commodore Amrik Singh was not just making idle conversation. A couple of weeks later I received a dinner invitation from Brigadier Gurbir Mansingh, an old acquaintance from the Yachting Association of India. He was Chief Engineer, West Coast, of the Military Engineering Service (MES) and as such responsible for naval projects. It would be his job to build the base. I was going to Nhava the next day and invited him to come along. He declined and said that Commodore Amrik Singh wanted to take him there. I told him, perhaps overconfidently, that there was no way the base could come up there.

In September, a few days after Commodore Amrik Singh's telephone call, at a meeting with Deputy Chief Minister Ramrao Adik, I met Bombay Municipal Commissioner B.K. Chougule. After asking me why I had opposed the cutting of trees on Linking Road, he said that the Coast Guard had wanted to have a base near the Strand Cinema at Colaba in South Bombay. It turned out that the proposed site was at Jamshedji Bunder. Chougule had refused and had suggested that they go to Nhava Sheva. Deputy Secretary R.B. Donald said that the Coast Guard had earlier wanted to set up their base at Backbay, perhaps the most expensive real estate in India. This showed a complete ignorance of ground realities, almost amounting to arrogance, since Prime Minister Indira Gandhi had written to Chief Minister V.P. Naik in 1974 expressing her concern at reclamation and construction in Backbay;

Ugly tree stumps scattered across Nhava provide evidence of large-scale environmental destruction. An ONGC shed and levelled hill in the background

reclamation in that area had since been banned and in fact reclamation in Bombay was against State Government policy.

I was told later that the BMRDA had said that with so much land in the military area in Colaba, the Coast Guard could surely locate its activities there – especially since a base had been set up at Karanja in Uran. As regards Nhava, while the Coast Guard wanted their local headquarters to be in Greater Bombay, they wanted to set up their Regional Headquarters on Nhava, which included offices, stores and facilities for servicing and repairing their coastal vessels. They had also wanted land from the Mazagon Docks area. Regarding office and residential quarters, the BMRDA had suggested, and CIDCO had agreed, that these should be located "behind" Nhava. However, quite predictably, ONGC had refused the use of their jetties to the Coast Guard, which would consequently have to build its own landing facilities.

Three weeks after my chance meeting with Commodore Amrik Singh, I discussed this issue with Admiral Cursetji on two occasions. He said that the Coast Guard probably had "incontrovertible" reasons to be located on Nhava. They needed to be near the Navy so that their development could be linked with that of the Navy. He went further and said that it might be a good idea to have them on Nhava, since they would be a good lobby for supporting the Nautical Institute and would have an interest in protecting Nhava. I did not agree.

I did not make the obvious point that there were other naval bases –

Vishakapatnam, Cochin, Goa and the proposed giant base at Karwar – where the Coast Guard base could be located. In fact, the bulk of the naval training establishments are at Cochin, which is the Headquarters of the Southern Naval Command and the Navy's Training Command. If they insisted on a Bombay location, there were other sites at Thana Creek and Panvel Creek. Also close to Bombay is Rewas on the left bank of the Dharamtar Creek, where there was already a civilian jetty for the ferry service from Bombay Harbour to the mainland and where a massive new port is now planned. Further up Dharamtar Creek, on the Amba River, are the Dharamtar jetty and the Mankule jetty, the areas adjacent to which had been earmarked for boat building and allied industries in the Regional Plan for the Bombay Metropolitan Region. Other options were Bassein Creek (where some shipyards are located), the jetty in the large naval establishment directly across Bombay Harbour from the Gateway of India at Karanja in Uran (which, though heavily silted up, could be examined for the suitability of locating at least small craft), and the naval jetty at Trombay in Greater Bombay (which though reportedly being used for the handling of explosives, could be examined). Outside Bombay were the many smaller ports which were not utilised or underutilised. Though I realised later that this would have posed its own environmental problems, another suggestion was Agardanda, which is upstream of the famous island fort of Janjira on a creek on the west coast, 40 nautical miles (77 kilometres) south of Bombay. At that time, the Maharashtra Government had decided to locate a base for large trawlers there and currently a large port is being planned in that area. It would surely be better to site the maximum number of facilities at one location, rather than ruining several places. A press report in the *Free Press Journal* in November 2006 quoted Coast Guard Director-General Vice Admiral R.F. Contractor as saying that three new stations were being planned on the West Coast – at Murud-Janjira, Dahanu and Ratnagiri.

One nautical expert made much more radical suggestions. He said that a logical site would be near the India-Pakistan maritime boundary, which would help prevent smuggling. He suggested Okha, Kandla and Porbunder, all in Gujarat. Kandla in particular had extensive harbour facilities which would provide berthing, repair and other facilities. He suggested Porbunder as the site of the Western Region Headquarters – but, however logical, few would prefer Porbunder over Bombay as a place in which to live. His assessment was not far wrong since Porbunder was selected as the site for the Gujarat District Headquarters, and Okha as the site for a base. Coming closer to Nhava, he said that every port had a defence component and that the Defence Ministry already had land on Sheva, which would therefore be a suitable site. By contrast, the Nhava location was ill-conceived, and a hazard to navigation.

I suggested some of these locations to the Shipping Ministry. I pointed out that the Coast Guard was operating initially with a small portion of the naval fleet, which had been transferred to it, and the *Pamban*-class vessels had reportedly been relocated to the east coast. The remaining vessels, together with other small craft which had been acquired, if based in Bombay, could easily function from the Naval Dockyard from where they were currently operating. The former naval frigates *Kirpan* and *Kuthar*, could in any case be based and maintained only in the Naval Dockyard. Furthermore, they had barely ten years left of residual useful life. If instead of the Coast Guard being constituted as a separate service, the alternative option of creating a Coastal Command of the Navy had been adopted, there would surely not have been this sustained pressure for a separate base involving heavy expenditure and severe environmental damage.

The Prime Minister's Directive was categorical that no other agencies should be allowed around Nhava and Sheva and that there should be no reclamation at Nhava. Both these should have automatically ruled out the Coast Guard base on Nhava; certainly Admiral Cursetji thought so. However, when dealing with the Government, matters are never that simple. I took this matter up at the Central Government level with the Ministry of Shipping, the DOE, the DOE Monitoring Committee, and the Prime Minister's Office (PMO). In Bombay I took up the matter with the State Government and CIDCO. I learnt that the Coast Guard had applied to CIDCO, and that the matter was being processed by the Maharashtra Government and the Ministry of Shipping. R.B. Donald told me later that the Maharashtra Government had referred the matter to the Government of India.

I raised this subject in December 1980 at the first meeting of the Monitoring Committee. At that meeting, Dr. Ramanathan of the DOE told me that the Coast Guard Base had received financial sanction in May 1980, before the Prime Minister had issued her Directives. He said that he would send a note to the PMO asking if the Coast Guard Base was covered by the phrase "no other agency". Shortly thereafter, I received a letter from M.C.K. Swamy of the DOE confirming the above. Swamy had earlier told me that the Coast Guard were themselves rethinking the Nhava location and had asked to be accommodated in the Sheva port scheme. He added that there was not enough draft at Nhava, and no reclamation could be carried out to reach deep water.

A curious aside was that in September 1980 one of the senior Coast Guard officers had told me that there would be a mutiny by his staff if it came to shifting to Nhava. In that case, why was there the sustained pressure for Nhava?

I raised the issue again and again for two and a half years. Apart from Sohrabji Godrej who gave his usual unstinting support, Dilnavaz Variava who wrote to DOE Joint Secretary Nalni Jayal whom she knew well, and several friends who gave their expert advice, I had to wage a lone battle. After Indira Gandhi's victory in the Lok Sabha general elections in early 1980, the Progressive Democratic Front government in Maharashtra had been dismissed. Hashu Advani, Prof. Varde and Nihal Ahmed were no longer in power and we were bereft of our strong local political support. The bureaucracy was hardly interested in environmental conservation, leave alone Nhava. Even more so than in the case of the ONGC base, the DOE acted as a neutral bystander, seemingly unconcerned about the environmental implications and content merely to ask for and await instructions from the PMO.

In mid-January 1981, my friend Rafiq Lala told me that the Planning Commission "Adviser" who had met us six months earlier had said that due to our campaign and the Prime Minister's Directive, the Coast Guard base was not coming up on Nhava. However, three weeks later, the news from the PMO was equivocal. On 10th February 1981, when in Delhi, I spoke to PMO Joint Secretary R. Rajamani, whom I was to get to know very well in subsequent years. He said that the PMO had conveyed their thinking to the Defence Ministry which was that there should not be any further development on Nhava. The Coast Guard had been asked to look for alternative sites, perhaps in Kulaba District, and they had been asked not to go ahead with the location of the Coast Guard base on Nhava. However, the Nhava location had not been stopped, but only stalled.

The Prime Minister's subsequent Directive of August 1982 was again categorical that "no further projects are taken up on the Nhava Island". In spite of that, there was no assurance that the Coast Guard base would not be allowed on Nhava. Eventually, on 11th March 1983 I wrote to Rajamani expressing my deep distress at the fact that in spite of the Prime Minister's Directives and in violation of several of them, the Coast Guard was still planning to set up base on Nhava. I requested that the Maharashtra Government be advised not to allow any land

Remains of hill levelling activity on Nhava

for this purpose and that this proposal be squashed once and for all. In response, I finally received a letter dated 31st March 1983 from Dr. Ramanathan which said: "At present, the Ministry of Defence have no such plans to set up Coast Guard establishment at Nhava". A large part of Nhava had been saved.

On Sunday 10th October 2010 there were press items which stated that a year earlier, the Coast Guard had requested that 40 acres be sanctioned to them at Marve, a lovely area in Malad (West), one of the northernmost suburbs of Greater Bombay. A Coast Guard officer was quoted as saying that other than Worli, where their regional headquarters is situated, they did not have any other location in the city from where they could operate, making them feel extremely handicapped in times of emergency. They did not explain why the large naval facilities in Bombay could not be used during emergencies.

The press items went on to say that the previous day, at the launching of Indian Coast Guard Ship (ICGS) *Samudra Prahari*, a pollution control vessel, Maharashtra Chief Minister Ashok Chavan had said that the Maharashtra Government had cleared the grant of 20 acres of land at Marve for the Coast Guard base, and had also given clearances to the Coast Guard to set up bases at Dahanu, Murud-Janjira and Ratnagiri. In fact, according to press items, the base at Janjira had been commissioned on 30th September, though it was operating from rented accommodation. With the new bases, Nhava seems, thankfully, to have been dropped off the Coast Guard radar screen.

As for the Coast Guard, after 1983 it has commissioned its own Seaward Defence Boats, Offshore Patrol Vessels which carry helicopters,

Fast Patrol Vessels, Extra Fast Patrol Vessels, Inshore Patrol Vessels, Interceptor Boats and so on. It has also built up its own air arm. In 2007, the fleet consisted of over 80 ships and watercraft and over 45 aircraft and helicopters, with a personnel strength of over 6,200 which included 1,000 officers. There were three regional headquarters – at Bombay, Madras and Port Blair. In addition, there were district headquarters in each of the nine coastal states and at Diglipur on the Andaman Islands , at Campbell Bay on the Nicobar Islands, and in the Lakshadweep Islands. There were several bases (including Vadinar, Okha, Tuticorin and Mandapam), two air bases (Daman and Madras), and seven air enclaves (Porbunder, Bombay, Goa, Cochin, Vishakapatnam, Calcutta, Port Blair and Campbell Bay). In Bombay, the Coast Guard vessels used the facilities of the Naval Dockyard and were based there, with its vessels having their distinctive white colour, with the "racing stripe" similar to that of the US Coast Guard – quite different from the Navy's battleship grey.

After the terrorist attacks on Bombay on 26th November 2008, the Coast Guard was given the responsibility of coastal security, with its jurisdiction extending from the shoreline to the limits of the territorial waters. In addition, the Coast Guard Director-General was designated as the Commander, Coastal Command with the responsibility of overall co-ordination between various agencies, state and central, in all coastal security matters. In response to its added responsibilities, the Coast Guard has been pursuing increases in its force level and its assets.

On 10th October 2010 Coast Guard Director-General, Vice Admiral Anil Chopra was quoted as having said on the previous day that by 2014, they were planning to acquire two offshore patrol vessels, 13 inshore patrol vessels, and 61 interceptor boats, which were under construction at different Indian shipyards. The current force level was 7,000, with plans to take it up to 15,000 within a couple of years, gradually increasing to 20,000 by 2020.

In early October 2010, there were news items about the commissioning of Coast Guard stations at Murud-Janjira in Maharashtra and in Veraval in Gujarat, on 30th September and 2nd October respectively. The other stations planned to be established within the next six months were at Dahanu and Ratnagiri in Maharashtra, Mundra in Gujarat, Calcutta, and Minicoy on the Nicobar Islands. Also planned was a Regional Headquarters at Calcutta. There was to be a full-fledged air station at Ratnagiri.

Hopefully, the new bases, most of which will be located at environmentally-sensitive locations, will be built with environmental considerations in mind. A senior Coast Guard officer was quoted as saying, regarding Murud-Janjira: "We are in the process of acquiring land for the building for which talks are on with the state government. However, due to some environmental problems, the land is not being sanctioned."

Ship Repair Yard

There was no shortage of agencies which coveted Nhava. On 4th December 1993 I received a call from Dr. Meka Papa Rao of Amma Lines Ltd. I knew him since he had been the civil engineering contractor for the Sassoon Fish Harbour expansion which we had strongly opposed in 1979 and thereafter. He said that he wanted some help from me. I was taken aback when he told me that he had bought some land on Nhava from the Maharashtra Government some years before and that he wanted to locate a shore-based ship repair yard there. He added that earlier the area had been earmarked for ship repair but was now earmarked for a Regional Park. He went on to say that while he had received the Maharashtra Government clearance, he would not go ahead if I said no: "I want your NOC." I pointed out that earlier the floating dry dock of Escorts had been located in the vicinity and had had to move out. Papa Rao replied that his proposal was for a land-based facility. I asked for a copy of the map and said that we could meet after that.

A few days later, he sent me a note prepared by Howe (India) Private Ltd., which were also the consultants for the Jawaharlal Nehru Port at Sheva. Though I had been told that their site would avoid the Nautical Institute, which was also what one of the outline plans indicated, another outline plan and the detailed map showed Site I for the yard as being bang on the premises of T.S. *Rahaman*. Site II was on the *bundh* connecting Nhava Island to the mainland and would have destroyed a substantial area of mangroves.

The Howe (India) note said: "The proposed ship repair facilities are located in an environmentally sensitive zone which is constantly being monitored by environmentalists who are concerned that proliferation of industries is destroying the air and marine environment around Bombay and making it unliveable for people." Knowing all that, it was amazing that this site was chosen. Their justification was that ship repair was a "relatively clean" industry, and did not release any toxic materials or obnoxious effluents. In addition, a large number of fast-growing trees of local varieties would be planted in the project area so as to give a green and pleasing appearance to the eye. Also there would be "large-scale employment for relatively unskilled labour".

The total land requirement was 40 hectares (100 acres), more than three times what the Coast Guard had wanted and almost equal to the land taken by ONGC. Of the 40 hectares, 25 hectares was firm land with 15 hectares being below the high water line. The facilities sought to be provided were jetties, dry docks, slipways, workshops, stores and administrative offices. They also wished to provide residential quarters, which even ONGC had not been allowed to have on Nhava. The 25 hectares of firm land could only be provided from the premises of T.S. *Rahaman*. Both sites involved a large amount of reclamation, with the first one involving the demolition of T.S. *Rahaman* and the second involving the destruction of large numbers of mangroves.

Papa Rao applied a lot of pressure saying that the closest ship repair facilities were at Dubai with a limited one at Madras. He added that Dubai was closing down since they wanted to move to commercial uses and he had just heard that Hong Kong was in trouble and people were moving away from there. We hear this argument all the time from businessmen who refuse to look beyond Bombay. As in the case of the port at Sheva, it seemed as if there was no other suitable site in India.

The sheer effrontery of the proposal took my breath away. What we had spent years fighting for, against ONGC, Mazagon Docks Ltd., the Coast Guard and the Bombay Port Trust, was now demanded from us on a platter. For a relatively minor commercial advantage, based on facts which were incorrect, we were being asked to surrender one of the most beautiful sites in the region and have several years of struggle washed away.

The situation was well described by Carol Andrade in the *Metropolis* on Saturday 19th February 1994. She wrote:

> NHAVA ISLAND, home to the country's oldest maritime museum and barely recovering from the environmental degradation imposed upon it by the Oil and Natural Gas Commission a decade ago, is still being eyed for private development.
>
> This latest phase of development is aimed at having a ship repair yard on 100 acres of land next to ONGC, right in the green belt marked out by City and Industrial Development Corporation (CIDCO). The developers, Amma Lines Limited, with offices in Bombay and in New Bombay, have even had a project report completed by Howe India Pvt. Limited, consultants to the Jawaharlal Nehru Port Trust, earmarking the most suitable area for the yard. According to Dr. M.A. Papa Rao, managing director

of Amma Lines, "provisional clearance" was given by CIDCO, provided environmental clearance was obtained.

Papa Rao was quoted as admitting that he had marked out the site without realising that there was a thriving institution already on the spot. Papa Rao was further quoted as saying that a location close by had earlier been earmarked by CIDCO for more or less the same purpose, but that the use had subsequently been changed to that of a green belt with an area beyond Karanja (in Uran) now being earmarked for the ship repair yard. He saw nothing wrong in asking that part of the green belt be used for the ship repair yard, since he claimed to have bought the land from the villagers five years earlier. This was odd since, as Rashid Yusuf pointed out, after CIDCO had moved in, all land transactions had been frozen and sale of lands without its permission was prohibited.

Papa Rao claimed that several alternative sites had been examined – Panvel creek, Uran flats south of Sheva, and Dharamtar Creek. These were ruled out on the stated grounds that, as the rock was at a fairly high level, substantial dredging was required and the area would be exposed during the south-west monsoon. At least the last point was, to put it mildly, incorrect.

The press item said that Papa Rao had been asked why he did not move to Dharamtar Creek where CIDCO was supposed to have earmarked land for a possible ship repair yard (and where the Regional Plan had earmarked areas for boat building and allied industries). He replied that that was too far since the ships and technologists were available in Bombay. He added that Dharamtar Creek was unsuitable for another reason as well, which was that the draft was inadequate, necessitating heavy dredging which would allegedly make the project uneconomical. He added that rather than move to Dharamtar Creek, he would go to Gujarat. All this sounds very odd, since less than ten years later, Amma Lines pushed hard for a large port at Rewas in Dharamtar Creek, just 16 kilometres south of Nhava where the project now seems to be under way.

Fortunately the Union Environment Secretary was R. Rajamani who had been Joint Secretary in the Prime Minister's Office when Indira Gandhi had issued her Directives; in fact it was he who had signed them. I knew him well and wrote to him and, at my request, so did S.P. Godrej. I met Maharashtra Government Urban Development Secretary D.T. Joseph, and gave him a dossier on the importance of Nhava and the need to protect it, together with the various committee reports and commitments made for its preservation. I also wrote to CIDCO Managing Director R.C. Sinha and Maharashtra Government Environment Secretary U.K. Mukhopadhyay.

Rajamani reacted quickly, writing on 3rd January 1994 to the Maharashtra Urban Development Secretary, the CIDCO Managing Director, the Maharashtra Environment Secretary, the Chairman of the Jawaharlal Nehru Port Trust and the Secretary, Union Ministry of Surface Transport. He pointed out the Directives of the Prime Minister, which specifically stated that no further expansion should be allowed on the Island, that no other agency should be allowed around Nhava and Sheva, and that no further projects be taken up on Nhava. In view of the above Directives, Rajamani requested the agencies not to permit leasing out or allotment of any land on Nhava Island for any type of industrial development.

On Republic Day 1994, D.T. Joseph visited Nhava. He noted that the Nautical Institute was doing excellent work and that it was a unique experience to see the Marine Museum. He congratulated the Chairman and all concerned for doing such a wonderful job on T.S. *Rahaman* and maintaining its high traditions. He added that once having visited the place, anyone would realise the importance of retaining and protecting such an enterprise in the existing surroundings and that it was necessary to ensure that these activities were not disturbed. He went on to say that the place was so cool and quiet that it was a pleasure to spend time in such peaceful surroundings.

Whether because of my representations, Rajamani's letter or D.T. Joseph's own visit, a week later, on 2nd February 1994, the Maharashtra Government's Urban Development Department wrote to the CIDCO Managing Director that no proposal for change in the Development Plan (Master Plan) for New Bombay should be initiated by CIDCO for the purpose of the ship repair yard at Nhava without getting a preliminary clearance from Government.

Carol Andrade summarised the situation saying: "Late last month urban development secretary D.T. Joseph, following a visit to Nhava Island, shot down the proposal. More important, CIDCO officials present on the occasion were told in unequivocal terms that the idea was terrible. For the present, the threat seems to have passed. Except that in a classic case of the left hand not knowing what the right is doing, the state environment department has only this month asked CIDCO's managing director R.C. Sinha, to look personally into the proposal, citing 'violations of the Prime Minister's Directives while granting environment clearance' as a reason."

Review Committee

While we blissfully thought that the ship repair yard was a dead issue, Union Surface Transport Minister Jagdish Tytler wrote to Environment Minister Kamal Nath requesting that permission be granted for a ship repair yard capable of handling ships up to 70,000 DWT on 20 hectares of land at Nhava. By now the Environment Ministry was aware of the Prime Minister's Directives, and Joint Director I.K. Kambhoj wrote to Jawaharlal Nehru Port Trust Chairman K. Nalinakshan asking for the project details. However, he cautioned that the proposal should not violate the Prime Minister's Directives, which, in effect, meant ruling it out.

The Environment Ministry officials said that subsequently Jagdish Tytler wrote to Kamal Nath saying that the Bombay Port Trust was not able to handle matters properly. He added that the Jawaharlal Nehru Port had opened in 1989, Rs. 3,000 crores of investment had been made, the traffic had grown and their future plans involved expansion of container-handling facilities, warehousing and ship repair facilities. He went on to say that initially it had been envisaged that the port would come up both on Nhava and Sheva, but following representations from environmentalists a Directive had been issued by the Prime Minister that there should be no port on Nhava. He asked for a review of the Prime Minister's Directive.

By this time, Rajamani had retired, and there was no one in the Environment Ministry who knew of or cared about the Prime Minister's Directives. However, they did not yield so easily to Jagdish Tytler. On 21st February 1995 the Environment Ministry constituted a Committee for an "in-depth review of possible developmental activities at Nhava". The Committee Chairman was Central Pollution Control Board Chairman, Dilip Biswas with other members being Bittu Sahgal (Editor of *Sanctuary* Magazine), Prof. Dinesh Mohan of IIT, Environment Ministry Joint Director K.K. Jain and me.

None of the other committee members were familiar with Nhava so the necessary background papers and briefings had to be given to them. What I did not know till Bittu Sahgal pointed it out, and which was mentioned in the Committee report, was that Nhava is frequented by several species of migratory and resident birds especially white-bellied sea eagles (*Haliaeetus leucogaster*), a species protected under the Wildlife Protection Act.

Far from recommending a review of the Prime Minister's Directives, the Committee made the opposite recommendation in their report of

May 1995. This is important enough to be quoted verbatim. It said: "Barring the campus of the Nautical Institute, the area of the Marine Museum, the villages and the areas occupied by ONGC/Mazagon Docks Ltd., **the rest of Nhava should be immediately declared as an ecologically sensitive area protected by sanctuary status under the Wildlife Protection Act 1972 (as amended in 1991)**. This ecologically sensitive area should include the mud flats, mangroves and shore line around Nhava and the 14 hectares of land made into a nursery by ONGC." (Emphasis mine).

The Environment (Protection) Act, 1986

The ship repair yard proposal and Jagdish Tytler's intervention were straws in the wind. By this time, following Indira Gandhi's assassination, there had been several governments in Delhi. The press widely reported that Prime Minister P.V. Narasimha Rao had scant regard for the Gandhi family. The Union Minister for Environment & Forests was Kamal Nath who had taken many anti-environmental decisions. Hence we could no longer be assured that Indira Gandhi's Directive would preserve Nhava.

The best way to protect Nhava would be to get Nhava declared as an environmentally sensitive area under The Environment (Protection) Act, 1986 (EP Act). We had been able to get similar notifications issued, first in January 1989 protecting the Dighi-Murud-Janjira area, and much more recently in June 1991 for Dahanu Taluka. Subsequently, in May 1992, a Notification had also been issued for the Aravallis. The Dahanu and Aravalli Notifications had both been issued during Rajamani's tenure as Secretary.

I took up the Nhava matter with Rajamani in December 1993, at the same time that I took up the question of the ship repair yard. I pointed out that in the Development Plan (Master Plan) for New Bombay, except for the area occupied by ONGC, the rest of Nhava had been designated as a Regional Park. In the light of many proposals for setting up units in and around Nhava, of which the ship repair yard was only one, the only sure way to provide protection was to declare the Regional Park area of Nhava an ecologically sensitive area under the EP Act.

With difficulty, I was able to get the Maharashtra Government to give their concurrence. However, a serious and unexpected glitch occurred when Dr. N. Bagchi, a Joint Secretary level officer of the Environment Ministry, wrote to the Maharashtra Urban Development Secretary D.T. Joseph on 12th August 1994 on the subject of Nhava and the EP Act. His letter said that it had been reported to the Environment Ministry that some private parties were approaching the Maharashtra Government for establishment of ship repair facilities on Nhava Island in violation of the Development Plan of New Bombay in which parts of Nhava Island had been classified as a "Regional Park". He added that the Environment Ministry had been requested to declare the area of the notified Regional Park on Nhava Island an environmentally sensitive area under the EP Act. He went on to say that as the Maharashtra Government had declared certain areas of Nhava Island a Regional Park, declaring Nhava an environmentally sensitive area would be a duplicating exercise.

This was an amazing communication, the like of which I have never seen before or after. Firstly, Dr. Bagchi had himself pointed out that violations of the Regional Park notification were likely to occur. Secondly, normally it is the state governments which resist Central Government Notifications on the grounds that they are infringements of their powers; here it was the Centre resisting an addition to their own powers. Another important point was that Dr. Bagchi kept referring to Nhava as an island; actually the original island was only a small portion of the total village of Nhava.

It took several months and several reminders from me for D.T. Joseph to reply. His reply of January 1995 was well worth waiting for and was the only one of its kind that I have seen from any state government to the Centre. He said that it was true that no development could be permitted on Nhava contrary to Regional Park uses. However, it was always possible that by an act of "minor modification", the Master Plan could easily be changed. Hence "if there is a second line of protection through the operation of the Environment Protection Act, 1986, it would ensure greater protection".

Matters progressed and in March 1995 I gave two alternative drafts of the notification to the Ministry.

On 17th May 1995, I got a very pleasant surprise when Kamal Nath came up to me during the tea break of a seminar at Nirman Bhavan in Delhi. He told me that he had agreed to declare Nhava as an environmentally sensitive area. Clearly the file had been processed and he had given his approval without even waiting for the Review Committee's report, which had yet to be finalised. Immediately after the tea break I went to Paryavaran Bhavan, the Environment Ministry headquarters. When I mentioned Kamal Nath's statement to one of the officers, he smiled. He said that Kamal Nath did so many things which did not please us, that he had to do some that did. The minister knew when to please me; it was a sort of telepathy. Telepathy or not, if Kamal Nath, or his personal staff had in fact intended to please me, they had certainly succeeded. I was jubilant.

However, the best laid plans of mice and men often go awry.

While following up on this, I was told that the Law Ministry, while vetting the draft Notification relating to Pachmarhi, had held up current pending notifications on the grounds that "Land and Land Use" is a State subject under the Constitution, on which the Centre has no powers to legislate. This was a severe disappointment. It was also extremely surprising as the Ministry had, at least since 1988, issued a series of Notifications covering different parts of India – Murud-Janjira, Doon Valley, Dahanu and the Aravallis – not to speak of the famous CRZ notification which covers the entire coastline of India. All these Notifications had been vetted and cleared by the Law Ministry. Since the Constitution had not been amended in this respect, what had suddenly caused them do an about-turn? I told the Minister's Private Secretary that we would seek legal opinion from our Senior Counsel, but he replied that there would not be much point in doing that, since the Government would be bound by their own Law Ministry's advice.

I did not know till years later that what had apparently transpired was that in March 1995, while examining the draft Notification for Pachmarhi, the Law Ministry had excised from it the provisions relating to the Zonal Development Plan, tourism, natural heritage and built heritage. In May 1995 the Environment Ministry asked the Law Ministry to reconsider these deletions. The previous Notifications were also shown to them. However, the Law Ministry stuck to its position. The matter was therefore closed and it seemed that the process of declaring areas as environmentally sensitive – a far bigger issue than just Nhava – was dead.

One fateful evening in December 1996, at the annual awards dinner of *Business India* magazine, of which my cousin Ashok Advani is the publisher, I was severely, if not insultingly attacked by several people around the table for the Coastal Regulation Zone Notification. My replies were drowned out in the volley of attack. I was furious at the extreme discourtesy and irritated with myself for not having replied in kind, and for not having walked away. It was just as well that I had not. One of those present went on and on to say loudly and repeatedly that those who had violated the Notification should not be penalised since "Land" is a state subject, that Government of India had no powers to enact such a Notification and that the Notification was unconstitutional. It did not occur to me to ask him why it had then not been challenged by any of his builder friends.

I was sufficiently upset to once again approach Senior Counsel Atul Setalvad who said that those who talked about the Constitution should first read the Constitution. His legal opinion stated that as per Article 253 of the Constitution, Parliament **does** have the powers to legislate on any subject whatever, regardless of whether such subject is in the Union, Concurrent or State List, provided that such legislation is required to implement an international treaty, convention, or a decision taken at an international conference. The Statement of Objects and Reasons and the Preamble to The Environment (Protection) Act 1986 said that the EP Act had been enacted to implement the Stockholm Declaration of 1972–which had been issued after the Stockholm Conference in which India had participated. Hence the EP Act, together with the rules and notifications framed under it, would be valid even if they related to subjects on the State List.

I knew Union Environment Secretary Vishwanath Anand very well. I do not now remember how the subject came up but during one of our periodic meetings, I mentioned this opinion to him and gave it to him in March 1997. I thought that he would just file it without taking action. However, to his credit, he did not follow the normal bureaucratic path of saying that he was bound by the Law Ministry's stand but passed Atul Setalvad's opinion to the Ministry staff for processing. The Environment Ministry took a long time to process the file and it was not till March 1998 that they wrote to the Law Ministry. In May 1998 the Law Ministry accepted the points made by Atul Setalvad. The way was now open to declare areas as environmentally sensitive. In July 1998 during one of my periodic visits to Delhi, both Vishwanath Anand and Additional Secretary Roy Paul informed me about the Law Ministry's concurrence. I was told that issuing of Notifications, starting with Pachmarhi, was under process. This was one of the most far-reaching environmental decisions ever, making the insult very well worth it.

However, by this time Kamal Nath was no longer in power. Environment Secretary Vishwanath Anand refused to move in the Nhava matter without once again getting the Maharashtra Government's written concurrence. I told him that their concurrence had already been received but he was adamant. His stand was illogical, since if State Government concurrence is necessary, what is the need for an EP Act Notification? My efforts to persuade him otherwise were fruitless. This was an unnecessary failure, a bureaucratic end to a promising start.

Though Nhava did not benefit from Atul Setalvad's opinion, other places did. The hill stations of Mahabaleshwar and Panchgani together with more than 200 square kilometres around them, the hill station of Matheran along with the surrounding hills, and the hill station of Mount Abu along with the surrounding areas have been declared as eco-sensitive zones under the EP Act, giving them the sort of protection we had tried to obtain for Nhava. Several other areas have also been given EP Act Protection, declared as eco-sensitive zones, and more such Notifications are on the anvil.

I have made a fresh attempt to get EP Act protection for Nhava. The areas suggested for protection include the non- ONGC parts of Nhava, the 800 hectares on Sheva which the JNPT had been directed to and had committed to afforest, together with Elephanta Island. If this works out, many of the constant battles over Elephanta would be reduced.

Regional Park

Dev Mehta, who had been Managing Director of the Maharashtra Tourism Development Corporation (MTDC), recalls that sometime in 1991-92 the MTDC took over that part of Nhava which had been classified as a Regional Park. The aim was to develop it as a park and divert picnickers from Elephanta. Subsequently, around 2004-05, some years after MMRDA constituted the Elephanta Planning Committee, CIDCO agreed to develop the park and took the land back from MTDC.

However, no action seems to have been taken.

Dev Mehta suggests that as part of the plan of the massive airport and related developments in New Bombay, some money should be set apart for conservation of Nhava.

Heritage Protection

In addition to preventing the acquisition of lands, the deforestation and the destruction of hills, there was a need to get statutory protection for the historic structures on Nhava. Since there were no heritage laws or regulations in place, the only way to do this was to have them protected under the Maharashtra Ancient Monuments and Archaeological Sites and Remains Act, 1960. Under this Act, protection can be given to any structure of historical, archaeological or artistic interest which has been in existence for not less than 50 years. I took Dr. Jamkhedkar, Director of Archaeology and Museums to Nhava. Since Archaeology and Museums at that time came under the Department of Education, I requested Education Secretary D.M. Sukthankar to come as well, and

A well wooded hilly island was flattened

he agreed. Both their reactions were extremely positive. Prof. Varde, the Minister concerned, gave his strong support but in spite of his personal interest, sadly no Notification for protection was issued. This is surely a failure of our system.

Quite independently, over 20 years later, in 2002, as part of a Listing project for the MMR Heritage Conservation Society, Sunita Dalvi and her team at the Pillai College of Architecture at New Panvel carried out a heritage listing of New Bombay which included Nhava. The Nhava sites listed by them were Training Ship *Rahaman*, the water tank, the Marine Museum, the Anchorage Bungalow and the Fatima Banu sanatorium, now the Sagaresh Suites. The Arogya Bhavan consisting of the five cottages was not included, presumably because it fell within the ONGC area. With this addition, efforts need to be made to get the Nhava Heritage List notified so that these lovely buildings finally get statutory protection.

Marine Museum

One area where some success was achieved was that of the Marine Museum. The most important achievement was the shifting, on 26th December 1978, of the alignment of the ONGC road which was to run through a corner of the Museum.

When I first visited the Museum in early 1979, it had a charming old-world appearance. An evocative description is given in an article appropriately titled "Marine Oasis" in *The Indian Express* of 6th January 1986:

> Conjure up the vision of a marine museum housed in an ancient building on a quiet, lushly wooded island. Sounds too good to be true? Well, such a haven does exist and very near the city too. The place is the Marine Museum, oldest of its kind in the country, on Nhava island, just an hour's ferry ride from Bombay.
>
> The Museum, established in 1912, is situated on that part of the island that does not belong to the Oil and Natural Gas Commission. It is managed by the Sir Mohammed Yusuf Seamen's Welfare Foundation, headed by Rashid Yusuf, a direct descendant of the family that owned the island. The white-painted stone-and-wood building, surrounded by trees and shrubs, is something straight out of a fairy tale. On the steps leading to the interior is a massive anchor that was in use more than a hundred years ago.
>
> The Museum was housed in a residence of the Wadia family, the famous ship-builders of Bombay. The rustic surroundings were close to the sea and overlooked mangroves. In its six rooms were housed a number of interesting exhibits, including a large collection of letters, arms and coins along with the original deed establishing the Bombay Steam Navigation Company. Swords and shields hanging on the wall gave it a romantic air.

The Indian Express added: "Wooden models of ships and boats of all kinds are encased in glass. There is a lot of literature, including some old, yellowing photographs, on the history of shipping in India. To top it all, there is a coin collection, including some Japanese money belonging to the times when the currency in use there was the rupee."

A prime attraction is the correspondence regarding Sir Mohamed Yusuf's desire to renounce his knighthood. A reply dated 22nd March 1937 to his letter to the Viceroy of India said "that his Excellency the Viceroy is unable himself to relieve you of the title of Knighthood, and that in the circumstances of the case it is not proposed to make any recommendation on the subject to His Majesty the King Emperor". Having then taken it up with the Secretary of State for India, Sir Mohamed Yusuf received a reply in December 1938 which said that "having once received the honour of Knighthood, it is impossible for you to divest yourself of that honour". He then consulted Rabindranath Tagore who replied saying: "In 1919, when I felt constrained to renounce my Knighthood as a protest against the Punjab atrocities, I was also informed like you that it was not possible to divest oneself of the said honour by merely returning the Letters Patent to the Governor General. One can be deprived of the honour by His Majesty the King Emperor but no resignation is possible. I do not myself use the title nor do I allow my friends to do the same. That was all I was advised I could do."

Admiral Awati was Chairman of the Committee of the National Maritime Museum. After his visit to Nhava in May 1979, he wrote: "Nhava's Maritime Museum should double as a place for storage and exhibition of artefacts of the National Maritime Museum, especially those of the Merchant Navy which has a long history. ...the Nautical Maritime Museum has recently made a beginning on the Middle Ground Island just off the Gateway of India. However, the area available there is highly restricted and an additional site is badly needed." Though this proposal did not fructify, it could now be revived, since the fortunes of the Nautical Institute have improved phenomenally.

Charming though the Museum was, there was an air of slow decay about it. The documents and photographs were left exposed and the exhibits were not being adequately looked after. The status was best described by *Mid-day* of 29th September 1979, in their article entitled "Decaying Museum":

> One of the most interesting aspects of the little-known nautical institute on Nhava Island in Bombay Harbour is a marine museum set up by the Sir Mohamed Yusuf Trust in 1912.
>
> To the casual visitor it offers a fund of interesting information in the form of old clippings, photographs, stamp and coin collections as well as poignant reminders of the founder himself.
>
> Set out on the ground floor of what used to be a residence, there are wall-hangings, works of art, furniture and personal belongings.
>
> Like the massive old desk at which Sir Mohamed used to conduct his administrative work. It still has the original, elaborately worked metal inkstand, a couple of ancient volumes pertaining to "Novha" island and personalised stationery, now yellow with age. And the "finest Baskerville vellum wove envelopes" still lie in their box on the table, near a hookah once used by the founder.
>
> The sad thing is the subtle odour of decay that hangs over everything. Peeling walls, damp furniture, crumbling documents all give off the same sombre sense of uncertainty, for it is still not sure whether the institute and the environs will be allowed to survive.

I took Sadashiv Gorakshkar, Director of the Prince of Wales Museum, to Nhava. His letter of 10th May 1979 to me speaks for itself. "As a Museum

person **I was very much impressed by the small institutional museum that has been maintained by the Institute ever since 1912, which is exactly ten years before the Prince of Wales Museum was thrown open to the public.** The foresight of the founders in establishing the museum is indeed commendable. Surprisingly enough this museum has never been listed in any of the directories of Indian Museums, the first of which was published in 1936". (Emphasis mine.)

Gorakshkar made several recommendations including that the exhibits and showcases be properly dusted and glazed, that the old newspaper cuttings along with the album containing original letters which were on display be kept in the archives, with only photocopies being displayed, etc. Swords and shields were cleaned and rust removed. Experts from the Prince of Wales Museum helped in the restoration and this assistance continued for many years. With the help of Dr. Jamkhedkar, the museum was accorded recognition and was able to obtain several grants over the years totalling Rs. 5.75 lakhs from the Union Government's Department of Culture.

Subsequently, over several weekend visits, Debi Goenka photographed many objects, and together with Heta Pandit, by then a writer

Picture gallery on the first floor of the Marine Museum

of repute, along with Dilshad Faroodi, helped in refurbishing the ecology section of the museum and in giving captions to its section on the Training Ship *Rahaman*. They also brought out pamphlets, fliers and a documentary on Nhava. Heta Pandit and Debi Goenka even donated a few artefacts from their personal collections.

With all these efforts, the museum was extensively reorganised and renovated. Even though the museum (at least to me) looks less romantic, the exhibits are now more likely to survive. The ground-floor galleries display the history of Indian shipping from the earliest days, along with a gallery on the famous Wadia ship-builders. There is also a gallery reserved for ecology and the marine food chain. The first floor galleries depict the histories of the Bombay Steam Navigation Company, the Training Ship *Rahaman* and the Scindia Steam Navigation Company, which became the premier Indian shipping company. Going back to a different age is the Durbar Hall on the top floor which brings back the days when almost like a nawab, Sir Mohamed Yusuf apparently held court, dispensed justice and received visitors. It is filled with period furniture, an armoury and some artefacts from the personal collection of Sir Mohamed Yusuf, along with the history of the Yusuf family.

CRZ Protection

IN CONSERVATION IT IS NECESSARY to have as many layers of protection as possible. With Nhava being on the waterfront, the Coastal Regulation Zone (CRZ) Notification is an obvious instrument for environmental protection.

The CRZ Notification divides coastlines (which include all waters such as rivers, creeks and backwaters which are subject to tidal action) into three categories of areas. CRZ I includes ecologically sensitive areas in which hardly any development is permitted within 500 metres of the High Tide Line. In CRZ II (areas which are substantially built up within municipal limits), by and large normal urban development is permitted with some restrictions. In CRZ III (areas which are not substantially built up), very restricted development is allowed.

In the Coastal Zone Management Plan of Greater Bombay which was to go to the Environment Ministry for approval, the Maharashtra Government had classified the whole of Greater Bombay and New Bombay as CRZ II. When I bumped into D.T. Joseph in the High Court in July 1993, I pointed out that the whole of Bombay could by no means be classified as "substantially built up", specially the very large green areas of Madh, Erangal, Marve, Manori, Gorai and the huge stretches of mangroves on the north-eastern coast of Bombay. I was a member of the Environment Ministry Coastal Zone Task Force and suggested to D.T. Joseph that rather than fighting in Delhi, we should settle matters amongst ourselves in Bombay. Even though he had already signed the file, he accepted the logic and over the next two-and-a-half years

Lime butterfly, one of Nhava's many living treasures

Contrived quarrying by ONGC contractors vertically slashing the hill

discussions took place. Eventually in November 1995, our point of view was accepted.

Once agreement had been reached for Greater Bombay, I asked that the same logic be applied to New Bombay and that the areas which had been classified in New Bombay's Development Plan as "Regional Park" be classified as CRZ III or CRZ I. D.T. Joseph eventually agreed that (except for the villages in Uran), Regional Park lands abutting the sea and also the creeks could be classified as CRZ III or CRZ I. This was a huge step forward and would protect all of Nhava. However, after D.T. Joseph was transferred, R.C. Sinha, his successor as Urban Development Secretary, tried hard to get this decision reversed but failed.

The Coastal Zone Management Plan (CZMP) for Maharashtra, as approved by the Environment Ministry on 27th September 1996, stipulated: "All areas marked in the Development Plan of New Bombay as Regional Parks are classified as CRZ III. These include Nerul and **Nhava.** In case of **Nhava**, the areas mentioned in the environmental clearance issued by this Ministry vide letter No.J-11013/21 / 88-IA, dated 16.9.1988 for Nhava Sheva Port project, viz., the green area of 500 metres all along the periphery of the port; **800 ha. Afforestation land inside the port and low-lying areas for mangrove plantation, along with mudflats and mangroves on the shoreline around Nhava, are classified as CRZ-I.**" (Emphasis mine.) In addition to protecting Nhava, this stipulation would also apply to the coastline of Uran which we had fought for long and arduously.

However, CIDCO once again tried very hard to get the whole of New Bombay declared as CRZ II. My colleague, Samir Mehta and I protested furiously over several years pointing out that these areas were not substantially built up and could not be classified as CRZ II and gave a large number of photographs to prove our point.

Eventually on 29th May 2000 the Environment Ministry constituted a committee to look into the issue. I was one of the committee members, the only NGO member, and had a very difficult time. I have described the whole process in my earlier book.

The reason CIDCO gave for wanting Nhava classified as CRZ II, was that they wished to develop roadside amenities and facilities along the 15- metre-wide stretch on the south side of the Nhava-mainland *bundh*. This proposal would involve the destruction of dense mangroves on both sides of the *bundh*. Another reason CIDCO gave was that the Sewri-Nhava road bridge would land there and attract illegal development. It was not clear how destruction of mangroves and construction of roadside amenities would stop illegal encroachment. One of the Committee members had missed this discussion and did not believe me when I told him of the proposal. CIDCO pressed for this proposal several times, especially after the Committee visited this area. This was turned down.

Perhaps more importantly, the classification of CRZ III and CRZ I for Nhava was not disturbed.

Fresh Threat

The latest threat is from Mazagon Docks Ltd, India's leading warship builder, which is expanding significantly, with projects to build frigates, destroyers and submarines. Because of shortage of space, they are setting up a new workshop at the Alcock Yard where they earlier did offshore fabrication work for ONGC, and they are also building extra storage space in a yard in Chembur, a north Bombay suburb. What is of great concern is their plan to try and lease 20 acres of land from ONGC on Nhava.

The Mazagon Docks' plan for Nhava would be in clear violation of Indira Gandhi's Directives of July and August 1980 which had said: (emphasis added) **"that no further expansion of the activity of any Central Agency should be allowed on this Island"**. "Ministry of Defence and Petroleum can go ahead with the setting up of off-shore facilities of Mazagon Dock and the supply base of ONGC **limiting it to the level and areas as now planned. No further expansion of activity of any of these organisations should be allowed on this island."** These directives had been reiterated in August 1982 when she had directed "that no further projects are taken up on the Nhava Island".

After a delay of a few months (part of which period I was overseas), I took this up with the Environment Ministry. The Environment Ministry immediately wrote to the highest level of the Defence Ministry, stating the reasons for Nhava's unique importance, the Nautical Institute, the Marine Museum and the fact that Nhava is virtually the only remaining green scenic area in New Bombay located on the sea front. The Environment Ministry added that apart from the above, with the exception of the area taken over by ONGC and Mazagon Docks, a lot of the rest of Nhava is a thickly wooded area warranting protection on that ground alone. The Ministry also mentioned the need to develop other green belts across the harbour so as to divert tourists from Elephanta, for which Nhava is ideal. Since the Mazagon Docks' proposal to set up additional facilities on Nhava would clearly violate the Prime Minister's Directives, the Environment Ministry suggested that alternative locations be considered.

Nautical Institute/ Training Ship *Rahaman*

What of Training Ship *Rahaman*, now the centre of Nhava?

In 1978 the Institute had dwindled to only a few score trainees, all of whom were ratings. Though charming, the Institute looked forlorn, not least because of the threat it was facing.

In 1978, the International Convention on Standards of Training Certification and Watch Keeping (STCW) for seafarers came into being. Two years later, in 1980 Rashid Yusuf was advised by the Nautical Adviser to the Government of India to start Survival at Sea and Fire Fighting Courses which were to become mandatory under the STCW Convention. This at the time all pleas had been rejected and the Nautical Institute had been told to vacate Nhava.

In 1981 T.S. *Rahaman* instituted Survival at Sea training which was inaugurated by Admiral Jal Cursetji (retired Chief of Naval Staff). It was the initiation of STCW training by *Rahaman* that enabled the Government of India to ratify the International Convention.

The same year, another Shipping Ministry Committee under the Chairmanship of retired Chief of Naval Staff, Admiral S.N. Nanda, was appointed to "investigate the unemployment among the Indian Seafarers." The Committee recommended a temporary suspension of all pre-sea rating training for sailors.

The Nanda Committee recommended that the training facilities of

Rahaman should be further augmented under Government auspices. One of the reasons given was the shortage of land with the Government of India. In 1984, Director-General of Shipping, B.K. Rao approached Rashid Yusuf to enquire whether he would consider handing over *Rahaman* to the Government of India. However, like his grandfather and father before him Rashid Yusuf again declined to do so. This was very fortunate.

Thereafter, the Shipping Ministry decided to scrap Training Ship *Rajendra* and set up Training Ship *Chanakya*, a shore-based establishment, which trained both officers and sailors. Another Committee chaired by C.P. Srivastava, in its final report recommended its preference for T.S. *Rahaman*, acknowledged its pre-eminence in the field of pre-sea training (it was the only one training pre-sea ratings in those days) and suggested that *Rahaman* be accorded recognition on a permanent basis as a Pre-Sea Training Institute for Ratings.

Their degree courses include a one-year diploma in Nautical Science which is affiliated to the Indian Maritime University and which, after the requisite sea service, leads to the B.Sc. degree for 160 deck officer cadets per year. Other degree courses include a three-year B.Sc. Nautical Science course for 40 Officer Cadets per year and a three-year B.Sc. course in Maritime Hospitality Studies for 40 Officer Cadets per year.

Courses at the higher levels include three-month courses for upgrading of Masters (Captains), 1st Officers and IIIrd Officers respectively, along with three-month courses for Chief Engineers, 1st Engineers and IIIrd Engineers.

For ratings, there is a six-month course which trains 120 General Purpose ratings at a time and a catering course which trains 40 Saloon ratings every six months. There are also a whole range of other maritime catering courses, including an orientation course for catering college candidates who desire to go to sea.

Very much in demand are several mid-career Sea Safety Courses such as Fire Prevention and both Elementary and Advanced Fire Fighting, Personal Survival Techniques, Global Maritime Distress and Safety Systems, Tanker Familiarisation, courses on radar and so on. There are also Medical Safety courses.

There are plans to include other courses such as a basic Offshore Course, Helicopter, Underwater Escape and Sea Survival, Helicopter Landing officer courses, Offshore Fire Fighting and Emergency Helideck Duties, etc.

In all, at any given time, there would be about 760 trainees, ranging from ship captains and chief engineers to ratings, with about 650 resident trainees on the campus. There is a faculty of over 40 and 80 staff members. The faculty includes 14 captains, eight chief engineers, five radio officers, one doctor and fourteen lecturers in physics, chemistry, mathematics, English and computer science.

Reverting to the old tradition, the Sir Mohamed Yusuf Seamen Welfare Foundation also runs a full-fledged school and Junior College up to the 12th standard with over 800 students (of which 105 are boarders) and 46 teachers.

The contribution of T.S. *Rahaman* was recognised in April 2009 by the Maharashtra Governor S.C. Jamir conferring on Rashid Yusuf the esteemed "Varuna" award of the prestigious National Maritime Celebrations Committee in appreciation of his outstanding contribution to the Maritime Industry for the last four decades.

On 27th November 2010 on the occasion of the Indian Maritime Human Resources Summit sponsored by the Indian Maritime University and Gateway Media at Chennai, Rashid Yusuf received an award at the hands of Union Shipping Minister G.K. Vasan, in recognition of his pursuit of excellence and yeoman service to the Maritime Community.

Training Ship *Rahaman*, larger than it ever was, has really become a leading maritime university. Its contribution to maritime training has been recognised by a rare honour.

On 20th September, which is designated as Founders Day, the Indian Postal Department issued a First Day Cover to commemorate 100 years of maritime training on *Rahaman*. The stamp was released by Post Master General Charles Lobo in the conference room of the Director-General of Shipping Dr. Satish Agnihotri.

Sheva (Jawaharlal Nehru) Port

In June 1980, the UNDP "Adviser" had gone on at great length about the fact that except for the little patch between Nhava and Sheva, there was no other suitable site for a port on the entire west coast. In July, Chief Minister Antulay had said the same thing. Maharashtra Urban Development Secretary, S. Ramamoorthi had gone further and said that there was no other suitable site on the entire Indian coast line. However, this was by no means a unanimous view.

In 1947, Vice Admiral Daya Shankar, then only a Commander, was appointed to the West Coast Port Development Committee. He wrote: "The Committee had many distinguished members, with the late Kasturbhai Lalbhai as the Chairman, leading shipping magnates, senior port engineers and other professionals. We visited many sites – Mangalore, Karwar, Jamnagar, Kandla and Bhavnagar" and "the Committee had a number of meetings to evaluate the ports we visited." The Committee was practically unanimous in favour of Kandla but his own preference was for Karwar and he wrote a dissent note. Nhava Sheva was not even mentioned. It only arrived on the scene later.

The eminent economist Dr. V.K.R.V. Rao, who was Minister for Transport and Shipping between 1967 and 1969, wrote in his memoirs that he had "got a lot of job satisfaction in the handling (of) the expansion of other major ports, especially Nava Sheva extension in Mumbai...." Kiran Mishra, V.K.R.V. Rao's biographer, also wrote that during Rao's tenure as Minister "the expansion of Nava Sheva was carried out." Rao and Kiran Mishra must have been referring only to the planning for the port expansion, since physical work commenced only in the 1980s. Sadly, neither Rao nor Mishra provided any further details.

The rationale for the port was well explained by the Regional Plan for the Bombay Metropolitan Region published by the Maharashtra Government in March 1974. In the section entitled "New satellite port at Nhava-Sheva", the Regional Plan said: "the present capacity of the Bombay docks was completely utilised and that the dock expansion scheme would provide only a limited relief. It added (emphasis added): "The Bombay Port Trust has therefore proposed to set up a **new satellite port** at Nhava-Sheva on the mainland across the harbour." Welcoming the proposal, the Plan said that this project would "help considerably in diverting the bulk cargo traffic with mainland destination directly into the mainland, bypassing the congested areas and communication routes in Greater Bombay."

There were, however, doubts in high places. Referring to the period from 1985 to mid 1986 when he was Maharashtra Government Chief Secretary, B.G. Deshmukh wrote: "This port should have come up years earlier, but our own cadre officer, M G. Pimputkar, in the Planning Commission did not agree that the cargo traffic warranted another port near Bombay. There was also a report that the sea breeze from the Thane-Belapur chemical industrial area would blow into the proposed JNPT area and make it difficult to live there." He added: "Strangely, when the project had to be cleared all these so-called difficulties just disappeared." Did they really disappear, or were they brushed aside?

There was absolutely no word in these discussions about the colossal environmental implications of such a port and the destruction of vast, badly needed, green areas, and the addition of yet more economic activity in an already over-concentrated region.

Over the decades, the port at Sheva had been planned as an extension of Bombay Port and had been strongly promoted by the Bombay Port Trust (BPT). However, there had been severe labour problems at Bombay Port. V.K.R.V. Rao recorded one occasion when he had "refused to be cowed down by the threat of strike, summoning the help of the Navy to run the Mumbai Port." Perhaps in order not to let the Bombay Port trade unions operate at Sheva, the Government of India decided that the port at Sheva would be a separate entity to be governed by a separate Port Trust, the Nhava Sheva Port Trust (NSPT) which eventually became the Jawaharlal Nehru Port Trust (JNPT). This was perhaps a fulfilment of the proposal made in the Regional Plan which was that: "while the new port may initially handle bulk and contain (sic) cargo traffic the port needs to be designed for its ultimate functioning as an independent port to handle all types of traffic."

Safeguarding Nhava

Forty-five acres on the southern part of Nhava Island had been earmarked for the port. Right from the beginning I had taken up the matter that the port should not touch Nhava. The Protection Committee, in their report of December 1979, had made a specific recommendation to that effect, saying that till that date, the Bombay Port Trust (BPT) had "undertaken no work whatsoever for their proposed Nhava Sheva Port". Hence the Committee recommended that the BPT should "confine their new port to Sheva, leaving Nhava alone". In May 1980 shortly, after C.P.N. Singh's visit to Bombay, the Protection Committee Chairman Ram Batra wrote to BPT Chairman B.C. Cariappa drawing his attention to this point but there was no reply. Joint Secretary (Ports) D.K. Jain, whom I approached on this subject more than once, also made no commitment.

However, this point was one of the safeguards suggested by us and Salim Ali. In response to that, the Prime Minister had directed: "No other agency (other than the existing military unit at Sheva) should be allowed around Nhava Sheva and areas around Nhava Sheva Port planned as a green belt." On 21st August 1980, Environment Secretary M.G.K. Menon wrote to Shipping & Transport Secretary Mohinder Singh, who on 30th August wrote to Maharashtra Chief Secretary P.G. Gavai. The Maharashtra Government was obviously very keen on the port project because they reacted virtually immediately. Gavai's letter of 4th September was followed by a telex the next day, which confirmed that the Maharashtra Government had accepted all the conditions stipulated. After that, on 10th August 1982, came the third Prime Minister's Directive which said categorically "that no further projects are taken up on the Nhava Island".

On 22nd April 1983, at the meeting of the Monitoring Committee, NSPT Chairman, Vice Admiral N.P. Datta said that for 20 years the port would not touch Nhava and even then, there would be only a wall or a fence with no structure being built on Nhava. Hence the development of the Regional Park, as directed by the Prime Minister, could be undertaken immediately. This was reiterated a few months later by the Shipping Ministry which, in a note to the Prime Minister's Office, said that no development had been proposed on Nhava Island and that there would be no structure on the island.

A confirmation was given in May 1985 by NSPT Chairman Anna Malhotra who, in her reply to INTACH Bombay Chapter Convener Anjani Mehta, wrote: "this Port Trust has no plans of any activity on the Nhava Island which is across the Elephanta (sic) Creek." Five months later, responding to pressure from the Monitoring Committee about adherence to the Prime Minister's Directives, in October 1985, Union Surface Transport Secretary P.M. Abraham wrote categorically to Environment Secretary T.N. Seshan that no port activity whatsoever had been planned on Nhava Island, and that lands on Nhava Island had been kept out of acquisition.

What's in a Name?

In order to clinch the issue of keeping the port activities away from Nhava, an effort was made to change the name from " Nhava Sheva Port" to "Sheva Port". At the Monitoring Committee meeting of 22nd April 1983, Dr. N.L. Ramanathan, Director in the Ministry of Environment & Forests recommended that the port be called "Sheva Port". CIDCO Managing Director L.C. Gupta said that three months earlier, on the Chief Secretary's instructions, the Maharashtra Government had written to the Central Government to call it "Sheva Port". Admiral Datta countered by saying that it was known as Nhava Sheva Port, and that the Detailed Project Report had been approved by the Union Cabinet on that basis.

I had got to know Admiral Datta very well over the past several years. After a clash which followed a suggestion made by me at the Annual General Meeting of the Yachting Association of India (YAI), I had been asked to join the YAI Selection Committee, which selected sailors for international events, including the 1981 Asian Sailing Regatta and the 1982 Asian Games. We had got on very well, generally saw eye to eye, and I used to do a great deal of the Committee's staff work. Our conflicting interests, both when he was MDL Chairman, and now when he was NSPT Chairman, had not affected this relationship. However, he was clearly very sensitive about the name of the port. The day after the 22nd April 1983 meeting, the Monitoring Committee members had been "gheraoed" by the villagers on Sheva. A few days later, at a party, Admiral Datta enquired about it and I mentioned the name change. He lost his temper, spoke harshly and said that he would never agree.

The matter was not allowed to end there. The Monitoring Committee chairman Dr. A.K. Ganguly was in full agreement with changing the name and said that he had started referring to it as "Sheva Port". On 1st May 1985 the Monitoring Committee made a categorical recommendation: "that the Port's name be changed to 'Sheva Port' deleting the word 'Nhava.' " However, NSPT countered this. The Project Manager, Brigadier P.S. Sethee replied that this was not a suggestion given by NSPT, "nor were they able to endorse it". He added that NSPT could "examine and attend only those recommendations" of the Monitoring Committee which had been approved by the Department of Environment. Regarding the name change, if the Committee wished to pursue it they could "approach the Government of India through the Department of Environment." All this became academic when the name was changed to " Jawaharlal Nehru Port".

Land Grab

I learnt from CIDCO officials that the port authorities had more than trebled their land requirements from the original 1,100 hectares to 3,400 hectares. On 2nd November 1981, CIDCO Chief Architect & Planner M.Y. Thackeray wrote to Dr. A.K. Ganguly, pointing out that the port's land requirement, as indicated in the Interim Report, was about 3,600 hectares, which was three times the area indicated in 1973 by the BPT as per the Master Plan prepared by their then consultants, M/s. Bertlin & Partners in 1972. The additional land sought and the suggested location would seriously affect the structure of New Bombay, its transportation network and the provision of land for housing. The port's plans would "literally divide" New Bombay into two parts, depriving the citizens of the southern part, where access to the jobs and facilities planned at Thana and Ulwe was easy. In addition, with the land allocation for residential and allied activities being halved, many of those working in the port and in port-based activities would have to commute for long distances "resulting in the undesirable repetition of problems being faced in Bombay."

I took this issue up repeatedly at the Department of Environment Monitoring Committee and received very strong support from Dr. Ganguly who had a phobia about agricultural lands being diverted for other uses. A transportation "expert" in BMRDA took the opposite stand, an amazing one for a Regional Planning Authority. Referring to the requests to the port authorities to give details of their land requirements he asked: "How can they and why should they?"

On 23rd April 1983, the Monitoring Committee visited Sheva where the port was then under construction. The villagers, who were, quite reasonably, upset about the acquisition of their lands, *gheraoed* the entire team for several hours. This was ironical since several of us were trying hard to minimise the amount of land to be acquired and I had been especially vociferous in arguing that the lands being acquired were hundreds of acres in excess of requirement. We mentioned that we were a Department of Environment team and had nothing to do with the Port Trust or with CIDCO. The villagers clearly did not believe us saying that there were no pollution problems on Sheva and hence no reason for us to have come to their village. One of the villagers referred to me as the *darhi wallah* (bearded one) and menacing glances were cast at my briefcase. It contained a number of my handwritten notes, of which I had no copies, which worried me considerably. However barring a few hours of hunger and fatigue, nothing happened to us. I have since learnt my lesson. Thereafter in tricky situations, or those which may turn violent, I have been careful about what I have taken with me, or worn, since comfortable old clothes and shoes are irreplaceable.

The Monitoring Committee kept pressing for implementation of the Prime Minister's Directives relating to decongestion of Bombay and release of Bombay Port Trust (BPT) lands for parks and gardens. However, having obtained the Prime Minister's clearance, the Shipping Ministry and the two port trusts kept stalling. They now took the stand that the Bombay Port Trust and Jawaharlal Nehru Port Trust were separate entities and hence the Bombay Port Trust was not concerned with the promises given for the Sheva Port. Figures were given of green and open patches maintained by the BPT but these did not pertain to the release of land as had been directed and agreed to. No action was taken regarding reducing the traffic going through Bombay Port.

Stretch of the Nhava coastline showing complete absence of trees and traces of quarrying activity

Prime Minister Rajiv Gandhi

I had made a series of representations to Prime Minister Rajiv Gandhi. During the summer of 1986, I was on a holiday in England when, out of the blue, I received a message saying that the Prime Minister had given me an appointment. I was extremely surprised, since I had not asked for one, and since Rajiv Gandhi was not easy to meet. When I telephoned the Tata Ltd. Office in London to send my reply, the Director in Charge said that they had been trying to locate me and asked when I was returning to India. He was very surprised when I said that I was not cutting short my holiday. I had come to England after nine years and did not know when I would next be able to do so. However, I was given another date to meet the Prime Minister, which I eventually did on 27th October 1986. When, armed with a number of representations on different issues together with photographs, I met Rajiv Gandhi, he was gracious and cordial, stepping forward from behind his table to shake hands. He asked: "How is the environment doing?" To which I replied: "Taking a battering." I told him that till recently, I had not been sure whether the Department of Environment was fighting for us or against us as they were clearing projects indiscriminately. In some ways it was worse than before the Department was created, since earlier we could have at least approached the Prime Minister's Office directly. He clearly had a high regard for Seshan and asked: "Even Seshan is letting things slip through?" At the end of our 15-minute meeting, as I was leaving, echoing the views of many people in the environmental movement, I said: "Please tell the Department of Environment that their job is to protect the environment." As he saw me to the door, he said he would do so.

Rajiv Gandhi asked me to meet his Secretary. It took a few seconds for me to realise that he was referring not to his Private Secretary, Vincent George, but that he meant his Principal Secretary, Mrs. Serla Grewal, one of the two most important officials in the Government of India. On my way out, I told George that the Prime Minister had asked me to meet Serla Grewal, and requested him to check and let me know when I should come. I thought that George would at least check back with the Prime Minister and obtain his instructions. He did not, and said that there was no need to come back again and suggested that I meet Serla Grewal then and there. A few minutes later, when I was with another officer in the PMO, the officer got a call and said that the Principal Secretary would like to see me.

During our meeting, Serla Grewal telephoned Defence Secretary S.K. Bhatnagar and told him that I had spent half an hour with the Prime Minister and asked him to meet me. She also telephoned Seshan and asked him if he could see me the next day with PMO Additional Secretary Otima Bordia, to which he agreed. The next day Otima Bordia accompanied me to the meeting with Seshan, and handed him all my representations. Seshan had taken the trouble to brief himself, and had with him a note entitled "Environmental Problems of Maharashtra". During the one-hour-long meeting, he did most of the talking and virtually spoke for us.

One of my representations was about the violation of the Prime Minister's Directives regarding Sheva Port. Whether because of Rajiv Gandhi's and the PMO's interest or otherwise, on 29th October 1986, Seshan wrote a strong letter to Transport Secretary P.P. Nayyar, asking for implementation of the Prime Minister's Directives.

Regarding the meeting of the Empowered Committee to be held the next day, T.N. Seshan wrote: "Since, the **raison d'etre for Sheva Port was the diversion of traffic from Bombay Port so that decongestion in Bombay could be achieved**, it is essential that both these projects – Nhava Sheva and Bombay Port – are considered together." (Emphasis mine.) He pointed out that little or nothing had been done to implement the Prime Minister's Directive, that no land had been released by the Bombay Port Trust for creating green belts or reducing congestion. On the contrary, it was envisaged to expand Bombay Port; this would be a total violation of the conditions laid down while approving the Sheva

Port. In addition, he pointed out that unauthorised constructions of buildings were taking place on Sheva hills. He said that if it was proposed to deviate from the assurances given, **"the project should be looked into de novo in full consultation with the local Environmental Groups."** (Emphasis mine.)

Working Group

Perhaps as a result of my meeting with the Prime Minister, in November 1986 I was nominated as a member of an Environment Ministry Working Group which was asked to study the environmental aspects of the port. The other members were M.A. Rashid, a retired Forest Department Officer, J.C. Daniel of the Bombay Natural History Society, S. Shiva Kumar of the Environment Ministry and Professor Katti. Shiva Kumar and I were familiar with the background. Professor Katti did not attend any of the meetings of the Working Group.

In the face of our repeated queries over the years, the Port authorities replied that out of the total land being acquired by them, 900 hectares were either hilly or low-lying marshy areas, consisting mainly of salt pans and silt mud flats. This figure was given by them several times in various permutations and combinations and there was no way that they could deny it. These lands could not be used and would be kept vacant. I argued that in that case these lands should be greened and this point was accepted. In their report of 25th December 1986 the Working Group recommended that the 900 hectares be afforested. To give some legal sanctity to the green areas, it was suggested that the area be shown as "green" in the long-term development plan for the port, be designated as Regional Park in CIDCO's Master Plan for New Bombay, and, most important of all, be declared as "Protected Forest" under the Indian Forest Act.

Regarding the broader aspects of the Prime Minister's Directives, the Working Group said: **"Work on the Nhava Sheva Port Project with its consequential environmental damage is proceeding at full speed and a fait accompli will be presented unless immediate action is taken perhaps by halting the work until the above and other environmental issues are resolved** and firm commitments are obtained from the concerned agencies on the interim recommendations suggested by the Working Group." (Emphasis mine.)

We had fought long and hard to preserve the hills and topography of Nhava. The hills and topography of Sheva were equally important. Regarding quarrying, cutting the hill in order to provide flat land for rail lines, etc, was one thing; but quarrying only for the purpose of obtaining fill material which could easily be obtained from less sensitive sites, was quite another matter. The port authorities had, after several years of prodding by the Monitoring Committee, been brought around to agreeing that there would be no hill cutting or quarrying above a "cut line".

Everyone wants to be on top – both metaphorically and physically. The Working Group had recommended that there be no structures on the hill and that "the location of the administrative block on Sheva hill must be reviewed, as its proposed location is undesirable." The Port Trust however went ahead with the construction on the hill and claimed: "this building on the proposed location was **essentially required at the proposed site from an operational angle**." This claim was difficult to understand. What was the operational imperative? Surely the Port Trust Chairman and senior officers don't sit with telescopes watching ships entering or leaving the harbour. None of the other major ports (Bombay, Calcutta, Madras, Cochin) have offices sited on hills. I wonder how many foreign ports have their offices on hill tops.

At the Environment Ministry's request, the Working Group made additional reports in October 1987, and again on 5th August 1988 in which the points made earlier were reiterated. The Public Investment Board (PIB) meeting, which was to consider this project, was reportedly scheduled for 11th August. Hence on 7th August, I wrote an urgent letter to Environment Secretary K.P. Geethakrishnan, requesting that the imminent PIB clearance be withheld till a time-bound programme was drawn up for implementation of the Prime Minister's Directive of more than eight years before. Geethakrishnan had come from the Finance Ministry. Civil servants in the so-called "economic" ministries view the environment as one of their biggest bugbears. Geethakrishnan was no Seshan, and when issues involving adverse locations of projects were raised, he used to keep saying that some deterioration in India's environment was inevitable, that India had 100 million cattle, which was unsustainable and so on. Hence I was not surprised when my request was turned down.

However, the final environmental clearance of 16th September 1988 did incorporate several key conditions. The total land area was restricted to 2,584 hectares. An area of 800 hectares was to be afforested. In addition, a green belt of 500 metres was to be provided all along the landward periphery of the port. Furthermore, suitable low-lying areas were to be identified for mangrove plantation. A total amount of Rs. 6.6 crores was to be included in the project cost to cover the costs of this afforestation. Regarding the recommendation that the green belt lands be classified as "Regional Park" and "Protected Forest", the Surface Transport Ministry had decided that the legal position would be checked. Sadly, in spite of this, no stipulation was made about classification of these lands as "Regional Park" and/or "Protected Forest".

Regarding the Sheva hill, which we had fought hard to preserve, several stipulations were made. The first was that the main administrative building under construction should not exceed the existing two storeys. No further buildings were to be built and the existing temporary structures were to be removed before the end of 1990. No further cutting of hill slopes, other than that already contracted, was to be carried out.

With regard to safeguarding Elephanta Island and the world-famous caves, it was stipulated that there should be no major blasting in the Port area and that adequate measures must be taken for protection of the caves, particularly from vibrations and from the sulphur dioxide emissions of ships. In addition, the operation of the berth which falls within the one kilometre Elephanta Protected Zone was to be controlled with adequate safeguards to ensure that the caves were not damaged.

The 500-metre-wide green belt on Sheva has not been created. As regards the 800 hectares of afforestation, while it is not clear if the full extent has been carried out, a great deal of planting has certainly been done. However, no progress has been made in getting the green belt lands statutorily protected. Part of the fault is mine since, though I have tried, my efforts have been spasmodic.

However, large amounts of land on Sheva have been afforested. A major victory is that Nhava Island remains free from the port. By a strange quirk of fate, an avoidable environmental disaster on 40 hectares of land caused by ONGC has resulted in at least 10 to 20 times the area being protected. This is one of several occasions in my conservation work where a major setback, sometimes because of my own ineptitude, has resulted in far greater environmental protection.

Bombay Port

B.G. Deshmukh complained: "The Central Government also took inordinately long to give approval to the setting up of the Nhava Sheva Port... In spite of State Government's repeated efforts the Central Government took its time to clear the Nhava Sheva Port." His rationale for the Nhava Sheva Port was (emphasis added): "The Bombay port was getting congested and needed relief, especially in the light of the growing container traffic. **Diversion of a good number of ships to the proposed new port was also necessary to give considerable relief to the road traffic congestion in the city.**"

This was the logic behind the Prime Minister's Directive, and the Environment Ministry's stipulations of 16th September 1988 directly relating to Bombay City. The latter are important enough to be repeated verbatim (emphasis added):

"(xi) With the operation of the Nhava Sheva Port, as a measure of decongestion of Bombay Port, the **traffic in Bombay Port must be gradually reduced** by steps to be taken by the Ministry of Surface Transport, Bombay Port Trust and NSPT, **so that the total general cargo inclusive of container cargo** handled at Bombay Port **comes down within three years to 6.5 million tonnes."**

(xii) **The Ministry of Surface Transport and Bombay Port Trust must take action to gradually make the land of Bombay Port, which is not required for operational purposes of the Port, available for greening and recreation."**

The time frame and action plans for bringing down the cargo traffic in Bombay Port and release of lands for greening were to be furnished by the Surface Transport Ministry within three months.

Over the years, no attempt was made to adhere to the conditions relating to decongestion of Bombay Port. Nor were the commitments to release land for greening and recreation implemented. The Environment Ministry had acted as a disinterested bystander.

Far from reducing the annual traffic of general cargo in Bombay Port to 6.5 million tons, the Port Trust did the reverse. As per their figures, they increased the general cargo (excluding Petroleum, Oil and Lubricants and crude oil) traffic to 11.4, 15.8, 16.4, 20.2, 20.0, 17.6 and 20.0 million tons, respectively in 2003-04, 2004-05, 2005-06, 2006-07, 2007-08, 2008-09 and 2009-10 – a far cry from the 6.5 million tons stipulated and agreed to. If Petroleum, Oil and Lubricants (POL) and crude oil traffic is added the figures would become 30.0, 35.2, 44.2, 52.4, 57.0, 51.9 and 54.6 million tons in 2003-04, 2004-05, 2005-06, 2006-07 and 2007-08, 2008-09 and 2009-10 respectively.

As if this is not enough, the Port Trust is planning to substantially increase the traffic and what is worse are their plans, as reported in the press, to set up a Special Economic Zone (SEZ) on Port Trust lands. The proposed projects include an Offshore Container Terminal to scale up

Site cleared for "development"

their capacity so as to enable handling of ships of 6,000 TEUS and construct four open sea berths with a deep draught of 14.6 metres. There is also a proposal for constructing a second Liquid Chemicals Berth at Pir Pau Pier at Trombay. What will be very harmful and virtually unprecedented is the filling up of the existing basins at Prince's and Victoria Docks. In other parts of the world, such basins are recycled for use by smaller vessels, pleasure craft and so on. This filling up will be irreversible and will be a gross violation of the CRZ Regulations. Surprisingly, the Environment Ministry seemed to have forgotten about the Prime Minister's Directive and their statutory stipulations and gave clearance to the Offshore Terminal Project on 9th November 2006.

Other proposed projects include an integrated passenger and cruise terminal which will offer facilities for berthing luxury liners, yachts, ferry terminal and shopping malls. The proposed locations are off Oyster Rock, Radio Club, Ferry Wharf and Sewree Mudflats. There are also proposals to develop the western waterfront facing the Arabian Sea. This is odd since there are no port facilities on this side except minor facilities at Mahim and some fishing villages. A bizarre proposal relates to Back Bay on the south-western corner of the Island City. The plan is to reclaim land at Back Bay and build a convention centre. This is a gross violation of the CRZ Regulations and will also violate the State Government policy of no further construction at Back Bay.

Another proposal in fragrant violation of the Environment Ministry's stipulations is the proposed development of a financial centre on 2.5

acres of vacant land at Masjid Bunder. At the presentation mentioned below, I pointed out that as per the Prime Minister's Directive and the Environment Ministry's statutory stipulations, lands were meant to be released for purposes of greening.

A presentation was made by KPMG Consultants (appointed by the Port Trust in 2006 for developing their long term business plan) in the presence of Port Trust Chairman Rani Jadhav, Maharashtra Environment Secretary Sharwaree Gokhale, Maharashtra Secretary (Special Projects) Sanjay Ubale, other Government Secretaries, Chairman of the Maharashtra Maritime Board and others. Some NGO representatives were also invited.

At the presentation, Rani Jadhav said that the main expansion would not be for container traffic but for dry bulk and liquid cargo. This was completely against what they had said when sanction for the Nhava Sheva Port had been sought, namely that they would be diverting traffic to Sheva. It was pointed out that the Port Trust expansion plans would greatly increase congestion and pollution in Bombay, to which the reply was that when a missing link of a 700-metre road was built, there would be no additional congestion. There would also be a dedicated freight railway line for cargo. Subsequently, they said that they were also depending on the Bombay trans-harbour Link which, however, is years into the future. What happens in the interim period? The congestion and pollution caused by workers, ancillary businesses and so on was brushed aside.

The Maharashtra Environment Secretary, Sharwaree Gokhale said that as far as her Department was concerned, the projects were fine and the Port Trust need not come to the State Government for approval at all. When Rani Jadhav pointed out that 60 percent of India's total container traffic passes through Bombay Harbour (namely Bombay Port and JNPT), Sharwaree Gokhale said the Maharashtra Government wanted an even higher proportion to go through Bombay Harbour. When Jamsheed Kanga pointed out the Environment Ministry stipulations, Sharwaree Gokhale replied that those had been imposed in 1988 and at that time they had not envisaged that the traffic would grow. She dismissed the environmental stipulations and commitments by saying: "This is all history". A retired Chief Secretary who was present said that the earlier commitments had been given when the economy was progressing only at the "Hindu" (very slow) rate of growth and had no relevance now. Adherence to prior commitments and statutory stipulations had been forgotten by those whose duty it was to enforce them.

Sanjay Ubale pointed out that Singapore Port handles 423 million tons of traffic by using only 532 hectares of land. In the case of Bombay, the traffic targeted was only one-third of that, with the same amount of land demanded. He asked whether space could not be conserved and also added that rather than expanding port facilities in Bombay, the Maharashtra Government could suggest that ports at other locations like Alewadi be developed. Jamsheed Kanga pointed out that as the Shipping Ministry was one entity, it was their responsibility to plan for the distribution of different types of cargo to different ports. Sharwaree Gokhale answered that all the ports needed to be developed and added proudly that environmental clearance to ports in Maharashtra were given in record time by her department. She forgot that her role was to defend the environment, and to grant clearances only after fully assessing environmental impacts.

Sanjay Ubale was very vocal about his concern regarding the expansion of Bombay Port. Senior bureaucrats and politicians took little interest and with Rani Jadhav being a Chief Secretary rank Maharashtra cadre IAS officer, his hands were tied, to some extent. However, eventually the Maharashtra Government came around to the view that the port expansion should not be at Bombay. Disregarding their request, the Public Investment Board cleared the project.

The Maharashtra Government then approached Prime Minister Man Mohan Singh. Yogesh Naik's article in *The Times of India* of 28th July 2007 was entitled: **"State to appeal to PM against port plan. Proposed Expansion Will Worsen Traffic Situation, Negate Infrastructure Investments."** Yogesh Naik quoted Sanjay Ubale as saying: "Throughout the world, ports are expanded in consultation with the city authorities. It is quite clear that this expansion will place certain demands on the city's infrastructure and it is not clear whether that has been taken into account. It is also feared that the expansion might negate the investments done by the state for infrastructure. At present, there is a massive congestion problem at Wadala due to trucks. This will increase with expansion."

However, what complicated the issue was that Sharad Pawar, the undisputed leader of the Nationalist Congress Party (NCP) (which is a major partner in the Maharashtra Coalition Government), has supported the project. The matter was referred to Planning Commission Deputy Chairman Montek Singh Ahluwahlia for his advice.

Montek Singh Ahluwahlia did not intervene in the matter, having reportedly said that the Shipping Ministry had already examined the project. The Planning Commission Member, Gajendra Haldea, who was handling shipping, also did not intervene in the project but did oppose the concession agreement, quoting a case study of JNPT which had said that the agreement was defective.

This is a clear case of a sectoral versus holistic approach and Bombay's future hangs in the balance.

Vice Admiral I.C. Rao who from 1990 to 1993 had been Chief of Material (the seniormost technical officer) in the Navy, wrote that normally irrational schemes of this type collapse of their own accord, but this time, the scheme was getting approvals at higher and higher levels, and it was felt that something needed to be done. Hence in October 2007 concerned citizens, activists, and marine professionals got together to form the Mumbai Docklands Regeneration Forum. The Convener, Major General S. 'Bobby' Dutta, a retired officer of the Electrical and Mechanical Engineers, and a well-known, experienced yachtsman, played an active role. A key member was Admiral I.C. Rao. Other members included Shirish Patel, an eminent structural engineer and Sharada Dwivedi, a prominent city historian, with retired Chief Secretary D.M. Sukthankar being the Chairman. Hema Ramani of BEAG was the liaison with BEAG and provided expert advice on environmental issues and the RTI Act.

The Forum started a campaign to convince the authorities that the Offshore Container Terminal Project was doomed to fail and to alert Bombay's citizens to the problems it would cause. The Forum held media briefings and wrote to Shipping Minister T.R. Baalu, requesting him to review the project. The Forum proposed alternative uses for the Prince's and Victoria Docks, for the benefit of the citizens of Bombay. A number of detailed technical reports, pointing out the severe adverse implications, were forwarded to Shipping Secretary A.V.P.N. Sarma, with a request for a professional review, but these remained unacknowledged and unanswered.

The Forum made a detailed presentation to Bombay Port Trust Chairman Rahul Asthana on 11th October 2008, soon after he took over from Mrs Rani Jadhav, the initiator of the ill-conceived project. The presentation brought out that the depths of 16.5 metres at the berths would be impossible to maintain due to rapid re-siltation in an area surrounded by mud flats at a distance as close as one nautical mile. Obviously worried about audit objections, Rahul Asthana replied that as the project was already under execution, it was not possible to modify or halt it. It was explained to the Chairman that though halting the project would incur some costs, these costs would be much less than the quantum of damages that the concessionaires would demand for not maintaining the designed depths at the berths.

In order to provide a land area (which comes to 55 hectares or about 135 acres) for stacking of containers, the Bombay Port Trust has commenced filling up the Prince's and Victoria Docks. To quote Admiral I.C. Rao:

> Filling up of docks which are being used by the coastal fleet is a diabolical idea. Users are offshore supply vessels, Coast Guard vessels, ocean-going tugs, and anchor handling vessels, including ships belonging to ONGC, Shipping Corporation of India, Great Offshore, and five other leading shipping companies.
>
> Filling up of Prince's and Victoria Docks will also result in permanent closure of the Merewether Dry Dock, access to which is through Prince's Dock. There are over 150 coastal vessels operating off Bombay and its adjacent coastline. These include Bulk Cargo Vessels, Cement Carriers, Offshore Support Vessels, Coast Guard Vessels, inland vessels for container trans-shipment, dredgers together with multifarious barges, including for coal and petroleum products. Each of these vessels needs to be dry-docked periodically for routine maintenance as stipulated by the maritime authorities, and for repairs. The hulls need cleaning, the underwater steel plates need replacement due to corrosion, shafting and propellers need inspection and repairs, and a host of other underwater equipment need attention in a dry dock.
>
> There are only two dry docks in Bombay capable of docking coastal vessels of up to 100 metres in length, namely Mogul Dry Dock of Mazagon Docks and Merewether Dry Dock of the Mumbai Port Trust. (Hughes Dry Dock of 270 metres in length is too large for short duration docking of coastal vessels). Mogul Dry Dock is rarely available due to the commitments of Mazagon Docks for major refits. Therefore the 150 coastal vessels have to depend on Merewether Dry Dock
>
> In obtaining approval for the OCT project, the Port Trust did not even mention in the Detailed Feasibility Report that filling of Prince's & Victoria for the Container Terminal Project would result in closure of Merewether Dry Dock. Regrettably, the ill-conceived Offshore Container Terminal project was pushed through the approval process by suppressing vital facts including the adverse effect of the closure of a strategic asset like the Merewether Dock. Shipping Ministry Officials in Distant Delhi assumed that any proposal coming from the venerable Mumbai

> Port Trust must have been vetted from all aspects, and raised no objections.
>
> The ONGC, a cash-rich organisation, can afford to send their vessels to Dubai for Dry Docking. The Coast Guard has been presented with a fait accompli. Several coastal vessels will default on maintenance hoping that it will be tolerated by the weak regulatory regime of the DG Shipping. Coastal shipping has received scant attention from the Government and this is one more instance of the lack of positive action to promote coastal shipping which most countries consider a life line of trade and commerce.
>
> Filling up of Prince's and Victoria Docks requires 2.7 million cubic metres of sand. Bombay Port Trust intends to obtain this sand from a shoal off Mandwa across the harbour. This shoal area protects Mandwa jetty and the removal of the shoal may well make Mandwa Jetty unsafe for public use. It will also probably cause siltation in Dharamtar creek, a busy waterway.

Alternative uses were suggested by the Mumbai Dockland Forum, to preserve the Prince's and Victoria Docks which are heritage structures built in 1888, and which deserve to be preserved in their own right, without having to lean on economic, technical or social compulsions. The uses suggested were:

- Marinas.
- Parks, waterfront promenades, and other 'green' areas.
- Passenger ferry terminal.
- A centre for the performing arts.
- Tourist facilities.

On 15th July 2008, Milind Deora, a young MP from Bombay, wrote to Shipping Minister G.K. Vasan. Taking over a year to reply, on 16th September 2009, Vasan merely repeated what the Port authorities had said earlier. He said that with the Eastern Express Freeway and the Bombay Trans Harbour Link (both of them years into the future), the port traffic would have more diversified routes; he ignored the impact on the other roads. Regarding Victoria and Prince's Docks, he merely said that these had been constructed in the nineteenth century and had outlived their utility. He did not deal with the alternatives suggested.

A desperate attempt was made by BEAG and the Mumbai Docklands Forum in April 2010 with Environment Minister Jairam Ramesh. We pointed out the violations of the Prime Minister's Directives and the Environment Ministry's stipulations regarding decongestion of Bombay, reduction of traffic in Bombay Port and release of land for parks, greening and recreation. Jairam Ramesh was requested to at least halt

Approach to the Nhava pier from the North

the filling up of Prince's and Victoria Docks. We pointed out that such filling up of docks is hardly if ever done elsewhere in the world. Land for stacking of containers could be made available from the land earmarked by the Port Trust for commercial purposes. We asked that at least this reclamation be kept in abeyance before it was too late. Jairam Ramesh wrote to G.K. Vasan on 23rd April. However, all these pleas seem to have fallen on deaf ears.

Admiral Rao has compiled an "Indictment" in which he says:

> The Mumbai Port Trust is not the only party to be blamed for trying to implement the flawed OCT project.
>
> The MMRDA, which is responsible for the development of the Metropolitan Region, should have, in 2001, halted plans to inject 3000 containers a day into a heritage *Ghadial Godhi* ('Clock Tower Dock' – the other name for Victoria Dock), in the very heart of *Amchi* Mumbai, grist for the Octroi mill.
>
> The Mumbai Municipality should have insisted that the Prince's Dock, which has been idle since 2001, be used for providing a sea promenade for the citizens of Bombay considering there is only standing room in the evening at Girgaum Chowpatty. A vibrant city-based waterfront will earn money for the Mumbai Port Trust rather than it being squeezed by a mounting Rs 100-crore maintenance dredging budget.
>
> The ONGC, which has been using Victoria Docks extensively for servicing its decaying OSV fleet, should have submitted a formal bid for leasing Victoria Docks in their backyard, while ex-

> ploring opportunities in Brazil, Sudan, Nigeria and Siberia.
>
> The Indian National Ship Owners Association should have halted the project for closing down Merewether Dry Dock which is the only commercial dock available to them for Coastal vessels of 20 to 95 metres. Their only alternative is Dubai or Goa. Ship repairers and shipyards have been silent about the loss of Merewether Dry Dock. Their alternative is Darukhana.

For that matter, why did the Coast Guard who call themselves the "Fourth Armed Service" keep silent in spite of persistent pleas to take up the issue?

The *Mumbai Mirror* of 10th November 2010 carried an article by Alka Shukla which was most alarming, entitled **"Draft policy may free up 50 hectares of port land: Prepared by Union Ministry of Shipping, it talks of allowing ports to lease out land outside custom bound areas for 99 years through bidding."** The article said that the Shipping Ministry had prepared a draft land usage policy and sent it to all major ports for recommendations. The policy talked of allowing ports to lease out lands for 99 years through bidding.

Saroj Tahiliani, Manager in the Mumbai Port Trust, was quoted as saying: "Once the policy is through, we will prepare a detailed land use plan for our vacant plots," including plots to be used for port purposes and "the ones that could be leased out to private players."

Alka Shukla wrote: "could mean windfall gains for the Mumbai Port Trust". They had **28 hectares** in the form of two large plots in Titwala, where the current rates are around Rs. 7 crore per acre. She added that another "**22 hectares are spread across around 120 plots from Colaba to Mahim, ranging from 24 square metres to 5,000 sq.metres.** This includes significant stretches along the Harbour Line – Sewri, Cotton Green and Wadala."

Leasing out these 50 hectares (125 acres) to private parties would be a flagrant violation of both the Prime Minister's Directive of 1980 and the Environment Ministry's stipulations of 1988.

I took this up with Environment Minister Jairam Ramesh saying that there have already been gross violations of the Directives to reduce the general cargo traffic in Bombay Port. However, at least the Directives regarding release of land and dock areas in the existing Bombay Port areas for parks, etc. (as directed by the Prime Minister), for greening and recreation (as per the Environment Ministry's statutory stipulations) should be implemented; the 28 hectares (70 acres) in Titwala and the 22 hectares (55 acres) in Bombay need to be released in a long overdue provision for parks and gardens in Bombay.

I was assured that the matter would be taken forward.

I subsequently pointed out that much of this land would fall within CRZ limits where the Environment Ministry could refuse development permissions.

B.G. Deshmukh described the Central Government mindset, writing (emphasis added): "The Central Government had the same narrow attitude towards Bombay Port Trust. When the BMRDA Bill went to the Central Government for approval, **they wanted to exclude port lands from its purview arguing that they should be the planners for their property**. This was ridiculous as the port lands formed an integral part of the city's land use and planning. Fortunately, Dr. Rafiq Zakaria, the Urban Development Minister, took a strong stand and got the matter cleared." Years later, Bombay Port Trust Deputy Chairman, Zafar Saifullah (who was to rise much higher to become Union Cabinet Secretary), asked us not to object to Port Trust lands being taken out of planning control. One of the arguments he used was that that would remove undesirable political interference. In the light of subsequent developments, it was very fortunate that the Maharashtra Government stood firm and insisted on retaining planning powers. This gives cause for some hope.

Use of an old lifebuoy

Shipping Ministry land policy

QUITE APART FROM BOMBAY, the new draft of the Shipping Ministry Land Policy will have ominous consequences for other major port cities where Port Trusts have substantial land holdings. Calcutta and Cochin are cases in point. It needs to be borne in mind that these lands were given to the Port Trusts for port purposes and not for real estate development. If the lands are in surplus of the ports' requirements, they should be used for civic amenities, specially parks and gardens.

The example of the Calcutta Port Trust (CPT) is relevant. CPT had planned very massive construction in the early 1990s. One of the schemes involved demolishing the Port warehouses, which are prime heritage structures located very close to the Hooghly River on Strand Road. On the 29 acres of land which the CPT owns there, they had planned to build a massive commercial complex with 15 lakh square feet of construction, and turn it into a second Dalhousie Square (Central Business District). It was planned that the Calcutta Stock Exchange would shift there from Lyons Range. Apart from destroying heritage, this would create enormous congestion and pollution in an area where it was (and is) already extremely difficult to move. Though the scheme included a two-kilometre-long pedestrian promenade along the river front, this was to be only five metres wide which was far too narrow; there would be no possibility of a Riverside Drive on the lines of Marine Drive in Bombay. The high-rise buildings would prevent the river front from ever being made properly accessible to the public. Simultane-

Land being cleared for "operational purposes"

ously, the CPT also planned on building another project on 100 acres of land in the Boat Canal area, in between the residential areas of Old Alipur and New Alipur. A colossal amount of construction (48 lakh square feet) was planned and it involved taking the existing *nullah* (canal) underground.

I heard about these schemes only by accident in 1992 and was appalled. I took the matter up strongly and repeatedly with the Environment Ministry whose clearance was necessary since the Calcutta Port Trust is a Central Government organisation. Except for PUBLIC, a local NGO (which included this in their writ petition challenging government construction in Camac Street), the other NGOs in Calcutta appeared to take no action. Neither did the State Government seem to be overly concerned. Though the concerned Environment Ministry official was not happy with the project, he seemed puzzled as to how to proceed.

I argued that the prime need for Calcutta was not more commercial or high-quality residential units, but decongestion, more open spaces, more public parks and more land for civic amenities. The construction projects would, once and for all, pre-empt land needed for the above purposes. I pointed out that the land had been given to the Port Trust for the operational purposes of running a port, and not for real estate development. I gave the example of the port at Sheva, when the matter had gone up to Prime Minister Indira Gandhi herself who had accepted our arguments and stipulated that the lands in Bombay Port which became surplus should be released for parks and gardens; the same should be done in the case of Calcutta Port if lands had become surplus due to the decline in port traffic, the development of Haldia Port or for any other reason. There were several other arguments.

Ashok Bhatia, Deputy Director in the Environment Ministry, was most receptive. The Environment Ministry accepted these arguments and Environment Secretary R. Rajamani took up this issue more than once with Calcutta Port Trust Chairman, Dr. A.C. Ray, Central Government Surface Transport Secretary, S.P. Bagla, the West Bengal Government and CMDA.

The Port Trust argued that the Port had been bearing a loan liability of over Rs. 500 crores on which the annual interest was more that Rs. 40 crores. In addition, there was the annual dredging cost of Rs. 50 crores to keep the 250-kilometre-long channel from Sandheads to Calcutta navigable throughout the year. Hence the construction project, which was expected to generate surpluses, was vitally needed by the Port.

In reply, Rajamani pointed out: "Building on Strand Road will preempt land vitally needed for the circular railway and other services." Regarding the 100 acres in the Boat Canal area, Rajamani wrote: "It would be desirable if the entire area is used for open spaces and gardens/parks and other civic amenities exclusively, which the city of Calcutta is desperately short of. These civic amenities can be charged for so that the Port Trust earns some revenue."

Rajamani added: "The best way of developing the land which is surplus, is to restore the land to the people of Calcutta in the form of open spaces, parks/gardens and if at all, any buildings are to be permitted, it should be only for vital civic amenities. Provisions to these services could be charged so that CPT has some revenue out of these." Regarding the Port's requirement for funds, Rajamani replied: "Surely, the intention should not be to raise funds at the expenses of the environment of Calcutta."

The Calcutta Port Trust Chairman was Dr. A.C. Ray who had been Additional Secretary in the Environment Ministry and whom I knew very well. In the Environment Ministry, he had taken the same stand in similar cases as the Ministry was now taking but I was told that now he was greatly upset by the Environment Ministry's stand. With the change in his job, there had obviously come a change in his perspective. However, Rajamani stood firm, and the Environment Ministry did not approve these projects.

Though the Calcutta Port Trust has not fully cooperated, the massive construction projects have not gone through either.

In an article entitled: "Promenade planned to beautify dying Calcutta Port", Subir Roy, in the *Business Standard* of 28th July 1997 wrote (Emphasis added):

> **Now that Calcutta Port is dying, the city has a chance to reclaim its waterfront.**
>
> The Calcutta Port Trust, which owns the land, has been persuaded to hand over close to 50 acres to six agencies of the state and central governments. They will look after what could become a long and pleasing stretch of landscaped waterfront, running alongside the Strand Road, so far known only for its endless lorry traffic.
>
> The Port Trust has agreed to hand over the land provided it is not commercially exploited. The corporation will abide by this and not 'develop' the land. But there is no question that a long waterfront promenade will add to the attractiveness of the city as a place to live and do business in.

A park, the Millennium Park, has been created on the river bank by the Calcutta Metropolitan Development Authority on land given by the Port Trust. Thousands of people pay an entry fee to enjoy this park and an annual river festival has been held here for the past four years. Thereafter, the Calcutta Municipal Corporation and Coal India Limited have extended the park. Reportedly one of the warehouses has been given heritage status.

What was done in Calcutta needs to be done in Bombay and all other ports. This can easily be ensured by the Environment Ministry since most, if not all, the land would fall within CRZ limits where the Ministry has full sway.

Right to Information – Landmark Decision

The one positive fallout of the Mumbai Port Trust imbroglio is **the landmark decision of the Central Information Commission (CIC) in which they ruled that Concession Agreements between the government and parties to any Public Private Partnership (PPP) projects cannot be concealed from the public and must be disclosed in their entirety.**

It took 20 months and a great deal of effort, including battles in the CIC and the High Court to obtain the decision.

On 17th March 2008 on behalf of the BEAG my colleague, Navroz Mody, aided by Hema Ramani, filed a Right to Information (RTI) application asking for a copy of the agreement signed by the Mumbai Port

Trust with Gammon Infrastructure Projects Ltd., for the construction of the Off Shore Container Terminal. On 16th April the Public Information Officer, Chief Engineer M.V. Patwardhan, refused to give us a copy of the agreement on the grounds that the contract was of commercial confidence.

On 28th April Navroz Mody went in for a First Appeal under Section 19(1) of the RTI Act 2005, with the Appellate Authority, the Deputy Chairman of the Mumbai Port Trust, who was Ashok Bal. On 12th June 2008, without even calling us for a hearing, Ashok Bal upheld the decision of the Public Information Officer of not providing us with the Licence Agreement.

Again on 17th July 2008 Navroz Mody went in a second Appeal to the Central Information Commission (CIC) to determine "whether Public-Private-Partnership Agreements can be disclosed to third-parties under the RTI Act."

Our arguments included: "A PPP Agreement involving the nation's physical resources and its infrastructure, which had critical environmental, social and human aspects, could not be a matter between the bureaucracy of the government and the private party alone. The people of the country are entitled to know the truth about the PPP Agreements, in general as well as in their specific details." Merely by inserting a bilateral confidentiality clause, public scrutiny could not be avoided.

This is especially important since a large part of the development process, affecting the lives of millions of people in the country, is now going the route of the PPP. If all such information was to be denied, then there would be little transparency over large areas of economic activity.

The Port Trust and the private parties had contended: "Furnishing such an agreement will have implications for various PPP projects being encouraged as a matter of government policy where the private parties need to be assured of confidentiality of their Business Plans, including Primary Design criteria, Financing Plan, operation and maintenance plan..."

On 12th January 2009 the Second Appeal came up for hearing before a Single Member Bench (of Central Information Commissioner A.N. Tiwari). However, he referred it to a larger bench: "as the matter related to determination of scope of disclosure of Public Private Partnership (PPP) Agreements, which are now becoming common."

The first hearing before the Full Bench (a Three Member Bench) took

ONGC fencing in front of the coconut plantation

place on 6th March 2009. The Port Trust was asked to clearly indicate which parts of the Agreement could be disclosed and which could not. The Mumbai Port Trust replied on 30th July "that, after consideration at 'the highest level' of the Ministry and the Port Trust Authority, it was decided that it was not necessary for the respondents to make such a determination."

The Central Information Commission also sought assistance from the Planning Commission and the Comptroller and Auditor General of India to clarify the points raised in our appeal.

The Planning Commission replied that they had published eleven Model Concession Agreements for use in PPP projects in different sectors of the economy. All these documents contained specific provisions relating to disclosure of documents including the Concession Agreement. Hence the Planning Commission was "of the view that disclosure of the concession agreement should not be withheld".

The Comptroller and Auditor General was of the view that there should be no objection in furnishing the concession agreements under the RTI Act. If there were clauses whose disclosure would harm the competitive position of the parties, these could be severed.

During the hearing, the Planning Commission and the Comptroller and Auditor General of India informed the Central Information Commission (CIC) that it was their considered view that no PPP Agreements should be held confidential and should be made available in the public domain.

The CIC asked the respondents: "to explain whether a mere arrangement between two contracting parties – one of which was the Government – to keep the document confidential was sufficient to decline its disclosure under the RTI Act."

The Commission noted (emphasis added): "**The position taken by the respondents** that the confidentiality arrangement they had entered into with the private entity as part of the PPP Agreement must be respected, the RTI Act notwithstanding, is **entirely untenable.** Any public document must stand the scrutiny of the RTI Act for a plea of confidentiality to be sustained. **Commission noted with dismay the uncooperative attitude of the respondents** in obdurately declining to share even with the Commission, the specific contents of the PPP License Agreement on which the plea of breach of commercial confidence under Section 8(1) (d) was based. The responsibility for taking such a plea is entirely the respondents' – or of the 'highest authority' they repeatedly alluded to."

The Commission had "pointed out to the respondents from the Bench that when this Agreement was concluded in the year 2007, the RTI Act was already in place. The respondents agreed to the confidentiality clause in regard to the License Agreement with the third-party-Private-Partner knowing full well that such an omnibus confidentiality provision had to be open to scrutiny under the RTI Act. Their plea, therefore, that the mere fact of the presence of the confidentiality provision in the License Agreement was a sufficient condition to keep the Agreement secret, was untenable."

After three hearings, the CIC Full Bench (of Shailesh Gandhi, Ms. Annapurna Dixit and A.N. Tiwari) decided on 3rd September 2009: **"It is therefore imperative that the PPP Agreements are made to embrace transparency rather than be cloaked in secrecy."**

The Port Trust filed Writ Petition 2071 of 2009 in the Bombay High Court seeking a stay on the operation of the CIC decision. We opposed their application. On 30th November 2009, the High Court (The Honourable Mrs. Justices Ranjana Desai and Mrudula Bhatkar) disposed of the Port Trust appeal and confirmed the CIC order on disclosure to the public of all Public Private Partnership Concession Agreements.

This decision now allows the public access to agreements and documents governing Public Private Partnership projects, bringing huge amounts of economic activity under public scrutiny. This will have a huge national impact.

A bridge too far

Even a small stone can sometimes cause a big ripple. One of the Directives of the Prime Minister regarding Nhava Sheva Port was: "Government of Maharashtra should be asked to give ... a categorical assurance that no bridges or causeway will be planned from mainland to Bombay." This condition was neither something that we had asked for, nor had it even occurred to us. It had probably been suggested by Dr. N.L. Ramanathan who had accompanied C.P.N. Singh to Nhava in April 1980. C.P.N. Singh's Report had pointed out that the construction of the port at Sheva would increase the circular flow of goods between the mainland and Bombay. Hence if there was a bridge from Bombay to Sheva, rather than the goods from the mainland going directly to Sheva to be shipped out from there, goods could come by road and rail into Bombay, and then be taken across a bridge or causeway to Sheva. Traffic within Bombay would increase and the professed aim of decongestion would not, therefore, be achieved.

This condition put me in the eye of a storm.

Chief Minister Antulay

A bridge from Colaba to Uran had long been one of Chief Minister Antulay's pet schemes. It fitted in with his idea of "development" of the Konkan within which his constituency was located. In 1970, the Maharashtra Government had appointed a technical committee under the chairmanship of the Public Works Secretary to study a bridge-cum-tunnel linking the island city of Bombay to the mainland. In 1972 the Committee, in its report, suggested two possible links. The northern alignment would be from Sewri via Pir Pau at Trombay to Nhava. The southern alignment would be from Sassoon Docks in South Colaba to Uran, between the Uran and Karanja hills. However, in 1974, Antulay, as Public Works Minister, directed that survey work be carried out only for the southern alignment – which is vastly more visible and, incidentally, costlier than the northern one. Six years later, when Antulay was Chief Minister, the Maharashtra Government justified this decision by saying that the **Sewri Nhava Sheva link was: "not considered desirable...on account of environmental reasons"**. Hence "this link will not be taken into consideration." The justification given for the Colaba Uran Link was: "The project is gaining more and more importance consequent to major investment decisions across the harbour such as Nhava-Sheva Port, New Bombay, ONGC Complex at Uran, RCF Project near Thal Vaishet." This was a very odd justification. Both Nhava Sheva

Port and the New Bombay developments were in the north, well away from Uran. The ONGC's gas and oil terminal at Uran and the RCF fertiliser plant had no relation with Bombay at all.

J.R.D Tata

The Colaba Uran Bridge was also a hobby-horse of J.R.D. Tata. Hence when he stressed its need to Antulay, the latter promptly appointed him in February 1981 as Chairman of a Steering Group to promote this link. This enabled Antulay to kill several birds with one stone. The first was to please India's top industrialist by a move that cost him nothing. The second was to actually try and promote the link. The third was best brought out in an article in a March 1981 issue of *New Delhi* magazine. This said: **"J.R.D. Tata's agreeing to head an autonomous corporation to consider and construct the link bridge is seen as Antulay's most impressive coup. Tata's presence has lent the whole project a tinge of credibility and viability.** 'I don't know how Tata got involved in such a senseless project,' says a member of the Bombay Environmental Action Group. Another offered the view that **even Antulay realises that the scheme won't take off and the setting up of a committee under Tata is a perfect alibi for him. He can always tell his constituency that he tried to do his best. If even Tata couldn't build the bridge what can Antulay do about it?"** (Emphasis mine.)

Other members of the Steering Group included N.M. Wagle, a prominent industrialist, and Ajit Kerkar, Managing Director of the Indian Hotel Companies Limited. It was not clear what the special expertise of these distinguished businessmen was and what contribution they could make to the study of this subject. Importantly, there were no environmentalists or urban planners in this Steering Group. It is also significant that more than 20 years down the line, the Steering Group report has not yet been made public. While writing this chapter in 2003, I asked a senior retired civil servant to lend me a copy, but he refused.

J.R.D. Tata got moving even before the Steering Group was formally constituted on 27th February 1981. When he met the Maharashtra Government officials, he was told that the environmentalists had objected and that the Prime Minister had put a stop to the project. This must have been an unpleasant jolt. He asked who was responsible and was told that it was Admiral Cursetji and me. He spoke to Admiral Cursetji who informed him that he was involved only in the campaign to save Nhava and had nothing to do with the Nhava Sheva Port. J.R.D. Tata then asked the officials who I was. On being told that I was employed in

Tatas, he apparently replied that Tatas was a big organisation and asked where I was working. On his return to his office in Bombay House, he had asked for me and had been told that I was in Delhi. This could not have improved his frame of mind. He had apparently said at the Directors' lunch table that as if there were not enough problems, the environmentalists had now objected to the Bombay mainland bridge. I was told later that he was irritated.

Of all this I was blissfully unaware; I was in Delhi trying, if memory serves correctly, to meet Rajiv Gandhi. On my return, my immediate superior, Noshir Soonawala, told me to contact the Chairman's office since he wanted to see me. I had no intention of doing that, at least till I had had a chance to brief myself. I was not given the chance. The next morning, 12th February 1981, I was told that the Chairman had not forgotten and that I should go up to him. Putting on my jacket, I went up. I had been advised to remain cool since J.R.D. Tata would try his best to rile me; I did not follow this advice.

J.R.D. Tata began courteously by asking me if I would like a cup of coffee. Perhaps a bit brashly, I replied saying that if he could organise it, I would love one. His eyebrows went up but he said nothing. He clearly treated the meeting as important since he refused all calls, including one from P.C.D. Nambiar, Managing Director of the State Bank of India – who, as head of India's largest bank, (in those days when the top 21 banks were in the Government sector), was a very important personage indeed.

Coming to the substantive discussions, I began, perhaps a bit tactlessly, by saying that he had allowed himself to be used by Antulay for the latter's own political purposes. He reacted sharply saying that whenever anyone tried to do anything good he was criticised.

J.R.D. Tata attacked me vigorously. When I said that building the Colaba Uran Bridge would convert Uran into a dormitory town for Bombay, he asked: "Isn't it cheeky for you to tell people where not to live?" I replied that town planning everywhere involved earmarking areas for residential and other uses. J.R.D. Tata said that we (BEAG) were tackling only peripheral issues. I answered back, but at all times respectfully. I said that his generation was at fault for today's mess; why did he not spend two or three hours a day on such issues? I said that Tatas should set a lead on environmental matters, that I could not possibly tackle all the issues. I added that as it was, I was on Calmpose tablets, had no assistance, and that I was shelling out from my own pocket for our environmental work. He repeatedly said that I was dogmatic, that I had fixed views, that I was an extremist, that it was no use talking to me and "wasting your time". I replied that I clearly could not contradict him, but at the same time, I could not accept what he had said. It was a hammer and tongs argument, which went on for an hour-and-a-half. I had a gruelling time. However, throughout, he conducted the meeting as between one gentleman and another and not as between a superior and someone vastly subordinate to him. He did not flare up when I replied to his strong statements in a similar vein. He even finally accepted some of my views. Few chairmen would have behaved like this.

The Bombay House bush telegraph clearly worked well. I was told later by a senior Tata director that J.R.D. Tata had said that I had "stood up to my riling quite well". In the evening, as I was leaving Bombay House, I bumped into another, more senior, director, Dr. Freddie Mehta. He knew of my meeting with J.R.D. Tata. He said that I should keep fighting, and not be frightened of important people, advising me to just be polite. All this concern for politeness seems most odd – it is almost as if my superiors thought that I behaved like a bull in a china shop.

During those more leisurely and spacious days, I used to go home for lunch. At lunch I told my mother what had happened and said that even if I got sacked, I could not change my views. She said that I should remain calm and nothing would happen. That afternoon at 5: p.m. while I was writing down my notes of the meeting, the telephone rang. When I mentioned my name, the voice at the other end said "Tata". I sat up; it was J.R.D. Tata himself, telephoning personally. He said that he had not meant to say that everything we were doing was wrong. However, he wanted to know why I held the view that the road link would increase congestion rather than decrease it. The next day I delivered at J.R.D. Tata's office a note enclosing Naeem Vakil's *Bombay Magazine* article referred to above. A couple of extracts from this article are given below:

> N.V. Merani, member-secretary of this committee and now the Chief engineer of the PWD, admits that no construction on this scale has ever been undertaken by the Government. The bridge-tunnel scores over the bridge because, 'In case of calamity, only one communication link would be cut off, and it would not block the whole harbour,' he explains. **The committee also suggested another cross-harbour link, from Sewree to Nhava. But for ecological reasons, this northern bridge was not feasible.**
>
> **New Bombay's architect Charles Correa feels that the**

Men, materials and machines were mobilised to destroy Nhava

> **bridge is being planned at the wrong point in the City. In south Bombay, the only place that it can connect with is the Marine Drive, and at peak hours that place already is a nightmare of congestion.** 'The cost of the bridge will be tremendous, and, I think, even more than what they have estimated. It will make New Bombay more accessible, but not if there is a bottleneck for traffic at either end.' Correa feels that finally the link will defeat its purpose. He feels that **instead of relieving the congestion of the City by siphoning off the population, there will be more people pouring in than ever before, a view shared by environmentalists.** Merani says that one of the reasons for delaying the project was because of New Bombay. 'We were waiting for New Bombay to be completed before establishing the link. This would minimise the risk of attracting more people into Bombay.

Continued Vakil: "...A.V. D'Souza, chief engineer at the Bombay Port Trust...is in favour of having a tunnel, rather than a bridge. **'In case of a calamity, if the bridge collapses, it will disrupt all the shipping in the port.'"** (Emphasis mine.)

My note to J.R.D. Tata came back from him the same day with a hand-written note from him thanking me, but saying that "the article makes no reference to the Sewri-Nhava Sheva alternative location and only mentions Charles Correa's mild objection". J.R.D. Tata also asked for “telling arguments” against the link. His reply was surprising since Charles Correa’s objections were anything but “mild” and the arguments given were “telling” enough. Nevertheless, I tried to formulate a reply.

There was a problem since I was told that the Save Bombay Committee might support the link. Cyrus Guzder reassured me that he would speak to the Save Bombay Committee straightaway asking them not to commit themselves to a position till he had discussed the matter with them.

I consulted various colleagues such as Darryl D’Monte, Cyrus Guzder and Govind Lalvani and prepared a detailed note. I was told, however, by a senior Tata officer that I would now be entering into a direct argument with the Group Chairman, an argument which could only end one way, and I should therefore let the matter drop. I consulted Dinshah Malegamvala, and showed him my note. He said that I should send the note saying that it was high time somebody stood up to the Chairman, since too many people were giving him wrong advice. This was in line with my own inclinations. I have always quoted the example of the Government, where, in spite of enormous political and other pressures coupled with the threat of transfers, there are still officers forthright enough not only to disagree orally when required, but also to record their dissents in writing. I therefore sent my note. Three weeks later, on 7th March 1981, I was contacted by Prasun Sengupta, a young TAS officer who was Executive Assistant to Ajit Kerkar. During a long late-night meeting at my home, before the first meeting of the Steering Group, I gave Prasun Sengupta my views, a third note on the subject and other documents. To all these notes and papers there was no comeback.

This time, there were no dinner invitations from Antulay. He must have felt that the handling of the environmentalists could be left to J.R.D. Tata.

I tried other channels. A couple of days after my meeting with J.R.D. Tata, accompanied by Abe Aboody, I met Pupul Jayakar, who, perhaps as Indira Gandhi’s closest personal friend, had considerable clout. I had been in touch with her for some time. I raised several issues with her, one of these being the Bombay Mainland Bridge. I said that I hoped that the fact that the Tatas and others were involved would not prevent our views from getting a proper hearing. She said that I should build a proper case, with the backing of proper experts, and send it. In the two decades to come, on this subject at least, I could not complain that we were not heard.

Colaba- Uran Bridge-cum-Tunnel

I was not the only one who felt that Antulay was using this proposal and J.R.D. Tata for his political purposes. Naeem Vakil, in her article which appeared in the *Bombay Magazine* of 22nd November 1980, said: **"Antulay's involvement has inevitably given rise to allegations that the whole scheme is no more than an election stunt.** His opponent at Shriwardhan, Datta Khanvilkar says: 'There is no doubt that he is doing the whole thing for personal gain.'" (Emphasis mine.)

Four months later, Surender Bhatia writing in *New Delhi* magazine commented: **"Political stunt:** Not surprisingly, most people view it as a political stunt rather than anything else.

"Antulay seems more intent on the Colaba- Uran link bridge than the other two proposed links: Sewri-Pau- Elephanta Island-Nava-Sheva and the rail link from Bandra to Mankhurd-Vashi-Belapur and Panvel. **'Like a true politician, Antulay has made the most expensive and so the most impressive choice,'** says a city executive." (Emphasis mine.)

Some of the arguments against the Colaba-Uran bridge were, firstly, that Greater Bombay is shaped broadly like a triangle with the base at the north, narrowing down southwards to the Island City which itself narrows down towards the tip at the extreme south in Colaba. For decades, the aim of official policy had been to decongest the over-crowded Island City, and more specifically, the southern portion. This was to be achieved by restricting, if not banning, the setting up of new commercial and industrial activities and encouraging them, by and large, to only come up in the northern part of the Island City and in New Bombay across the harbour. Building a bridge from Colaba to Uran would result in the current northbound traffic shifting direction and coming southwards, making the roads even more congested.

Secondly, there was the question of access to the proposed bridge. I can't do better than to quote from a note of 13th February 1981 prepared by Shirish Patel, one of Bombay's leading structural engineers.

> The road link from Apollo Bunder to Uran would need to be at least about 60 metres above high water in order to permit liners and other shipping traffic into the harbour. This means that it would start at Apollo Bunder at the height of a 20-storeyed building and ramp down into Colaba for its approaches. **It is estimated that approximately 100 acres of land would be required for the approaches to the bridge at this height and this would mean demolishing half of**

> **Colaba.** The bridge would be costlier than the other options indicated above, partly because of its great height and partly because of the depth of seawater over which it has to run. It would not be possible to establish a rail link at this location. As far as the road connection is concerned, the Fort area in Bombay is at the tip of a long and narrow island, and the number of approaches to the Fort area is consequently restricted. The Uran bridge would add a further approach from the South, but it would mean that all traffic from Greater Bombay towards Uran would have to be pushed through the Fort area. The traffic congestion in Fort would be many times more severe than it already is on this account. It is not only cars but also trucks which would then be going through the Fort area to approach Uran.

Thirdly, the bridge would convert Uran, in the southern part of New Bombay, into a dormitory town of Bombay, whereas New Bombay was supposed to be an independent city with people working and living there.

Fourthly, any accident to the bridge could well result in blocking the narrow shipping channel of Bombay Harbour, thus immobilising India's premier commercial port and by far its most important naval base.

Most informed opinion was against the link; in particular, the Colaba Uran bridge faced virtually unanimous opposition. *New Delhi* magazine called it an "outlandish proposal" of Antulay's, comparing it to "several of his actions, cancelling all farmers' debts, personally visiting Bombay's red-light area, to mention a few".

Trenchant criticism was expressed in an article entitled "A Bridge Too Far", which appeared in *The Indian Express* of 26th March 1981 under the provocative pen name, "Bhavani Talwar". The pen name needs some explanation. Antulay was the first, and so far the only, Muslim Chief Minister of Maharashtra and an extremely controversial one. He made a number of token gestures hoping to appease the dominant Maratha community. One of these concerned the Bhavani Talwar, the famous sacred sword of Shivaji, the founder of Maratha power, whose name is an emotive one amongst Marathas. In fact, on what was widely perceived as a wild goose chase, Antulay had gone to England with the avowed aim of retrieving the sword, which was reportedly in the Royal Collection in London, and bringing it back to Maharashtra. Antulay did, apparently, succeed in bringing a sword back from London, but retired Maharashtra Chief Secretary N. Raghunathan, quoting the official historian of the Maharashtra Legislative Assembly, says that this was not the Bhavani sword.

I can't do better than to quote a few paragraphs from Bhavani Talwar's article:

> It seems that the recent utterances of Chief Minister Antulay on a **new bridge across the harbour are meant to be taken seriously. Initial reaction was to dismiss them as part of those image making and vote-gathering statements which public men are so accustomed to spew. But recurring press reports and the association of Mr. J.R.D Tata's name with the proposal clearly indicate that the threat is real, not imaginary.**
>
> Those who believe that this brave new bridge can be more than just a flight of fantasy or a piece of escapist fiction would be well advised to ponder over a few propositions before committing personal reputations or public funds.
>
> The first proposition is that the bridge, or perhaps the bridge-cum-tunnel, is currently talked about as likely to cost Rs. 500 crores. That, by any reckoning, is a lot of money.
>
> **The second is that for the bridge to make any kind of economic sense it must necessarily generate toll-paying vehicular traffic of a magnitude that is truly mind-boggling.** If the cost of money is taken at 12 per cent and depreciation and maintenance at another three per cent the annual revenue would have to be Rs. 75 crores for the project to break even. Assuming a recovery of Rs. 10 per vehicle crossing (and that is not a small amount), **the number of vehicle crossings at break-even point would be 75 million per year or a little over 200,000 per day.**
>
> Even if only half this traffic is to be handled during five peak traffic hours we get peak-hour traffic of 10,000 vehicles per hour in each direction. As one lane of traffic can be expected to carry 1,500 to 2,000 vehicles per hour **about six lanes would be required in each direction – double the capacity of Marine Drive!**
>
> In order to cope with this additional load a whole new network of roads will have to be created in Bombay, especially in the south, which is both physically not feasible and economically prohibitive, even if we ignore the fact that a bridge with six lanes in each direction will cost vastly more than Rs. 500 crores!
>
> A third proposition for consideration is that the cost of the bridge should be reckoned not only in terms of rupees but also in terms **of the alternate uses to which the money could be**

put. For instance, consider the number of basic dwelling units, which can be created with the same amount of money. Assuming that a minimal house can be constructed for Rs. 10,000 and that related land development costs would be another Rs. 10,000, Rs. 500 crores of rupees could finance 2,50,000 of such minimal homes. With six persons per home, **it means a new life for as many as 1.5 million people if not more.**

No doubt, one cannot hope to achieve a 15 per cent return from the occupiers of such dwellings if the return is reckoned in monthly cash payment alone. But the return would be more than adequate if one takes into reckoning the physical and social costs of crowding people into inhuman slums and assigns a monetary value to the benefits and savings which accrue to society from a major urban renewal scheme. (Emphasis mine.)

Colaba-Uran Bridge Shelved

J.R.D. Tata echoed some of our arguments in his letter which appeared in *The Times of India* of 25th June 1981, extracts from which I repeat below:

> Sir, – With reference to your editorial entitled 'Need For Caution' (April 27/28) in which you set forth the case **against government's alleged proposal to connect Colaba with Uran by a bridge-cum-tunnel** across the southern end of the Bombay harbour, you may be interested and reassured to know that there is **no such proposal at present and that the project** under active consideration by the steering group of which I am chairman, appointed by the government of Maharashtra, **is not for a link from Colaba to Uran** but for one between a more central point on Bombay's harbour front and a point adjacent to the Nhava-Sheva port across the harbour.
>
> The possibility ultimately of establishing **a second link from Colaba to Uran**, first mooted many years ago, will depend on the nature and extent of the developments that may take place across the harbour in the years to come after the proposed link is built, **and when this second link is established, effective means of avoiding further congestion in south Bombay will undoubtedly have to be provided**, possibly through the creation of a new western highway which would enable most of the traffic to and from the Konkan and south India to bypass that part of the city. (Emphasis mine.)

Two points stand out in J.R.D. Tata's letter. Firstly, the proposal for the Colaba- Uran bridge-cum-tunnel is described as an "alleged pro-

Nhava forests stood silent spectators to the destruction

posal". Secondly, the Sewri to Nhava Sheva link, earlier deemed to be environmentally undesirable, had suddenly become environmentally benign.

Kumar Ketkar, in *The Economic Times* of 2nd December 1981, wrote that the Colaba Uran Link project "has been ruled out at present, in view of the fear that it would aggravate traffic congestion in South Bombay. It would have also created restrictions in the navigational channel approaches at Bombay port."

A press item in the *The Economic Times* of 20th July 1983 stated that the report of the Central Road Research Institute "does not favour a link with the mainland from the Gateway of India as there would be a traffic bottleneck at Apollo Bunder. Instead, it has called for a link between Sewri and Nhava."

Social Conflict

My stand on the bridge involved me once in a totally unnecessary fracas. One Saturday night at a party at the home of my journalist friend Gautam Vohra, one of the guests asked me why I had opposed the bridge. That whole day I had been preparing for a trip to Delhi, for what threatened to be a major battle at the Petroleum Ministry Advisory Committee. I was exhausted and in no mood for environmental discussions. I said so, but the lady said that she was particularly interested and would really like to hear my views. It would have been discourteous not to comply. While I was speaking another guest asked me, rather aggressively: "Why do you always oppose everything that is tall and high and beautiful?" I replied that everything that was tall and high was not necessarily beautiful, and that in any case we did not oppose everything that was tall and high. In a sentence which I hoped would conclude the argument, I said that all the experts were against the bridge. He asked: "Who are all these experts – corrupt government servants earning two hundred or three hundred rupees per month?" I was very angry at this typical businessman's reaction to the ill-paid Civil Service which I have always felt is the guts of a stable society. I lost my temper and gave a rude reply.

I have always felt that one has enough battles in real life, and does not need any more waves in social situations. The next day, I contacted Gautam Vohra, rechecked the guest's name and obtained his telephone number. I telephoned him and apologised, which apology he accepted. Many years later, when I bumped into this gentleman at the Bombay Gymkhana bar, I was wary. Before I could say anything he said: "You apologised to me when I should have apologised to you." I have never forgotten this.

Bridging Problems

It was probably because of J.R.D. Tata's persistence that on 5th December 1981, the Centre's Department of Environment constituted a high-powered Study Group chaired by B.B. Vohra, Chairman, National Committee for Environmental Planning. It included as its members Secretaries of the Union Ministries of Shipping and Transport, Works & Housing, Railways and of the Planning Commission. The Maharashtra Government was represented by Bombay Municipal Commissioner D.M. Sukthankar.

The Sewri Nhava-Sheva link ran into problems. The take-off point on the Bombay side could not be south of Sewri since it would interfere with the existing port activities on the waterfront. If the take-off point was located north of Sewri, it would be difficult to provide suitable express feeder roads due to the existence of the two large refineries, the Tata Electric Company's thermal power station and the Bhabha Atomic Research Centre nuclear establishment (BARC). The alignment crossed the various oil pipeline jetties and also the water intake jetty of BARC. This was unavoidable because of the shipping approach channel to the Pir Pau jetties at Trombay. However, the BARC authorities objected to any alignment which came within a one-kilometre radius of their installations, including the water intake jetty. The Consultants pointed out that BARC's objections were not consistent with the International codes of safety of atomic energy establishments. The matter was therefore taken up by J.R.D. Tata with Prime Minister Indira Gandhi.

On 28th June 1984 Union Environment Secretary T.N. Khoshoo accompanied by Dilip Biswas, (then a Director in the Department of Environment) visited Bombay and had meetings with J.R.D. Tata's high-powered Steering Group and with several environmental groups. They said that information would be made available to the environmental groups who were each asked to nominate a contact person for this purpose. They were very keen that I should be the contact person for BEAG.

However, when I consulted a Tata director, he advised me not to be the contact person since J.R.D. Tata was personally committed to the link and felt that all our objections were silly. Characteristic of the best Tata traditions, he gave me no orders. He said that the decision was mine, but added that J.R.D. Tata was "not that democratic" and would make my life miserable about this, even though I was only acting as a conduit. The director said that in fact, regarding the Tata Electric Companies projects at Trombay (to which BEAG had raised strong objections), J.R.D. Tata may have been more sympathetic, though he would have said that he could not interfere. I decided that discretion was more advisable than fruitless valour. In any case, Debi Goenka was fully conversant with this subject and I therefore nominated him as BEAG's contact person.

To conclude, in my interaction with J.R.D. Tata on this subject, years later, at a TAS Officers' gathering at the Taj Mahal Hotel, he jocularly told me that he would get the link through. I replied "Over my dead body!" Few chairmen would have taken open opposition this way.

Elephantine Problem

The statutory Regional Plan for the Bombay Metropolitan Region showed the bridge as being via Elephanta. Much more seriously, in June 1984 we saw that one of the proposed alignments, from Sewri in Bombay to the Nhava Sheva area across the harbour, showed the bridge as resting on Elephanta Island. This would desecrate the island and be a monumental threat to the World Heritage monuments and sites. It would add to the noise and pollution and be the thin end of the wedge, since where bridges and roads enter, concretisation and other undesirable developments often follow.

When we expressed our concern, we were assured that the bridge would "only touch Elephanta". We also came to know that high-level meetings were being held in Bombay to discuss this project. In spite of our sustained efforts, we could not get precise information about the alignment nor could we get an assurance that the bridge would not touch Elephanta. Frantic SOS appeals were made, and on 22nd June, I wrote to Pupul Jayakar, the founder of the Indian National Trust for Art and Cultural Heritage (INTACH). She must have been extremely exercised about this issue since her action was very swift. Just five days after my letter, on 27th June 1984, Rajiv Gandhi (then an MP, General Secretary of the All India Congress Committee, and Chairman of INTACH) wrote to Union Deputy Minister of State for Environment, Digvijay Sinh of Wankaner. Though Rajiv Gandhi was not yet Prime Minister, he commanded a great deal of clout.

There was some mention of the fact that the bridge pier would not be on Elephanta but on Elephanta Spit. A spit is a projecting bank of sand which runs out from a point. Elephanta Spit extends one mile north-eastward of the north-eastern end of the Island, is uncovered at low water and is an extension of Elephanta.

Either because of Rajiv Gandhi's intervention or otherwise, the latest alignment of the bridge shows it as bypassing Elephanta. However, transport planners have a habit of shifting proposed alignments and hence vigilance is absolutely essential.

Record Keeping

With the environmental clearance still not having been obtained, and with Prime Minister Indira Gandhi no longer on the scene, fresh attempts were made to get the project cleared. Environment Secretary T.N. Seshan came to Bombay on 31st December 1986. I suggested to him that he postpone his visit by at least a few days; the pressure on him must have been considerable since he said that he did not wish to postpone his visit to 1987.

One of the things I have always been derided for – even by most of my colleagues who should know better – has been my obsession with keeping notes, maintaining files and multiple copies of documents which, for reasons of safety, are stored in different locations. As a result, my home resembles a disorganised godown of files. It has been impossible, for the last 15 years, to hold the large monsoon parties, that I used to host annually. My sister says that I have transformed a lovely family home with beautiful memories, into a junkyard. My nieces, who grew up there, refuse to visit. One of them says that with my love for files, I should have been a government servant.

However, record keeping and archiving are crucial. They proved to be very important on several occasions, not just for historical reasons, but for operational purposes as well. They had very beneficial results in one incident, simultaneously amusing and potentially disastrous. In 1992 the link proposal was revived – reportedly for a bridge-cum-tunnel from Colaba to Uran – the very alignment that had been rejected ten years earlier. I reiterated our objections to Environment Secretary R. Rajamani. However, the Environment Ministry could not trace their file on this subject; I received requests, both written and oral, to send them whatever earlier documents I had. I sent them all the papers I could; more importantly two years later, from one of the Ministry's letters to me, **I gave them their own file reference number.** I received a warm letter of thanks from Advisor M. Parabrahmam, a Joint Secretary level officer. He wrote: "But for the extremely good gesture from your office it would not have been possible to compile such information in such a short time. I convey my grateful thanks to you and your colleagues."

Reportedly, after J.R.D. Tata's death, the link was once again mooted, this time by Tatas and as a partly Tata funded project, planned as a memorial to him. However, it was not found feasible. As of August 2004, environmental clearance had still not been obtained. This project was included in a list of projects taken up by Maharashtra Chief Minister, Sushil Kumar Shinde, who went along with an all-party delegation of MLAs and MPs to Prime Minister Atal Bihari Vajpayee for sanction. The proposed alignment is from Sewri to Nhava, landing on the east of the island. The need for such a bridge is extremely questionable, especially in the light of the already existing road and rail bridges (one of which was built fairly recently), and the flyovers which have been constructed during the last few years, all of which have greatly reduced travelling times to New Bombay.

On 7th August 2004 the Maharashtra State Road Development Corporation Ltd. (MSRDC) published an advertisement of a global tender for "Implementation of India's longest Sea Link Expressway between Mumbai and Navi Mumbai". The advertisement talked of "A spectacular two-way, six-lane, Sea Link connecting Sewree in South Mumbai to Nhava in Navi Mumbai over the sea." The bridge is to be 22.5 kilometres long, 28 metres wide, with a six-lane dual carriageway and will cost Rs. 2,600 crores. It was surprising that bids had been invited when environmental clearance had still not been obtained.

The Indian Express MUMBAI *Newsline* of 26th August 2004 carried an article by Rajshri Mehta, entitled "Nhava-Sewri link will not have railway line – **Study indicates poor passenger numbers.**" The article said inter alia:

> "**However, urban planners are unhappy with the current plan.** They point out that rail travel is a preferred mode of transport for the common man.
>
> "**An internal MSRDC report has also said that the Rs. 2,600 crore project will be unviable if it depends only on toll revenues.**" (Emphasis mine.)
>
> If there is no railway line, if there will be poor passenger numbers, and if the bridge is not going to pay for itself, one wonders why and for whom it is being planned.

Environmental Clearance

Since then, clearance from the Environment Ministry has been obtained, even though the bridge that will take off from Sewri will affect mangroves and flamingos and also the dense mangroves on the bundh going to the mainland, just a kilometre away from Nhava Island. What the impact on Nhava will be is anybody's guess.

Other Islands

It all started with a small portion of Nhava Island. Captain Vijay Shivdasani, writing in October 2006, said that he remembered Nhava as a delightful island even a quarter of a century after he had visited it. He drew a parallel with Chep Lak Kok, a small island to the north of Lantau in Hong Kong, which he had visited and walked around 10 years after his visit to Nhava. He recalled Chep Lak Kok as being a lush wooded island which had on it the Romer's Tree Frog, a unique species of finger-sized frogs found only in Hong Kong. Also close by is the mouth of the Pearl River where 'pink' dolphin frolic and swim in the muddy waters. In spite of a hue and cry in the media, Chep Lak Kok and the island of Lam Chau were both levelled and now form part of the new Hong Kong airport. A question comes to mind, namely, would such massive environmental damage have been permitted by the British in their own country?

However, a far better comparison would be with Compton Mackenzie's fictional island of Little Todday, which was off the north-west coast of Scotland. In his *Rockets Galore*, he has described how the Ministry of Protection, the Royal Air Force and the Ballistic Regiment had decided

Coconut palms form a backdrop to mudflats where mangrove tress once stood.

to remove the crofters and take over the whole island for the purposes of building a missile base. Just as Rashid Yusuf was told by the CIDCO Managing Director that he should be proud to surrender the Trust's land free of cost in the national interest, so were the Little Todday islanders told by the Parliamentary Under Secretary of State for Scotland, Andrew Wishart, that they were the spearhead of the Free World and that it had once been the privilege of the MacDonalds to fight on the right of the line of battle.

Like ONGC, the Ministry of Protection was adamant. Just as the ONGC had made their promises applicable "for the present", so had the Protection Ministry. Just as ONGC were made to fight every inch of the way in India, so were the RAF and the Ballistic Regiment. Just as Salim Ali described the ONGC's actions as vandalism, Father Macalister, the Roman Catholic priest who led the islanders, described the Protection Ministry officials as "barbarians from the outer darkness". I often felt the same way about the ONGC officials. Just as the villagers on Nhava and Sheva protested, so did the inhabitants of Little Todday. The latter however went much further. Father Macalister vowed to resist even if he had to go to prison for it. The inhabitants moved the markers and a 90-year-old farmer on another island hid a theodolite in a byre full of long-horned Highland cattle from which retrieval was difficult. When the contractors arrived, their tools disappeared; the surveyors' measurements were changed five times and removed four times. The lorry of a local merchant suddenly careered off and violently hit a bulldozer rendering both unfit for use. Local witnesses said that the lorry jumped up on its own. A few months later, two bulldozers were landed but on their first night on the island their vital parts were removed and in Father Macalister's words, they became "oxdozers" incapable of ferocious behaviour.

Most important was what happened to a missile which, going astray, landed on the island. The RAF officer, Group Captain Oakenbotham, told Father Macalister that it was his duty to report on the condition of the missile, to which the reply was that the missile would shortly be in no condition at all. The missile was soon surrounded by a mob who, to the accompaniment of highland music provided by bagpipers, were dancing and smashing the missile with axes and other weapons. When Group Captain Oakenbotham suggested that Father Macalister be arrested, the police sergeant said that if that was attempted, they would all be thrown into the sea.

Some of the inhabitants initially favoured the project because of the additional business possibilities, but the bulk of the local opinion was against them. When the owner of the lorry complained to Father Macalister, he was surprised to get a strong reproof. The police sergeant was so upset by the coldness shown to him that he requested a transfer to the mainland.

The Little Toddday story, however, had a far happier ending than that of Nhava. Hugh MacInnes, Wishart's Parliamentary Private Secretary, resigned from his job in order to fight for the island and joined his father's wool business. This gave him an excellent vantage point for a brilliant idea. He approached the wool company's dyers and asked for a rose coloured dye which could be used on birds. He obtained that, along with a promise of complete confidentiality. Together with some of the local islanders, he went to the island of Pillay close to Little Todday and dyed some herring-gulls. He was then able to persuade a friend of his, a popular broadcaster on birds, to visit Little Todday. The latter saw some "pink" herring-gulls and though initially sceptical, was excited by his "discovery". His reports led to a popular agitation to preserve the rare species of "pink" herring-gulls and Little Todday. Eventually the government capitulated and abandoned their plan. However to save face, they did not mention birds, but said that the island was unsuitable, thereby binding themselves for all time.

Sadly, I have never been able to pull off an environmental coup of this nature.

Sequel

Whenever I used to complain, my mother used to say in Sindhi "Sabha mein changai aahe (There is good in everything"). It was so in this case. Though 40 hectares on Nhava had been cruelly ravaged, at least there were some benefits.

On Sheva, several hundred hectares have been afforested. To understand the scale of the afforestation, a comparison could be drawn with the "Colaba Cantonment Heritage Precinct" whose area is about 200 hectares and also with the much admired Bombay Port Trust Gardens in Colaba which have an area of 4.75 hectares.

A landmark decision, having national implications, regarding Right to Information has been obtained.

Though so far not implemented, the Prime Minister's Directives and Environment Ministry stipulations regarding Bombay Port give scope for several hundred acres of land in the congested heart of Bombay to be converted into parks and recreational uses.

Coming to Nhava, in spite of my failure to obtain protection under the Ancient Monuments and EP Acts, the Nautical Institute and Marine Museum are still intact, are flourishing, and have, in fact, been renovated and greatly expanded. The beautiful venerable buildings still stand and the romantic memorial water tank still survives. Much of the greenery still remains, though is subject to threat, and the mangroves remain, statutorily protected, though also under threat. Out of the 54 hectares of land with ONGC, 14 hectares were made into a tree nursery which, though neglected in recent years, is still green. Fourteen hectares of beautiful mangrove lands were saved from takeover and destruction by ONGC. The port has left Nhava alone. The rest of Nhava has been classified as a Regional Park in New Bombay's Master Plan. This area needs to be greened and made accessible to the public. We are pushing for enactment of heritage regulations in New Bombay within which Nhava falls. Once these are enacted, this area of history and beauty will receive further protection.

If it was not for the fact that environmental victories are never permanent, if there was only one activity which justified my life, it would be the saving of the lovely island of Nhava, the institutions within it, and the hundreds of hectares on Sheva.

ANNEXURE – I

MOST IMMEDIATE

Prime Minister's Office

Secretary, Science & Technology, may kindly refer to the report on the visit of Minister of State for Defence to Bombay on the 8th & 9th April, 1980, in Colaba near the existing Sassoon Dock, and the ONGC's supply base and fabrication of offshore platform by Mazagaon Dock in the Nhava Sheva Island.

2. Prime Minister has ordered that in respect of the first issue relating to Sassoon Dock, Agriculture Ministry may be requested to find an alternate site for augmentation of facilities above the existing level which can be handled without affecting the environment. The number of mechanised boats, which can be handled at the existing harbour, should be fixed. Arrangements for greater cleanliness will have to be made here by taking care of the environment including air and water pollution and sanitation. The alternative accommodation for additional facilities for additional fishermen may be surveyed in any of the sites mentioned in the report of the Minister of State for Defence and a decision taken urgently in consultation with the Government of Maharashtra and Department of Science & Technology. The land already reclaimed could be considered for conversion into a botanical garden as suggested by the Minister.

3. With regard to the second issue relating to setting up of offshore facilities at Mazagon Dock in the Nhava Sheva Island and ONGC's supply base, the Prime Minister has ordered that Ministry of Petroleum may be asked to go ahead with the project limiting it to the level now contemplated and they may be informed also that no further expansion of the activity of any Central Agency should be allowed on this Island. Further they should constitute a Committee of Central Government, ONGC, State Government and Department of Science & Technology to ensure that the safeguards for planting of trees, etc. are observed.

4. Prime Minister has also concurred in observation about the need to preserve Elephanta Island and that trees should not be allowed to be cut there and its development should be part of the regional plan. The suggestion of the Minister of State for Defence that the Central Department of Tourism should take over the development of Elephanta Island should also be examined.

5. Minister of State for Defence has also made a reference to the pollution caused in the Bombay area by the thermal power station of the Tatas which was approved without obtaining the clearance of the Central Agency in regard to environments. This may kindly be verified and note sent separately to Prime Minister on this.

6. Action on this may kindly be followed up with the Ministries wherever necessary.

Sd/-
(R. Rajamani)
Joint Secretary to the Prime Minister

Secretary, Science & Technology (Prof.)
P.M. Office u.o. No. 17 (1723-A)/80-PMS dated 4.7.1980

Copy to Secretary, Agriculture
(for action on paras 1 & 2)

(ii) Petroleum (Shri B.B. Vohra)
for action on para 1 & 3)

(iii) Defence Production

Sd/-
(R. Rajamani)
Joint Secretary to the Prime Minister

ANNEXURE – II

Excerpts from the directives of prime minister on environmental and related aspects of the respective projects

1. NHAVA ISLAND

As already instructed, Ministry of Defence and Petroleum can go ahead with the setting up of off-shore facilities of Mazagon Dock and the supply base of ONGC limiting it to the level and areas as now planned. No further expansion of activity of any of these organisations should be allowed on this island. Bombay Port Trust also should not have any activity on this island that would endanger the environment or result in any further reclamation. The village, picnic spots, Nautical Institute, Museum etc. should be left untouched and no further area should be taken from any of these activities. Department of Science & Technology should monitor closely the adherence to the environmental safeguards (including planting of trees) suggested by M.O.S. Defence and Maharashtra Government by ONGC as well as Mazagaon Dock and the project estimates should specifically provide for Expenditure on these safeguards.

2. NHAVA SHEVA PORT

Project feasibility report for which is being processed by Ministry of Shipping & Transport should be scrutinised to ensure that it would significantly decongest Bombay. The NCEPC should scrutinise environmental aspects and the suggestions of NCEPC should be built into the feasibility report and financial outlay to carry them out specifically provided. The feasibility report should provide for the release of land and dock areas in existing Bombay Port area for parks etc. No other agency (other than existing military unit at Sheva) should be allowed around Nhava Sheva and areas around Nhava Sheva Port planned as a green belt. Government of Maharashtra should be asked to give commitment in this regard and a categorical assurance that no bridges or causeway will be planned from mainland to Bombay.

3. SASSOON DOCK

As already intimated, Agriculture Ministry should not augment facilities beyond requirements of 700 boats (now operating for fishermen already settled there). The area can be made more clean taking anti-pollution steps already suggested but extra facilities for storage, docking, etc., should be started only after alternate sites and facilities are located for the boats over and above 700 which used to touch Sassoon Dock..

4.

The work on Thal Vaishet fertilizer factory plant itself may go ahead but no work on the township or residential or other tenements other than plant should proceed until Department of Science & Technology resolves the correct site for them keeping in view environmental factors. The decision said to have been taken by RCF in consultation with the Maharashtra Government about location of township should not be implemented now.

ANNEXURE – III

PRIME MINISTER'S OFFICE

NHAVA AND ELEPHANTA ISLANDS

(Received with the demi-official letter No. 5-28/82-FRY (Cons), dated 30 August 1982 from S.P. Mukherji, Secretary, Department of Agriculture Cooperation)

Secretary, Environment, may kindly refer to the decisions relating to Nhava Island near Bombay in July 1980 wherein safeguards for preservation of environment in Nhava Island were mentioned and it was clearly directed that no further activity should be allowed to be taken up on the Island. In the light of a recent inspection of the area from our office, Prime Minister has directed that the activities of ONGC should be strictly limited to the present area taken up by them and the Environmental Committee should visit the place at least once in three months to ensure that the safeguards prescribed are being implemented according to the agreed plan. Also the workers quarters should be dismantled as soon as the work is over. These matters may be followed up with the Ministry of Petroleum.

Prime Minister has further directed that in order to ensure that no further projects are taken up on the Nhava Island. It may be suggested to the Maharasthra Government to take over the rest of the Island and convert it into a park and also ensure that the Nautical Institute is not permitted to give up its operations in future to allow buildings to come up. Maharashtra Government should be asked to ensure that on the Nhava and Elephanta Islands no commercial or building activity of any description is allowed and positive steps are taken to green them and if necessary convert them into parks with birds, wildlife, etc. This may kindly be taken up with the Maharashtra Government immediately and confirmation of action being taken reported within one month.

Sd/-
(R. Rajamani)
Joint Secretary to the Prime Minister
10-8-82
Secretary, Environment (Dr. T.N. Khoshoo)

P.M.'s Office, U.O. No. 17 (1923) (A) 82-PMS, dated 11-8-1982

Copy to:
1. Secretary, Petroleum
2. Secretary, Shipping and Transport
3. Secretary, Agriculture
Sd/-
(R. Rajamani)
Joint Secretary to P.M.

ANNEXURE – IV

No.J-11013/21/88-IA

September 16, 1988

OFFICE MEMORANDUM

Subject: Environmental clearance to Nhava Sheva Port Project

The undersigned is directed to refer to Ministry of Surface Transport D.O.No. PD/17023/1/86-NSPT, dated the 28th August, 1988, on the subject mentioned above.

1. In a directive dated August 8, 1980, the Prime Minister instructed that Nhava Sheva Port Project must significantly decongest Bombay and that environmental safeguards and necessary financial outlay to carry them out must be provided for in the Project. The Prime Minister also directed that the feasibility Report of the Nhava Sheva Port should provide for release of land by the Bombay Port Trust for Park, etc. Pursuant to the Prime Minister's directive, a Monitoring Committee and later a Working Group were set-up. After deliberations of the Committee and the Working Group and the discussions with the Standing Committee of the Ministry of Surface Transport, a general outline of environmental safeguards and decongestion of Bombay was formulated. On the basis of these discussions and on the basis of commitment of the Ministry of Surface Transport given in the letter referred to above, environmental clearance to the Nhava Sheva Port project is hereby accorded, subject to the following conditions: -

(i) The total land area of the project must not exceed 2584 hectares, as approved by the Government. Any re-appraisal of land requirement may be only towards reduction and not for additional land.

(ii) No further cutting of hill slopes would be under taken by the Nhava Sheva Port Trust (NSPT) except in the areas already contracted for terracing along the cut line as of 4.8.88.

(iii) Administration and operation buildings built on the hill feature at Sheva Island should not be more than what is existing now, i.e. two storeys. No further buildings be built on hill feature area. All temporary structures built in the area must be removed before the end of 1990.

(iv) The NSPT must not have major blasting in the Port area.

(v) Dredging will be limited for operation and maintenance only. Disposal of dredged material will be done in consultation with Environment Division of NSPT. Such material must not be used for filling up any waterbody.

(vi) No large-scale dumping of wastes shall be undertaken by NSPT without clearance from environmental angle. This is to ensure that marine ecology of the area is not affected by dumping in the marshy lagoon/low level areas.

(vii) A green belt of 500 metres must be provided all along the periphery of the Port excluding the water areas. The approximate cost of the greening – initial cost and cost of maintenance for 5 years will be Rs.3.5 crores at present day cost. A provision for this amount has to be made in the Project cost for the NSPT. Annual financial requirement after initial 5 years has to be provided in the annual budgets of the Port.

(viii) Inside the Port, 800 hectares of land must be afforested. This may be spread in pockets of hill and vacant areas and need not be concentrated in one area. The cost of such afforestation approximately Rs. 1.6 crores, spread over a period of 5 years, must be included in the project cost of the NSPT. Thereafter, annual fund requirement must be provided for in each year's budget.

(ix) Suitable tidal low-lying areas should be identified for mangrove plantation and provision of the required amount – approximately Rs.1.5 crores, must be made for this purpose in the Project cost of the NSPT.

(x) Six Air Pollution Monitoring Stations and six Water Pollution Monitoring Stations must be set-up, in the Port area and in the neighbour-hood, susceptible to pollution arising out of the Port's functions and port related activities. The capital cost of these stations, approximately Rs.1 crores, must be provided for in the Project cost of the NSPT. Annual recurring expenditure must be provided for in the annual budgets.

(xi) With the operation of the Nhava Sheva Port, as a measure of decongestion of Bombay Port, the traffic in Bombay Port must be gradually reduced, by steps to be taken by the Ministry of Surface Transport, Bombay Port Trust and NSPT, so that the total general cargo inclusive of container cargo handled at Bombay Port comes down within three years to 6.5 million tonnes. The schedule of reduction and the action programme in this regard should be forwarded to this Ministry by the Ministry of Surface Transport within three months.

(xii) The Ministry of Surface Transport and Bombay Port Trust must take action to gradually make the land of Bombay Port, which is not required for operational purposes of the Port, available for greening and recreation. A time frame and an action programme in this regard should be forwarded to this Ministry by the Ministry of Surface Transport within six months.

(xiii) The NSPT must draw up a Disaster Management Plan and get it approved by the nodal department of the State Government and forward it to this Ministry for approval.

(xiv) There must not be any cutting of trees in any area of the NSPT.

(xv) The operation of the berth of the NSPT which falls within 200 metres of the protected zone of the Elephanta Caves should be controlled with adequate safeguards so that there is no damage to the Elephanta Caves.

(xvi) Adequate measures for protection of Elephanta Caves, particularly from SO_2 emissions from the vessels funnels and from vibrations must be taken. Regular monitoring in the Elephanta Caves must be done for this purpose at the cost of the NSPT.

(xvii) An Environmental Division must be set up in the NSPT which will consist of one Environmental Manager, two Environmental Engineers, two Forest Officers, four Laboratory Assistants and 13 Forest Guards. An Environmental Laboratory for water, air and solid waste monitoring must be set up with adequate equipment and qualified staff. The approximate capital cost for the Laboratory which will be Rs.50 lakhs must be provided in the Project cost. The annual recurring cost for the Laboratory and the Environmental Division must be provided for in the Annual budgets of the Port.

(xviii) The minimum financial requirements for meeting the above conditions, that is Rs.8.1 crores besides the annual recurring cost, must be provided for in the Project cost. The annual recurring cost for the different items for environmental protections must be provided for in each year's Annual budget of the port.

2. The implementation of the above conditions of the environmental clearance must be monitored by a Standing Committee to be set-up for the purpose with the representatives of Ministry of Surface Transport, Nhava Sheva Port Trust, Government of Maharashtra and the Ministry of Environment and Forests. The Ministry of Surface Transport will take action for setting up of this Committee.

3. The enforcement of the conditions stipulated in this Office Memorandum will be under the provisions of the Environment (Protection) Act, 1986.

(A. C. RAY)
Additional Secretary

To

(1) Secretary,
Ministry of Surface Transport,
Parliament Street,
New Delhi

(2) Chairman,
Nhava Sheva Port Trust,
Bombay

(3) Chairman,
Bombay Port Trust,
Bombay

(4) Secretary,
Department of Culture,
Ministry of Human Resources,
New Delhi

(5) Director General,
Archaeological Survey of India,
New Delhi

(6) Chief Secretary,
Government of Maharashtra,
Bombay

2.12.2010

Bibliography

1. Ali, Salim *The Fall of a Sparrow*, Oxford University Press, New Delhi, 1985
2. Arunachalam, B. *Essays in Maritime Studies*, Maritime History Society, Mumbai, 1998
3. Bhate, G. C. *Isle of Nhava*, G. C. Bhate, Poona, 1932
4. Blake, George *B.I. Centenary: 1856-1956*, Collins, London, 1956
5. Bombay Metropolitan Regional Planning Board, *Regional Plan for Bombay Metropolitan Region 1970-91*, Director of Town Planning, Town Planning and Valuation Department, Government of Maharashtra, Poona, March 1974
6. Bombay Sailing Association – Booklet
7. Carter, Lionel *Chronicles of British Business in Asia 1950 – 1960*, Ajay Kumar Jain for Manohar Publishers & Distributors, New Delhi, 2002.
8. Chainani, Shyam *Heritage and Environment – An Indian Diary*, UDRI (Urban Design Research Institute), 2007
9. Chainani, Shyam *Nhava Island as Private Beach – A Comment*, Article in Economic and Political Weekly, August 9, 1980
10. Daji, Cawas N. (Editor) *The Coronation Souvenir*, D.D. Kanga
11. Deshmukh, B. G. *A Cabinet Secretary Looks Back – From Poona to the Prime Minister's Office*, Harper Collins Publishers, New Delhi 2004
12. Deshmukh, B. G. *A Cabinet Secretary Thinks Aloud*, Bharatiya Vidya Bhavan, Mumbai, 1998
13. Deshmukh, B. G. *A Cabinet Secretary Looks Around*, Bharatiya Vidya Bhavan, Mumbai, 1998 (Check)
14. D'Monte, Darryl *Temples Or Tombs? Industry Versus Environment : Three Controversies*, Centre for Science & Environment, New Delhi, 1985
15. D'Souza, J. B. *No Tumpets or Bugles: Recollection of an Unrepentant Babu*, Allied, 2002
16. Fox, Loren *Enron The Rise And Fall*, John Wiley & Sons, New Jersey, 2003
17. Fraenkel, Peter & Partners *Oil And Natural Gas Commission: Bombay Offshore Project: Nhava Sheva Development – Feasibility Study and Master Plan*, January 1977
18. Fraser, David *Alanbrooke*, William Collins Sons & Co. Ltd., London, 1982
19. Hailey, Arthur *Overload*, Michael Joseph Ltd., 52 Bedford Square, London, 1979
20. Jog, N. G. *Saga of Scindia – Struggle for the Revival of Indian Shipping and Shipbuilding*, (Golden Jubilee Volume) 1969
21. Mackenzie, Compton *Rockets Galore*, Chatto & Windus, London, 1957
22. Maharashtra Government Committee for the Protection, Preservation and Beautification of Greater Bombay and its Environs, *First Interim Report on Nhava Island*, December 1979

23. Mishra, Kiran *V. K. R. V. Rao: His Life and Times*, Vikas Publishers, New Delhi, 1996

24. Naravane, M. S. *The Maritime and Coastal Forts of India*, APH Publishing Corporation, New Delhi, 1998

25. Pandit, Heta *Yusuf's idyllic dream becomes a nightmare – Nhava in turmoil*, The India Magazine February 1984

26. Peters, Thos. (Editor) *Who's Who In India, Burma & Ceylon*, 1939

27. Piramal, Gita *Business Legends*, Penguin Books India (P) Ltd., 1998

28. Raghunathan, N. *Memories, Men and Matters*, Bharatiya Vidya Bhavan, Mumbai, 1999

29. Rao, T. S. Sanjeeva *Indian Shipping & Shipbuilding*, January 1978

30. Rao, S. L. *The Partial Memoirs of V.K. R. V. Rao*, Oxford University Press, New Delhi, 2002

31. Russel, Wilfrid *Merchant in a Mirror*, Asia Publishing House, London, 1961

32. Shankar, Vice Admiral Daya *Memoirs and Memories*, Nitin Shankar, New Delhi, 2003

33. Sharma, Lt. Col. Gautam (Retd.) *Indian Army*, (A Reference Manual), Dr. S. K. Bhatia for Reliance Publishing House, New Delhi, 2000

34. Singh, C.P.N. Report on the visit of Shri. C. P. N. Singh, Minister of State for Defence, to Bombay on 8th and 9th April 1980 in connection with the location of a new fishing harbour at Colaba near the existing Sassoon Dock; ONGC's supply base and fabrication of offshore platforms by Mazagon Dock in the Nhava Island; and the implications of setting up a new Port at Nhava-Sheva across the Bombay Harbour, Government of India, Ministry of Defence, April 1980

35. Sridharan, Rear Admiral K. *History of the Naval Dockyard Bombay: Two Hundred and Fifty Years (1735 – 1985)*, Admiral Superintendent, Naval Dockyard, Bombay, 1989

36. Srinivasan, Kannan *Nhava Island as Private Beach* article appeared in Economic and Political Weekly, May 3, 1980

37. Srinivasan, Kannan *Reply* an article appeared in Economic and Political Weekly, August 9, 1980

38. Subramanian, T.S.R. *Journeys Through Babudom and Netaland – Governance In India*, Rupa & Company, New Delhi, 2004

39. Wadia, Ruttonjee Ardeshir *The Bombay Dockyard and The Wadia Master Builders*, Khursetji F. Guard, Bombay, 1955. Quoting Lishman N. (on page 325, Appendix A)

40. *West Coast of India Pilot* (Ninth Edition) Hydrographic Department, Admiralty, London, 1950

Acknowledgements

When Shyam Chainani passed away, this book was almost ready to be published. However, it took several of us time to re-start where he had left, and publish the book.

Publishing the book was a labour of love by several people, who were committed to ensuring that Shyam's legacy lives on.

In addition to those thanked by Shyam earlier, the editors of the book would like to add their additional and very hearfelt thanks to:

Bertie D'Souza for designing the book

Aurobindo Patel, who gave his input on the design

Perveen Mahoney who proof read the manuscript

Carmen Kagal who created the editing guidelines

Fred Poonawala of Comart Lithographers Pvt Ltd for processing the cover of the book

Cyrus Guzder, Statira Wadia and Ashok Advani for helping steer the book forward in many different ways

Sir Mohamed Yusuf Seamen Welfare Foundation and The Heritage Network for their generous contributions to the Heritage and Environment Protection Association (HEPA) that Shyam Chainani founded

They were extremely generous with their time and their invaluable inputs after Shyam's demise, ensuring the book was published.

Editors